Directions in Euripidean Criticism

Directions in Euripidean Criticism

A COLLECTION OF ESSAYS

EDITED BY PETER BURIAN

Duke University Press   Durham, 1985

The chapter by Charles Segal, "The *Bacchae* as
Metatragedy," is adapted from chapter 7 in his book
Dionysiac Poetics and Euripides' "Bacchae".
Copyright © 1982 by Princeton University Press.
Chapter 7 is adapted and reprinted by permission of
Princeton University Press.

Library of Congress Cataloging in Publication Data
Main entry under title:
Directions in Euripidean criticism.
Bibliography: p.
1. Euripides—Criticism and interpretation—
Addresses, essays, lectures. I. Burian, Peter, 1943–
PA3978.D59 1985   882'.01   84-25950
ISBN 0-8223-0610-7

WAR

Contents

Preface

The title of this collection means what it says: the essays gathered here illustrate a number of ways of thinking about Euripides, the most enigmatic and controversial of the three Attic tragedians. Among the plays discussed are recognized masterpieces and neglected problem children, and pieces that run from early to late (or even beyond, if one does not accept the authenticity of the *Rhesus*). There is no party line other than a willingness to take Euripides seriously as an artist.

Directions in Euripidean Criticism began as a conference sponsored by the Department of Classical Studies at Duke University in March 1977. The essays published here differ substantially from the papers presented then, but all of the original participants are represented, with the exception of Pietro Pucci (Cornell), whose memorable lecture on "Justice in the *Medea*" was incorporated in his book *The Violence of Pity in Euripides' "Medea"* (Ithaca, N.Y. 1980). Bernard Knox's conference lecture has become part of his contribution to the first volume of the *Cambridge History of Classical Literature*, soon to appear. He has kindly supplied a new and luminous essay to serve as the introduction to this volume. Froma Zeitlin's lecture appeared as "The Closet of Masks: Role-playing and Myth-making in the *Orestes* of Euripides," in *Ramus* 9 (1980) 51–77. I am grateful that she has allowed me to include in this volume an equally stimulating and perhaps even more probing essay on the *Hippolytus*. Charles Segal's lecture, in the form printed here, is a shorter, independent version of the chapter "Metatragedy: Art, Illusion, Imitation" in his magisterial *Dionysiac Poetics and Euripides' "Bacchae"*

(Princeton 1982). Anne Burnett's and my own essays are revised and expanded versions of our lectures. Only Kenneth Reckford's retains the form and flavor of the actual lecture he delivered on what was both a pleasant and a most rewarding occasion.

Unless otherwise indicated, all translations from the Greek are by the authors of individual essays. I owe thanks to many: to my department and its former Chairman John F. Oates for their whole-hearted support of the conference; to Mrs. Mary D. B. T. Semans and former Dean of Faculty Harold W. Lewis for their encouragement, and to the Mary Duke Biddle Foundation for a generous grant to help defray the cost of publication; to Douglass Parker (Texas) and Wesley D. Smith (Pennsylvania) for their strong endorsement of this project at a critical juncture; and to Louise Pearson Smith for her indefatigable assistance in compiling the Selected Bibliography. To my colleagues whose essays appear here at long last I am grateful above all for patience and unflagging commitment.

One participant in the lively concluding panel at the Duke conference is no longer here. Harry L. Levy warmed our hearts and cheered our days through the very active years of his "retirement" in Durham. His encouragement, his guidance, his example have meant more to me than I could easily say. This book is dedicated to him in fond memory.

Peter Burian
Durham, North Carolina
March 1984

Directions in Euripidean Criticism

Euripides: The Poet as Prophet
BERNARD KNOX

He was a many-sided poet; even in the fraction of his work that has come down to us—about one-fifth—we can hear many different voices: the rhetorician and iconoclast of Aristophanic travesty; the precursor of Menandrian comedy; the realist who brought the myths down to the level of everyday life; the inventor of the romantic adventure play; the lyric poet whose music, Plutarch tells us, was to save Athens from destruction when the surrender came in 404; the producer of patriotic war plays—and also of plays that expose war's ugliness in dramatic images of unbearable intensity; above all, the tragic poet who saw human life not as action but as suffering. The essays of this collection explore in detail many different aspects of this protean dramatist's work; this introductory note is concerned with one aspect of Euripides' tragic mood, its prophetic vision.

We have nineteen of his plays—almost three times as many as the seven of his contemporary and competitor Sophocles, the seven of his predecessor Aeschylus. We know him better than the other two and yet we find him more difficult to understand, to accept, to love. He seems unable or perhaps unwilling to resolve the discords his plays inflict on our ears; even his masterpieces leave us full of disturbing questions. If he were not so great a dramatist we would suspect him of lack of direction, of faulty construction, of exploitation of dramatic effect without regard to structure, of rhetoric without regard for character; in fact many critics have tried him and found him guilty on some or all of these charges. But a man who could conjure up out of iambic lines and a mask such awesomely living figures as Medea, Phaedra, and Pentheus, who could round off the action of a play with final scenes like those of the *Trojan Women* or the *Hippolytus*, clearly knew his business as a dramatist. He must have intended to produce this unsettling effect, which disturbed his contemporaries as it disturbs us: to leave us with a sense of uncertainty, painfully conscious now, if not before, of the treacherous instability of the world in which we live, its utter unpredictability, its intractability. It might be said of him what the Corinthians in Thucydides say of the Athenians, that he was born never to live in peace himself and to prevent the rest of mankind from doing so.

Nearly all the plays we have were written in the last twenty-five years of his life, the years of the Peloponnesian War. One of the most famous, and shocking, of them, the *Medea*, was first produced at the very start of that disastrous war, in the early spring (end of March–beginning of April) in the year 431 B.C. This was the spring festival of the god Dionysus and the Athenians looked forward to it eagerly, for it marked the end of winter.

It had been a tense winter. Thucydides, who watched carefully the events of those months, intent, as he tells us, on writing the history of the war that was in the making, describes the atmosphere of that spring of 431 B.C. "Although war was imminent, the contending powers maintained diplomatic relations and exchanged representatives, but without confidence. For the preceding events were in fact a renunciation of the thirty years' peace treaty and anything now might provoke open hostilities" (1.146). We know this atmosphere very well; we live in it and have lived in it since 1945—the Cold War we call it. It has not yet, mercifully, turned into a hot one, a full-scale general conflict. In Greece it did and the spark that set off the explosion was, as usual, an insignificant episode in itself—the Theban attack on the small city of Plataea on a rainy night in March 431 B.C., the month and the year in which the *Medea* was produced.

This spring was the last spring of peace, of the Golden Age of Athens, the Periclean age, that period of enormous creative activity in every field of endeavor, political, scientific, intellectual, artistic. This was the last spring: two years later Pericles, speaking of those who died in the opening battles, was to say, "the spring has gone out of the year."

In the *Medea* the chorus sings the praises of that Athens of the great, the Golden Age. "The Athenians . . . rich and happy from of old, sons of blessed divinities, inhabitants of a land which is holy, and undamaged by enemies; their diet is wisdom, which brings them honor; they walk luxuriously through air which is brilliantly clear, a land where once, the story goes, the nine Muses were born to golden-haired Harmony" (824–32). This description of an ideal Athens, set in a play in which a husband cynically betrays a wife and a mother murders her children, was sung in the theater of Dionysus at the very moment when what it described was about to disappear forever. "Rich and happy"—the wealth of Athens stored as golden plates on the Phidian statue of Athena in the Parthenon was to be poured down the sink of nearly thirty years of war; the happiness, the Periclean sense of mastery of the environment, of control and balance, of unlimited horizons—all this was to go up in smoke, the smoke of the burning farmhouses and orchards in the Attic country-side. The "land undamaged by enemies" was to feel the ax of the Spartan invader chopping down the olive trees. And wisdom was to go too—that sense of proportion, that bold initiative which yet recognized proper limits, the moderation of real understanding—all this was to die and fester in the plague that swept through the besieged, crowded city. The "brilliantly clear air" was to be clouded not only with the smoke from burning trees and houses but also with passionate hatred, anger, greed, partisan accusation, ambitious demagoguery—"golden-haired Harmony" was to be replaced by serpent-haired Discord.

And this is what the *Medea*, the *Hippolytus*, and Euripidean tragedy in general are about. It is a vision of the future. In it we can see at work the poet as prophet, as seer: *vates* the Romans called him, a word that means both poet and prophet.

The prophet is not a familiar figure in our modern civilization but ancient Greece had many prophets human and divine who foretold the future, Apollo at Delphi the greatest among them. In the museum at Olympia one can see, among the figures on the pediment showing Oenomaus and Pelops about to run their chariot race, the figure of the prophet—a bearded old man whose tense and tragic face shows that at this very moment he foresees all that is to come from that fatal charioteering: the children eaten by their father, the husband slaughtered by his wife, the mother cut down by her son. Though prophets play a prominent role in Greek art and literature, as they did in everyday life, all this seems foreign to us. Yet we have our prophetic writers too, not only those who deliberately try to foretell the future, like Huxley in his *Brave New World* or Orwell in his *1984*, but also those greater writers who, without consciously trying to, create in their writing the shape of things to come—such as Dostoyevsky, who, in his nineteenth-century novel *The Possessed*, creates a character who describes with terrifying accuracy and with apparent approval the theory and practice of Stalin's rule by terror and purge.

The writer as prophet is not someone with a lucky gift of foresight but someone who foresees only because he sees, sees clearly, unmoved by prejudice, by hopes, by fears, sees to the heart of the present, the actual situation. He knows where he is. And if you really know where you are, you can see where you have been and also where you are going. The poet as prophet is no vague, dreamy seer but on the contrary a man of hard analytic vision who sees the here and now truly and exactly for what it is. His face is not that of the young Shelley in the idealized portraits but the face of the prophet on the Olympia pediment, worn, sad, and loaded with the burden of terrible knowledge. The poet as prophet lives not in the past, as most of us live—our attack on reality made with weapons that are already out of date—nor, as others live, in dreams of the future which turn away from the world as it is, but in the present, really in the present, seeing the present.

And this is what another poet-prophet, Arthur Rimbaud, meant when he said, "il faut être absolument moderne"—one must be absolutely modern. This is what Euripides was, as he still is: absolutely modern.

But it is a dangerous thing to be. Rimbaud gave up poetry, left France to become an unsuccessful gun-runner in Abyssinia, and died of gangrene in a hospital in Marseilles, unknown, unrecognized. Euripides left his beloved Athens and went to spend his last years in the half-savage kingdom of Macedonia, where he died. The trouble with being absolutely modern is that you are ahead of all your contemporaries. You are, in fact, like all prophets, rejected and scorned by the present, to be acclaimed and understood by the future. It is the story of the Trojan princess Cassandra again: the divine gift of true prophecy and the condition that the prophet will not be believed. The prophet is rejected. With Euripides, in fact, begins the tradition of the poet not only as prophet but also as outcast and rejected. His career is a modern career. Unsuccessful throughout his life (he rarely won first prize and was the constant target of the comic poets), he became after his death the most widely read and most frequently performed Greek dramatist, eclipsing, and on the stage at any rate almost entirely extinguishing the fame of his competitors. Euripides was understood not by his own generation but by the next and the generations that came after. Stendhal, when he published *La Chartreuse de Parme* in 1839, said, "je serai lu vers mille huit cent quatre-vingts." He was right. It was just around 1880 that the modern adoration of Stendhal began.

This was the fate of Euripides too. The tragic world he created in the *Medea*, the *Hippolytus*, the *Trojan Women*, and many other plays is an image of the world in which he lived, but few recognized the accuracy of that image. It shocked his contemporaries because they had not come to realize the nature of the world they lived in; still less could they imagine what sort of a world their sons and their sons' sons were to live in. One can forgive their dismay. The world Euripides created in the theater of Dionysus is one of disruption, violence, subversion, uncertainty, discord. The keenness of his vision of reality cut him off from his fellow citizens. He "saw beyond," as Aeschylus says of the prophet Calchas. "You cannot see them, but I can" says Orestes to the chorus—he is talking about the Erinyes. And the chorus replies to Cassandra's visions of the future: "we seek no prophets in this place at all."

The democratic regime established in Athens at the close of the sixth century had emerged triumphant from its trial by fire and sword, the Persian invasions of 490 and 480–479; the next half-century saw the system consolidated at home on an increasingly egalitarian base and supported by the tribute from an Aegean empire which made Athens the dominant power in Greece. These were the years of confidence, of an outburst of energy, political, military, intellectual, and artistic, which astonished the world. There seemed to be no limits to what Athens—and Athenians—could achieve. It was in these years that Aeschylus produced his final masterpiece, the *Oresteia*, and Sophocles moved into his place to succeed him as the foremost poet in the theater of Dionysus. They spoke, through their actors and chorus, to a citizen body which, for all its diversity of income, status, and opinion, was fundamentally united on essentials; it was not until a long war had taken its toll and a disastrous defeat in Sicily had inflicted enormous losses that the democratic regime was overthrown in 411 B.C. It was soon restored, but Athens was never the same again; the ideal city of the Periclean funeral speech, a vision of creative order, tolerance, and freedom, was now a fading memory.

And Euripides is the poet of the crack-up: the *Medea*, the *Hippolytus*, the *Orestes* are visions of a divided city, a disordered universe, the nightmare in which the dream of the Athenian century was to end. Small wonder that Euripides was rejected by the majority, passionately admired by a few, but liked by no one. No nation, no society, welcomes the prophet of its own disintegration, any more than Belshazzar, at the feast, welcomed the writing on the wall.

They drank wine and praised the gods of gold and silver, of brass, of iron, of wood and of stone. In the same hour came forth fingers of a man's hand and wrote over against the candlestick upon the plaster of the wall of the king's palace; and the king saw the part of the hand that wrote. Then the king's countenance was changed and his thoughts troubled him . . ." (Daniel 5.4–6)

The words on the wall were words of a language the king did not understand: MENE MENE TEKEL UPHARSIN. The prophet Daniel interpreted them: "Thou art weighed in the balances and found wanting." Euripidean tragedy is the writing on the Athenian wall. It numbers and weighs; it understands and pities. It does not condemn, for the situation is beyond judgment; it does not propose reform, for it is beyond action. Euripides attempts to understand and to sympathize; but he offers no comfort, no solution, no explanation, only sympathy. And this quality is perhaps what made Aristotle say that in spite of his defects he was the most tragic of the poets.

In his time and place he was a man apart. Sophocles served as general, as ambassador, as one of the treasurers of the Delian League, and even on the emergency committee set up to guide the democracy after the Sicilian disaster. For Euripides we have not the slightest hint that he ever held political office or took part in political activity. Aeschylus fought at Marathon and probably at Salamis too; for Euripides we have no record of military service. Like the incomprehension of his audiences, this apparent withdrawal hints at a modern situation: the alienation of the intellectual writer. And many passages in his plays suggest that he was familiar with that situation. Medea, for example, defends herself against the charge that she is *sophē*, an intelligent woman. Such a reputation, she says, is a dangerous thing to have and she goes on to claim that no one should have his children too highly educated; it will only earn them the hatred of their fellow citizens. Young Hippolytus, an ascetic and religious intellectual, explains himself to his father along similar lines. "I don't have a talent for explaining myself to the crowd; my intelligence is best displayed in converse with a small group, men of my own generation. That's quite natural. The people who charm a crowd usually make a poor showing among intelligent people" (*Hipp.* 986–89). The tone is familiar; and so is the reaction to it. "Go on," says his father Theseus, the public man. "Go on, sing your own praises, pick and choose your vegetarian food, claim Orpheus as your mystic priest and study the cloudy doctrines of those many books of yours. But I have seen through you" (*Hipp.* 952–55). We can recognize in these characteristic passages a modern phenomenon, that alienation which seems to be the inevitable mark of the artist and intellectual in modern society. In fact Euripides is the first European to whom the modern term "intellectual" could with some exactness be applied. We know for example that he had a private library (perhaps the first in European history); he read many books and this was rare in fifth-century Athens, where literature and even philosophy were an oral, rather than a written, affair; where Homer was recited by professional rhapsodes, not read, dramatic and lyric poets performed, not read; where Socrates talked incessantly but wrote nothing. The library of Euripides could almost have been deduced from the titles of his plays—many of the plots come from out-of-the-way stories, legends from the periphery of the Greek world, local myths that deal with minor figures rather than the great heroes of the central Greek tradition. The Thessalian story of Alcestis is one example and the tale of Iphigenia as a sacrificial priestess among the barbarous Taurians another, but there are even more striking examples in the tragedies that have been lost. The *Aeolus* for example dealt with the love of brother for sister in the strange family of the king of the winds on his floating island; its high point was a lyric aria by the heroine which was interrupted by cries of pain as her birth pangs came on. The *Pasiphae* dealt with the passion of a Cretan queen for a bull and the *Auge* with one of the many loves of Heracles, but one who happened to be a priestess and who gave birth to his child in the temple precincts (a place where birth and death were tabu). The choice of subjects we can recognize as modern too. They seem to have been chosen, like those of Faulkner or Sartre, for their shock value.

One feature we know did shock his contemporaries was the predominant role in his drama of what the Greeks called Eros, the irresistible force of sexual passion. The chorus of the *Hippolytus* finds it strange that this powerful deity ("tyrant over mankind") has no cult at Olympia and Delphi; in the play Eros brings about the deaths of Phaedra and Hippolytus and in many another Euripidean tragedy it "comes down on mortals with destruction and every shape of disaster." In the debate between Aeschylus and Euripides in Aristophanes' *Frogs* the elder dramatist is made to claim that he never put on stage a woman in love; he accuses Euripides of producing women "who act as go-betweens, who give birth in temples, sleep with their brothers—and say life is not life." Aeschylus had, of course, created the powerful figure of Clytemnestra, who conspired with her lover to murder her own husband, but, though her speeches are shot through with sexual imagery, no emphasis is placed on her feelings for Aegisthus. And in the scheme of the trilogy, though she is victorious in the first play, she is in the end defeated, rejected by gods and men. In the *Hippolytus* there is no such rejection of Phaedra; in the *Medea* it is Jason who appeals in vain to men and gods. Conservative expectations are disappointed, traditional relationships reversed, and this reversal is not confined to the domestic sphere. In the *Trojan Women*, for example, there is no question about where our sympathy is directed—it is to the defeated, the enslaved. In Euripidean tragedy old certainties are shattered; what seems solid cracks and melts, foundations are torn up, direction lost. "The waters of the holy rivers flow uphill," sings the chorus of the *Medea*. "Justice and everything in the world is turned upside down."

The subversive force turning the world upside down was something the intelligent moderation of the Periclean funeral speech had failed to reckon with, which the belief in human progress under divine tutelage built into the fabric of the *Oresteia* had relegated to the past, which Socrates, as we see him in the early Platonic dialogues, underestimated: the blind passions and ambitions native to the human soul which reason may for a time control but never entirely subdue. For Socrates, man's ethical and political problem is an intellectual one: if a man knows what is really good he will do it— goodness is in essence knowledge, evil merely ignorance. Euripides seems to have no such belief in the human capacity to make the right choice. Phaedra in the *Hippolytus* states the human dilemma in words that have been considered a specific Euripidean critique of the Socratic program:

τὰ χρήστ᾽ ἐπιστάμεσθα καὶ γιγνώσκομεν / οὐκ ἐκπονοῦμεν δ᾽

We know what is right, we distinguish it clearly, but we don't achieve it. (380–81)

The irrational elements in our human nature can overwhelm our reason.

Among those forces Eros has pride of place. But Euripides studies them at work not only in individuals but also in groups—war fever in armed mobs, as in *Iphigenia in Aulis*, Dionysiac frenzy in the Maenads of the *Bacchae*. Eros, in any case, is not a deity confined to the loves of men and women. When Achilles in *Iphigenia in Aulis* describes the mood of the army which demands immediate departure for war, he says:

οὕτω δεινὸς ἐμπέπτωκ᾽ ἔρως / τῆσδε στρατείας Ἑλλάδ᾽ . . .

So fierce a desire (*erōs*) for this expedition has fallen on the Greeks. (808–9)

Writing, probably, at just about the same time, Thucydides (6.24) proposed an identical explanation of the Athenian expedition to Sicily: "a passionate desire fell upon them all (*erōs enepese tois pasin*)." The historian who had so meticulously explained the causes, real and professed, of the outbreak of the war could find no other word to describe this irrational and, as it turned out, fatal decision.

Thucydides cites *erōs* as a psychological factor, a human impulse, but Achilles, in his speech at Aulis, is careful to qualify his explanation. To the statement that *erōs* for the expedition has fallen on the Greeks he adds the words (809) "not without the gods." The gods are in fact regularly adduced, in Euripidean tragedy, as wholly or partly responsible for irrational behavior in human beings. This is of course a commonplace of Greek epic and tragic motivation but in Euripidean tragedy it is given such impressive dramatic form that it must be taken as more than metaphor. Aphrodite begins the *Hippolytus* (28) by explaining how she has driven Phaedra mad with love for her stepson—"her heart was seized with a terrible passion for Hippolytus—it was my decision (*tois emois bouleumasin*)"—and, when Phaedra comes on stage, we see the goddess at work in her victim, Racine's "Venus toute entière à sa proie attachée." In the *Heracles* we see Hera's deadly ministers, Iris and Madness, appear on stage on their way to take possession of the hero's mind and direct his murderous hands against his wife and children. And in the *Bacchae* we watch Dionysus himself transform Pentheus into a simpering transvestite victim, crazed with megalomaniac visions as he dances off to his hideous death.

Pentheus' fate might be considered no more than the appropriate punishment for his opposition to the god's cult and the insults offered to his person. But no such defense can be offered for the unspeakable calamity that falls on Heracles; Hera has hated him from the moment of his birth and now chooses the point at which he has completed the great labors for mankind to bring him to ruin. Hippolytus has offended one great goddess by the purity of his devotion to another, but even if his attitude exhibits a reprehensible pride, there is no moral justification possible for the destruction of Phaedra and in fact Aphrodite announces: "she is noble—but she shall die just the same." Agave, too, is cruelly used by Dionysus as an instrument of divine revenge and Cadmus, whose offense was venial and who begs for mercy, is driven into exile together with his wife and daughter. There seems to be no correlation between divine intervention and human ideas of justice.

Divine intervention in fact is always, in Euripidean tragedy, motivated by considerations of personal prestige. The gods act like jealous sovereign states, which will go to any lengths to maintain that prestige, no matter what the cost in human life. In the *Trojan Women* we see Athena and Poseidon, bitter opponents in the Trojan War, negotiate an alliance against the Greeks; Athena's change of sides is in retaliation against the whole Greek fleet, for an insult offered her by one Greek chieftain. And in the *Hippolytus* we learn from Artemis that she cannot intervene to save her favorite because of the rules of the game: "This is law and custom (*nomos*) for the gods; no one is willing to oppose the will of another who has a wish; we stand back always" (1328–30). All she can do is destroy some human favorite of Aphrodite, which she promises to do at the first opportunity. Mortal lives count for little or nothing in the alternating friendships and enmities of the powers that rule the universe. These powers are in their relationships no more rational than the human beings in whose destinies they intervene so cruelly; the creatures whose passions are too much for their reason are in any case unwitting victims of tyrannical, amoral forces intent only on manifesting their power. In such a world there is little place for heroic action: what is called for is heroic endurance—Heracles' resolve to go on living (*egkartereso bioton*, *HF* 1351), Talthybios' advice to Andromache to bear pain and sorrow with nobility (*eugenos*, *Tro.* 727) and be silent.

Even in his own time some of his audience must have felt that his plays were images of a new Greek world in the making. But to the audiences and readers of the next century Euripides spoke directly, as if he were their contemporary; the world had finally caught up with his vision. The Greek city-states exhausted their material resources and their spiritual potential in endless, indecisive struggles for hegemony—all Greece became the theater for the mindless violence of the *Orestes*, the irreconcilable hatred of the brothers in the *Phoenician Women*. Too weak and too divided to resist successfully the pressure of Macedon, the city-states lost that jealous independence which had been the source of their creative energy and also led to their downfall. As Alexander's conquest opened up the East for Greek settlement, the cities, no longer sovereign states, became the cultural and administrative centers of the huge Hellenistic kingdoms. And as the Hellenistic kings, like Euripidean gods, fought out their everlasting dynastic disputes with sublime indifference to the fate of the victims sacrificed in a quarrel not their own, men faced the unpredictable with Euripidean attitudes: the Epicurean withdrawal from the world of action, foreshadowed in Hippolytus and Amphion; the Stoic acceptance of suffering and the will to endure whatever comes that Heracles proclaims as he renounces suicide. All through the Hellenistic and Roman centuries, in the theaters of Asia Minor, Palestine, Egypt, and farther east, it was Euripides who held the stage—even in the non-Greek court of Parthia there was a performance of the *Bacchae* going on when a general arrived from the battlefield of Carrhae carrying the head of Marcus Licinius Crassus. Even the triumph of Christianity did not put an end to Euripides' presence in the minds of men. The writings of the Greek Fathers of the Church, Clement of Alexandria especially, are studded with quotations from Euripides. And the reason is not hard to understand. They found exposed in his tragic plays the desperation of the human spirit, the misery of the human condition, in a civilization which had reached the end of its spiritual reserves and, as it looked foward, saw, like the prophet on the Olympia pediment, nothing but disaster to come.

Rhesus: Are Smiles Allowed?

ANNE PIPPIN BURNETT

In recent years scholars have proved that the play called *Rhesus* comes from the fifth century B.C. (unless it stems from the fourth) and that it was not written by Euripides (unless perhaps it was). The disputes that were necessary to the nice establishment of these points have, however, left neither space nor time for appreciation of the piece in hand.[1] The authorship game has been played on the settled ground of the play's inferiority, and the gamut of response has stretched only from scorn to embarrassment as disbelievers asserted that Euripides could never have written such trash,[2] while believers apologized, pleading the poet's youth or his special political intention to explain the "unevenness" of this tragedy.[3] Everyone sees that the *Rhesus* is not like other classical plays, but hardly anyone has been willing to suppose that its differences might be due to something other than mediocrity or muddle on the part of the author. Not since Gilbert Murray has anyone asked himself what kind of drama this was meant to be, what sort of experience it tried to offer to its spectators, and what set of principles allowed its playwright (whoever he was) to feel that it was a finished and poetic whole when he had brought it to a close.

The almost unanimous refusal to take the *Rhesus* seriously as a work of art is surprising because the play has an extraordinary surface glamour about it. It concerns itself with doomed Trojans, a spy in wolf-skins, a golden barbarian prince, two Greek bravos, and the most beautiful horses in the world. In addition, the drama offers a stage spectacle unique in surviving tragedy, as an unparalleled action of darkness is played out in front of a rare army-camp decor—an action in which temporal unity is defined by the succeeding hours of a long and fearful night. Indeed, its exoticism extends to basic philosophic assumptions, for this odd play shows a moment when a single mortal might balk the general will of all the divinities. In the Trojan camp that the *Rhesus* proposes, the central question is whether an interloper, Fortune's man, can live through the next few hours, for if he can he will tomorrow reverse the expectations of heaven when he enters the battlefield. The plot produces his assassins and arranges events in the interest of the gods, but we are nevertheless assured that there was a chink in the armor of the Olympians. Things might have gone otherwise, and if they had the Achaeans would have been driven from Troy, taking their defeat not from their traditional and honorable adversary, Hector, but instead from a barbarian king who would then have led Thracian hordes in an invasion of Greece. Such is the unthinkable proposition that the spectator must entertain, as he watches this peculiar tragedy.

In spite of these arresting attractions, almost everyone feels uncomfortable with the *Rhesus*, and the reason for this discomfort is not hard to find, for as the play proceeds appalling discrepancies between poetic intention and poetic performance seem to appear. The play depicts a crisis that determines the course of the war, but the simplicity of its action is dissipated in lurid spectacle and destroyed by a complex dramatic structure. What is worse, the seriousness of the tragic deed is attacked by an intermittent levity of tone that flickers inextinguishably throughout almost every episode. Even as the Thracian completes his fall from high fortune to gruesome death, moments come when a spectator must fight back a smile (or even a laugh), and frequently he finds himself entertaining responses that are cynical and disorderly rather than unquestioning and filled with awe.

Because of such lapses, the *Rhesus* is dismissed as a "bad play," but the fact is that these dubious moments are so egregious that they cannot have been mere careless errors overlooked by the dramatist. Even Verrall's "botcher" could not have been so blind and in any case there is no question of "botching" here, for the poet's care is everywhere evident. The laughable instants are perfectly wrought bits of comedy, and they are placed in conjunction with traditional passages that are likewise brought off easily by an author who is, scene by scene, in perfect control of his powers. Consequently, before we say that this is a "bad" play, we ought to ask whether these inner contradictions, and in particular this flirtation with the ridiculous, might not be contrived aspects of a drama whose temper is other than that of conventional tragedy. Perhaps the play is dominated by a purpose that demands just such a disturbing juxtaposition of the awesome and the absurd.

Materials

The poet's choice of materials suggests that this hypothesis may at least be entertained, for he has taken his fiction from the lightest book of the *Iliad*.[4] The Doloneia is a tale of outlaws, a rogue's comedy in which Athena is fairy-godmother to a pair of murderous horse-thieves. It is also a self-contained whole; nothing in the rest of the epic depends upon it, and it describes a perfect happy overturn with an almost tragic unity. Book 10 begins with a restless and anxious Agamemnon and ends, amid general rejoicing, with the laughter of a satisfied and successful Odysseus (*Il.* 10.565). The movement is from an initial sleepless discomfort to the final luxury of baths (10.576; note the ritual preliminary cleansing in the sea) and banqueting (578), and there is even, in Nestor, a kind of chorus—a figure who registers this change and directs the listener's attention to it. The raid into the Trojan camp is recorded as a case in which human activity not only succeeds, but finds a divine reward beyond all expectation, and the emblem of this unearned felicity is the wonderful pair of horses that the Greeks bring back with them to the Achaean camp. Men who set out on foot to face death come back alive, their mission accomplished, and riding on horseback. As Nestor says, the steeds must be the gift of a god (546, 551), and though Odysseus pretends to belittle this idea, the whole exploit has taken place under Athena's aegis. It was proleptically dedicated to her in the departure prayers (272ff.) and it is offered again, retrospectively, when the spoils are hung up at her door (571; cf. 460) and a libation is poured out to her, at the very end of the song (579).[5]

Once this story of the raid into the Trojan camp had been given its position in the sequence of the *Iliad*,[6] it was able to serve as a *teras* for the whole, a happy sign that Hector's successes could not continue and that the Greeks would eventually enter Troy on another, much larger nighttime expedition. It is thus generally similar to the torn hare of Aeschylus' *Agamemnon*, and like that portent it has touches of the animal fable about it, for nowhere else in the *Iliad* are men so consistently given animal accouterments. Agamemnon wears a lion's skin (10.23) and Menelaus a leopard's pelt (10.290); Diomedes becomes a second lion who attacks goats or sheep (10.297, 485), and Odysseus puts on a boar's tusk helmet to catch a wolfish Trojan spy who behaves like a doe or a rabbit (10.361) when he is chased by a pair of Greek dogs (10.360).[7] Unlike the *Agamemnon* portent, however, and unlike anything else in the *Iliad* except perhaps Aphrodite's tears, this tale borders on farce. When Diomedes falls upon Rhesus' sleeping men and slashes wildly left and right while Odysseus deftly stacks the corpses up—an even dozen of them (490ff.)—the moment is pure Goscinny. (A more correct comparison would be to the Cabiric or the South Italian vases, with their gross parodies of heroic scenes.) There is no sense of fate in Book 10, but on the other hand neither is there any suggestion that the Trojan ally who came so conveniently to hand might have changed the course of the war. Instead, for deeper meaning, we get a kind of wisdom tale about the predator who is preyed upon, coupled with an almost Aesopic lesson from the two pairs of horses: how the Trojans lost the ones they had by coveting an immortal pair that belonged among the Greeks.[8] The Homeric story, then, is essentially a comic one of god-favored heroes who by violent means gain rewards from an enemy both cowardly and unwise (10.552–53, cf. 245).

This was the material that the *Rhesus* poet (tempted probably by the nighttime action[9] and the emblematic power of the two pairs of horses) chose for adaptation to a tragic form. He kept the two Greek ruffians and increased the animality of their first victim; he exploited the obscuring darkness and the leitmotif of fires in the night; and he put on stage the opening mood of confusion and anxiety that had allowed for a comic overturn in the Doloneia (*Rhes.* 56–57; cf. *Il.* 10.109). In a sense he even intensified the farcical tone of Book 10, for he refused to provide any direct description of the killings, and for the sordid scene of Dolon's capture he substituted a silly one of Odysseus' near capture and escape. On the other hand, however, he made a formal preparation for a negative overturn by shifting his setting from the camp of the destroyers to that of the destroyed. He found his chorus in a few epic lines about the Trojan watch (*Il.* 10.416ff.), and he took the thirteenth of Diomedes' corpses,[10] added the power and gold that the Homeric Dolon had said belonged to the Thracian chief (*Il.* 10.434ff.), and made of this creature a titular tragic principal.

The Principal

With Rhesus at the center of his drama, a poet could discover a negative arc of fortune in the Doloneia's comic episode and so make a tragedy, but this is not precisely what the present poet has done, for the single most evident fact about the *Rhesus* is that it proposes not one but three figures as potentially central to its *praxis*, while it makes no one of these figures a responsible focus for its staged action.

Hector is most on stage; furthermore, his ethos is studied through decisions that are analyzed scenically, and he suffers a slanderous accusation, then is cleared of it. Nevertheless, Hector undergoes no external reversal of fortune, nor is he the cause of one; he walks offstage in the end the same man, both in situation and in understanding, that he was when he burst out of his tent in the prologue. He is thus not the hero of this piece. Next comes Rhesus, who gives his name to the show, and who enters in majesty and exits as a maimed corpse lamented by his mother. Certainly the explicit overturn is his, and yet this prince is given only one scene (the third episode, 388ff.), and in that scene he is allowed no deed whatsoever. Except in the theatrical sense he does not act, for not even in mind or spirit does he move; he takes no decision, defends no resolve, gives no command, imposes his will upon no other man. He meets with Hector's insults but he does not even grow angry; instead he makes excuses about his past and boasts about his future, which only makes us more aware that in this staged present his one visible "action" is passive, for all he does is allow himself to be led away to bed. Later we learn that his one invisible action was the inaction of failing to post sentries around his camp (764–66; in contrast, see *Il.* 10.418). It is very hard to see Rhesus as a hero of tragedy.

The third potential hero is Odysseus, one of the comic principals of the matrix version of this tale. He enters stealthily with a

companion, as a vengeance principal might;[11] he is set a task of violence by a divinity, and after its accomplishment he is at the center
of a visible drama as he escapes by his own wit from men who would
capture him.[12] In brute action, he thus outstrips Hector and quite
eclipses the inert Rhesus. In addition he can be said to experience a
peripeteia, since his initial dejection at failing to kill Hector is replaced by his final escape and his success in the murder of Rhesus.
And yet of course he is not the principal (he is not even the actual
"doer" of the tragic deed, for Diomedes kills while Odysseus only
steals, as in the Doloneia), nor is this in any sense a vengeance tragedy. How could it be, when it ends with a lamenting Muse and the
ritualistic display of the body of the Thracian king, quite as if he
were another Agamemnon?

The Prologue

The three-headedness of the *Rhesus* plot amounts to a structural
proclamation of some extra- or ultratragic purpose, and in fact the
boundaries of tragedy are crossed in almost every scene. The prologue, with its shouting, its panic-stricken guard, and its understand-
ably cross Hector, can only be paralleled in comedy (cf. Ar. *Ach.* 570)
or in the "Hilferuf" scenes of satyr-drama,[13] and it inaugurates a
senseless bustle which proves to be characteristic of the whole play.[14]
It does not, however, inaugurate the stage action, as a tragic prologue
should, for instead of preparing for the coming of the Thracian who
gives his name to the piece, it focuses all our attention upon Hector.
There is no reference even of the most oblique sort to the absence of
Rhesus or to any need for help. There are no portents, no signs, no
longing for someone's coming, nor is any attention given to supernatural forces or agents interested in the eponymous hero.[15] No one
knows anything about Rhesus at this point in the night, and what
the prologue shows is a camp full of activity and a Hector who believes that the war is already won. He is at the crest of success, and
he wishes for nothing but the dawn of a new day, so that he can
finish the previous day's work by setting fire to the Achaean ships.
All of which means that Rhesus cannot enter this place like a long-
desired Heracles or a decisive Oedipus—not even like a stern Pentheus or a maddened Ajax—for nothing in the situation calls out to
him.

Hector and Aeneas

The first episode begins as a prince-and-counselor scene of a sort that has two conventional functions: it may establish the prince as wise and moderate (a Theseus),[16] or it may prove him to be stubborn and ready for disaster (a Prometheus or a Creon). In this case, however, the encounter discloses a prince whose purposes merely waver in a subtragic and indeed a submilitary way. Hector has been hot for battle in the prologue and when he begins now with an almost Promethean arrogance, he is scolded by Aeneas as having a talent only for battle. Hector feels that Night has stolen his victory from him (56ff.) and he means to defy nature and steal Night's usual prerogatives by mounting an attack in the dark (109). One speech from Aeneas, however, is enough to alter this Titanic resolve and make of Hector an ordinary and cautious human being, and it is just here that we meet the first major breach in the tragic tone of the *Rhesus*.

What are we to think of the swiftness and the extremity of Hector's about-face?[17] The parallels of Theseus in Euripides' *Suppliants* and Eteocles in *Phoenician Women* only serve to emphasize the alarming speed and ease of this change of mind, and once doubt has been cast on the soundness of Hector's judgment, a devilish fact obtrudes itself. This commander has called for a general arming in the prologue (70; cf. 90), and he seems to have followed his own order at once, for Aeneas asks him why he has put on his arms (99).[18] Greaves, breastplate, and shield seem to have stood just within his tent ready to be brought out, and evidently he has begun the awkward process of actually assuming them, a process that he continues in the first moments of Aeneas' questioning. This means that when he gives his most swashbuckling speech ("I shall fall upon them as they retreat and hit them heavily . . ." 100–101), he will be dressed for the part and able to gesture with lance or sword. Unfortunately, however, it also means that when he suddenly becomes prudent, he will be most inappropriately dressed. He will either have to play through the rest of the scene as a dove in hawk's clothing, or else he will have to accompany his reversal of policy with a new stage business of *dis*arming, which will be disastrous to his dignity.

The confusion over Hector's panoply will embarrass the beginning of this episode to some degree (even its nonappearance would make Aeneas' line 99 a patent absurdity), but it is impossible to tell just how much the Trojan prince loses in tragic authority. When Aeneas leaves, the scene is still formally one that gives a positive color to Hector and his actions, for his courage, as it was tempered by the prudence of his friend, has been its overt subject. Daring and caution have combined to bring forth the idea of a spy, and this new plan presumably proves that a moderate but manly *euboulia* now inspires the Trojan forces. If this spy were to appear next as the personification of bold reason, all of Hector's volatility could be dismissed as mere poetic accident, but that of course is not what happens. Instead, it is Dolon who is proposed as the fruit of Hector's wise leadership, and as soon as he takes the center of the stage, the fiction of Trojan military wisdom collapses.

Dolon

Dolon is a nobody. The son of a herald, Eumedes, in the Doloneia (*Il.* 10.315), he has no patronymic here, and he appropriately comes from nowhere. There is no telling how he got on stage; probably he came in with Aeneas and has stayed behind, but at any rate he steps forward now with no introduction, in answer to Hector's call for a volunteer. He is the only figure in surviving tragedy to materialize in this way,[19] and his anomalous eruption into the action is only the start of his unprecedented behavior. First and most strikingly, since he was fixed in tradition as an ugly creature (*Il.* 10.316), Dolon doubtless wears an "ugly" mask,[20] just as a traditionally old character would wear an "old" mask. Next, he begins with excessive brashness (he will "dice" with danger, 155, 184, but he does not admit the possibility of losing his throw)[21] and then, as soon as Hector calls him "patriotic" (158; cf. 151, 154, 194) he contradicts his commander by showing himself to have no interest at all either in cause or in country. What he wants is a reward, and suitably to his class he reduces his mission to a form of physical labor (*ponon*, 157; *ponein* and *ponounta*, 161) for which he demands a wage.[22]

The notion of repayment now takes possession of the stage and produces a sequence unlike anything else in ancient drama as Hector probes, in a kind of guessing game, for the price he must offer to Dolon.[23] It is as if the old Greek priamel of worth had taken to the boards, for the ostensible achievement of the exchange is to display this recruit's hierarchy of values. What is so dear that he would risk his life for it? With Hector's help, Dolon develops his demand after the fashion of a poet making a rhetorical figure, saying that he does not want power (166) or a great marriage (168) and that he has gold enough already (170, 178). Ordinarily this tripartite *praeambulum* would lead on to the assertion of a new sort of value, and Hector hints at this when he asks, "What then do you want, that is within the gift of Troy?" (171). The man seems to be about to ask for health or courage or happiness, and Hector cannot of course bestow any of these. When Dolon says that his reward can wait until the Greeks are defeated, Hector at first assumes that the new value is Vengeance or perhaps Piety, but there is no Greek chieftain Dolon wants to torture, no piece of enemy property he has promised as an offering to a god. The priamel seems to have run down, but at last a final term is produced and after such an introduction it suffers from inevitable comparisons. The cap to such a series ought to be abstract and generally instructive—something like Beauty or Youth or Good Reputation—and consequently Dolon's pair of immortal horses strikes an emphatically false note. On the one hand it is much too specific to be edifying, and on the other it is much too immodest, for this desire betrays a vainglory that is almost irreverent.

It is clear that Hector reacts with a start when Dolon makes his demand (184), and this reminds us that Odysseus, in Book 10, was so struck by Dolon's oafish arrogance in wanting these horses that he broke into a rare battlefield smile (*Il.* 10.400). Here in the play, Dolon presumes to set himself beside Hector, who has coveted the same pair; his presumption, indeed, is even greater than this, for he wants to sit where Achilles has sat, driving the horses that Poseidon gave to Peleus on his wedding day. It is pointedly unkind that Peleus, the handsomest and most virtuous of men, should be named to this notably ugly and treacherous creature, but the poet is insisting on the grotesque quality of this base man's astonishing ambition (186 and 188, reemphasized by the chorus at 240). Just as Hector's talk of patriotism allowed Dolon to display his greed, so the philosophical search for value has permitted him to show his total lack of moderation and self-knowledge.[24] It has also, incidentally, allowed us to find out that even Hector is not motivated exclusively by love of Troy, for he too has been dreaming of a reward. We see him pass a kind of test of *aretē*, as he promises Dolon the very prize that he himself longs for, but unfortunately, by wanting the same thing, he has somehow likened himself to this despicable man. Indeed, a phrase from his own mouth makes him the equal in bestiality of this wolflike creature, for he says that he and Dolon are "rival suitors" for the same pair of steeds (184).

The reward of Dolon is decided, and he has the audacity to praise Hector for his honorable promise (191). When he goes on to gloat over the fact that he will have the finest prize of all the Phrygians because of his "courage," Hector can bear him no longer. The commander evidently makes a gesture of protest or disgust (one that inspires Dolon to accuse him of being envious) and then he turns his back and moves away without a word, while Dolon has the effrontery to call consolations after him.[25] With his chief gone, Dolon at once shows the chorus the exact nature of his "courage," and we understand why he has called it "strength of gut" (a tragic *hapax*, *eusplagchnia*, 192) instead of "strength of soul" (*eupsuchia*).[26] He is not going out to win the divine horses of Peleus as a warrior; he is not even going out as a man, but instead he will perform the exploit that is to make him Achilles' equal, Hector's superior, disguised as an animal! The epic Dolon carried bow and spear, wore a dog-skin cap, and walked upright in a wolf-skin that may have been a cape, but the poet of the *Rhesus* has put his Trojan spy into a full wolf-suit[27] and has made this costume the mark of his depravity, wickedly causing him to say that he will dress himself "appropriately" (202) in the pelt. Of course the spectator does not actually see Dolon wearing this outfit (though Gilbert Murray caught a glimpse of him, crossing the stage in it, while the next choral ode was being sung),[28] but the spy himself urges us to picture him in his disguise, and doubtless his words are accompanied by gestures as he explains how he will "imitate the four-footed walk of the wolf" (211–12). Whether or not he actually drops to the ground to demonstrate, this undignified stance becomes Dolon's insignia, and the chorus insists upon it with a phrase especially invented for the occasion, calling his whole exploit a "four-footed mimicry" (256).[29]

Even in his bestiality, however, Dolon overrates himself, for a wolf is not only a devious outsider, he is also a ferocious animal. Alcaeus in exile, Aegisthus in Argos, and Pindar at court are all proper wolves, dangerous and proud, but Dolon is about to fall blubbering into the arms of the enemy. The tragic unity of place keeps the *Rhesus* poet from staging the beast-man's cowardly surrender (he shows its doublet, the near capture of Odysseus, instead), and he chooses not to dignify the death of such a creature with any kind of report, but he nevertheless urges his audience to remember how the Homeric Dolon squirmed and informed and then died in humiliation, as a traitor should. With his initial emphasis upon the wealth of Dolon's father (170, 178), he brings back the epic lines in which this sobbing spy promised that his father would pay the Greeks well to spare him (*Il.* 10.379–80), and as the staged scene closes he makes Dolon himself remind us of his coming fate. Though it is completely contradictory to his mission, the foolish spy confides to the chorus that he means to do some killing while he is inside the Achaean camp, and the first name he mentions is the all too relevant one of Odysseus. Worse yet, he boasts that he will cut off Odysseus' head, thus forcing even the dullest spectator to remember the grotesque line from the Doloneia in which Dolon's severed head continues to beg Odysseus to spare him, craven even after death (*Il.* 10.457).[30]

The irony of this last speech of Dolon's is distinctly comic because the man is base and the fate that he misknows but we foresee promises to be appropriate for him and crudely enjoyable for us. Dolon will get what is coming to him, and so he is akin to all the upstart braggarts who are tortured and humiliated in folktales. He is also like Cyclops and Syleus and other rude creatures that satyr-drama punishes, but he has nothing in common with a Pentheus or an Oedipus. Of course he is not funny, any more than a pig at a pig-sticking is funny, but he arouses the nontragic emotions of scorn and satisfaction, and in this way he confounds any spectator who has come to the play expecting to admire men better than himself. What is more, Dolon's essentially comic quality works backward into the scenes that preceded his entrance, for if *this* is the product of Hector's courage and Aeneas' counsel, then those men and their virtues must also have had something inappropriate and exaggerated about them. Dolon seems to prove that we were right to wonder about Hector's variability and Aeneas' self-righteousness, and the poet sees to it that the chorus that follows his exit shall work a subtle confirmation of our worst suspicions.

The watchmen unwittingly display the fullest measure of Dolon's bestiality by mentioning it in immediate conjunction with the manly and glorious heroes whom he would rival, Peleus and Achilles. They also, without realizing it, give the coup de grace to any talk of

Dolon's courage by locating this virtue in the Trojan spear that the four-footed spy so conspicuously will *not* carry (250–51). Their enthusiasm leads them to exaggerate the ignoble (and nonexistent) ferocity of this man who is less than a man as they cry out, "Which of the Greeks might he not kill in his bed, this crawling assassin who creeps four-footed on the ground and imitates a beast?" (253ff.). They treat themselves to a delicious vision of the bloody corpses of kings slain by such unheroic trickery, and in so doing they prepare for the bathetic collapse of Dolon's despicable claim to importance. In actuality this would-be murderer of Odysseus, Menelaus, and Agamemnon will not kill anyone. Instead, he will be killed and furthermore his death will be of no more significance than his silly boasts have been. He will fail the army and he will also in a sense fail the play, for the collapse of his mission will have no consequence and no influence whatsoever upon the major event to come, the destruction of Rhesus.

Dolon has taken the center of the stage, but Dolon is a meaningless figure and he has been made so by the poet's express contrivance, for the man who composed this play robbed his spy of the single crucial function that he had had in the Homeric tale. There Dolon informed Odysseus and Diomedes of the coming of Rhesus and so prepared for the killing of that prince, but here the spy cannot even act as informer, because the arrival of the foreigner has not yet been announced. On this stage all Dolon can do is go forth in his pelts to fawn upon the enemy and die; he plays the traitor, it is true, but all he has to give up are the position of his commander's tent and the Trojan password for the night. His information destroys no one; rather, in good comic fashion, it rescues, for it is the betrayed password that finally saves Odysseus' skin. In sum, then, Dolon is a greedy braggart, according to his own words; he is a beastly fellow, judging by his chosen costume; he is a cowardly imitator of ferocity, if we listen to the unintended information of the choral song; and finally, he is a figure of futility, when tested by the pragmatic achievements of the action. The Trojan watch prays for his success, calling upon a barbarian Apollo who is named as Thymbraean and Lycian; he is their particular divinity, but evidently even this Trojan "wolf god" cannot tolerate a Dolon, for the man disappears ignominiously.[31]

The machine of the *Rhesus* plot will run without a Dolon and yet the poet has built his entire complex first episode as a display case for this no longer functioning part—why? If he were interested merely in the sensational, he would surely have shown us the animal imitation, just as he would have favored us with a grisly account of Dolon's death. There must have been a reason of another sort, and anyone who judges the poet's intention by what he has wrought will say that Dolon has been brought forward to erode our sense of the value and the magnificence of the Trojan cause. Verbal confirmation of such a function is to be found in the watchmen's song, for when the men announce that Dolon represents the true "temper" (245; cf. 499, where the same word is used negatively of the sly temper of Odysseus)[32] of the Phrygian race, when they congratulate themselves upon belonging to that bold group, what are their words but a general confession of "Dolonism" from the mouths of the Trojan host? Their temper is Dolon's temper, and Dolon's is mean, despicable, brutish, and wholly ineffectual.[33]

Rhesus

The Trojan temper is further described in the next episode, and curiously enough its new representative is yet another fellow dressed in skins—a shepherd who has come down from the mountains with news for the commander. The scene begins with a bit of comic business as Hector mistakes the purpose of the man, thinks him a bother, and orders him away, much as Alcmena does with the servant at the opening of a semicomic scene in *Children of Heracles* (648ff.). When the rustic is finally allowed to begin his speech, it turns out to be a flamboyant description of Rhesus' arrival, but in the course of the message we learn that Trojan countryfolk are as much given to panic as Trojan soldiers are (*Rhes.* 286), and also that they are ready to worship a stranger as a god, if that stranger is adequately covered with gold (302–3). The essential function of the scene, however, is to instruct the audience in how it is to receive the character who is about to enter, and so it is important to observe exactly what is said about the prince who will next appear. Rhesus' first identification is as a Thracian, his next as the son of the River Strymon (279), and for a moment this prince seems to be proposed as far more heroic than his epic original, for his father, in the *Iliad*, was a very ordinary mortal (Eioneus, or Shoreman, 10.435; it is a stock name, cf. *Il.* 7.11). The next point, however, works to undermine this grandeur with an effect that is almost bathetic, for we are told that this wonderful hero has come the wrong way, by the mountains and at night instead of by the plain and in the day (282–83). We are also reminded that he is literally a barbarian, one who does not speak Greek (294), and this was a quality that Hellenes always found just a little funny (cf. e.g., Ar. *Thesm.* 1001ff.). Nevertheless he has appeared in a golden chariot, dressed in gold-dight armor and driving snow-white horses; he is much like a god (302), and his army is beyond description and beyond counting—"many, many, many . . ." (311–12).

The vision is dazzling, in spite of the misjudged arrival, but it is immediately tarnished by a huffy Hector, who accuses the Thracian of coming to the banquet after staying away from the fatigues of the hunt (325–26). He, Hector, is Troy's savior and the city needs no other. All the same, having concisely called Rhesus a greedy coward, and having been approved in this judgment by the chorus (327), Hector hears three lines from the rustic messenger and three from the watch and then turns himself about. Two minutes ago he meant to refuse to recognize the Thracian in any way; now he announces that "this golden-armed Rhesus will be the ally of the land" (340–41) and at this the chorus forgets all recent history, all honor to Hector and his leadership, and indeed all moderation, and breaks into a fulsome hymn which by its own label is excessive (343). They greet the arriving Rhesus as worshipers might greet a god in epiphany ("You come, o child of river, you come . . . !" 346–47); they mention his miraculous birth and its place (351ff.), they give him special cult names (calling him Zeus Phanaios and Zeus Eleutherios, 355 and 359), and they mention his chief attribute, his horses (356). As *dunamis* he has the power to defeat Achaeans and bring them death, and the watchmen imagine him in particular in the act of slaying Achilles (370ff.). In the end he is invoked directly as if this were a cletic hymn ("Come! Appear!" 370), and then the Trojan soldiers artfully turn to an apostrophe of Thrace, his motherland, before they finish by calling this foreign king "Ares" (386) and a god who will resurrect a fallen Troy.

A hint of blasphemous praise can set a tragic hero up for a magnificent downfall, but a full-blown hymn must necessarily turn its object into a parody of an Oedipus, a Xerxes, or an Agamemnon. The mere surface of this present song is outrageous [34] because it addresses a mortal as if he were a god, and it proceeds with such a mad confusion of ritual motifs that even the opening placation of Adrasteia seems to be another example of excess. No Olympian could feel envious of such tasteless praise as this, especially as two negative tendencies can be perceived just below the laudatory surface of the "hymn." One of these identifies Rhesus as barbarously Thracian, the other makes him almost comical, and both are extremely important to the final tone of this play.

The final phrases of the watchmen's "hymn" have an oxymoronic quality, for they greet Rhesus as an Ares who has come to resuscitate Troy. The notion of Ares the life-giver is unnatural in a Hellenic context, but it reflects two of the commonest Greek convictions about the Thracians, because those people were thought of as frenzied warriors, but also as believers in immortality (Hdt. 5.3–11). Greeks associated Ares with the Thracian Enyalios and Enyo, and when Herodotus visited the north he naturally recognized the chief of the gods of Thrace as the same Ares, naming him even before Dionysus (5.7).[35] On the other hand, Thrace was also the homeland of the strange figure of Zamolxis, and of men who claimed to be able to escape death (Hdt. 4.92).[36] Orpheus had come from there, and in the fifth and fourth centuries one frequently met with magicians from the north who had spells for cheating the grave (Pl. *Chrm.* 157a, 176b; cf. Eur. *Alc.* 966; Ar. *Ran.* 1034). Because of these double associations a Thracian Ares who resurrects is an exotic but not an inconceivable figure, especially when we remember that these are stage Phrygians who sing of him. Nevertheless, a certain sense of anachronism creeps in when the resurrected Troy is envisaged as a paradise of drinking and masculine love (360ff.), for it is impossible not to think of Plato's complaint that the Thracian orphics made of the afterlife nothing but drink and debauchery (*Resp.* 2.363c–d).[37]

When the chorus names Rhesus' river-god father (in emphatic enjambment at the opening of an antistrophe, 351),[38] they touch again upon esoteric matters, because in Thracian religion there was a particular interest in the cults of such gods, with Strymon first among them.[39] Rhesus himself seems to have been a river-god in certain localities, for there were rivers with his name in the Troad and in Bithynia, and it was on the banks of one of them that he died, according to one ancient tradition.[40] Another bit of Thracian local color is supplied by the heavy identification of Rhesus with his animal double, for traces of animal worship were still to be found in the

Thrace of classical times. Sabazios, the Thracian Dionysus, was tended by priests who dressed themselves in fox-skins,[41] and Zamolxis was thought of as wearing the bear-skin of his animal form.[42] Of course the horses of Rhesus belong to the epic tradition,[43] but the Trojan watchmen manage, as they sing, to subsume the rider into his steeds in a barbarian way, calling him a "Strymonian colt" (387, cf. 381), and singing of the clangor of his harness bells. Again they touch upon a Thracian actuality, for Herodotus reports that white horses were sacrificed at Pangaion, where Rhesus had his sanctuary (7.113).

In actual northern cult Rhesus was worshiped as a form of the mysterious Hero, or Zagreus, to whom animals offered themselves willingly, and one of whose epithets was *sotēr*. He was usually pictured in St. George fashion, on his horse and using his long diagonal lance to kill a bestial enemy on the ground,[44] but he was also in Anatolia identified with the sun.[45] The theatrical battlefield scene makes it impossible for our Rhesus to come as a hunter (though Hector makes bitter reference to hunting, in connection with him, 325–26), but the chorus does suggest his heliacal aspect by calling him *phanaios* (355) and by making an icon for him in which he attacks Achilles by sending a beam from his golden shield into the enemy's eyes. (Their phrase is so curious that it must have been meant to attract attention: "holding thy shield aslant, cast its golden gleam into the eye of the Peliad," 370–72.)[46] And finally it should be noted that the first word of their hymn announces its Thracian flavor. About to sing what they know is an improper panegyric, the men of the watch ask that their song should escape the usual punishment of such exaggeration, and this allows them to address Adrasteia, a goddess whose northern cult was known.[47]

The potential blasphemy of the hymn to Rhesus is thus excused by its patent barbarism, but it is also neutralized by a streak of sheer foolishness, as are the blasphemies of comedy and the satyr-plays. It may be merely Thracian to call a god-king a horse because that is his attribute, but it is downright Aristophanic to chant: "Oh hear the jangling boasts sung by the bells of his harness-clasps!" (384–85). A hero in horse-trappings is absurd, and the poet has fixed this absurdity with a sevenfold repetition of the kappa sound: *klue kai kompous kōdōnokrotous / para porpakōn keladountas.* As if that were not enough, he has also invented a showy pseudo-Aeschylean compound (*kōdōnokrotous*) that Aristophanes found funny enough to echo when he was describing the martial excesses of Lamachus (*kompolakuthos, Ach.* 589).[48] The comic poet, in fact, evidently admired the ode to Rhesus, for he held its exaggerations up to further ridicule by making the chorus of the *Acharnians* call upon their general with a prayer-parody all too much like this one. (Gorgon on his shield: *Ach.* 574, 567, 964–65, 1095, 1124, 1131, 1181, see *Rhes.* 306; likeness to Zeus: *Ach.* 566, see *Rhes.* 355, 359; address as friend: *Ach.* 568, see *Rhes.* 367; call for epiphany: *Ach.* 567, see *Rhes.* 370.) Hector has already charged Rhesus with being a greedy shirker, and the choral hymn now suggests that he is a prancing, pretentious creature as well—all pomp and noise.

The latent ridicule of the phrase about Rhesus' boastful trappings invites the listener to smile at other parts of the song as well, and the passage about the hero's conception seems almost to ask for a titter. A proper prayer mentions the birthplace of its divinity, sometimes even the "mixing" of the god's divine parents, but a prayer does not usually dwell upon this engendering. In their prayer to Rhesus, however, the Trojan watchmen forget all reticence and sing:

> You're come, o river's child,
> you're come! You arrive at this camp
> most welcome, now your Pierian mother
> sends you at long last,
> she and the well-bridged river
>
> Strymon, who in a fluid guise
> once swirled through the undiluted womb
> of that melodic Muse,
> engendering your youth! (346–54)

When Rhesus enters[49] after such an introduction, his mere mortality is bound to create a bathetic drop, and this particular Rhesus has been made so as to intensify the anticlimactic effect, for he is built on a subtragic scale. His first words contain an admission of tardiness ("at this late date," 389),[50] and apologizing and boasting are the only two kinds of expression that the following scene allows him. Hector at once makes him as small as possible by reminding him of a time when he was only a "tiny tyrant" (406) and by taking all the credit for Rhesus' present strength upon himself. He treats this "Ares," this "Zeus in Epiphany," as a vassal who is late with his dues, and as a soldier who does not understand military honor. How can he, one bound by kinship and gratitude, dare to come late and unscathed among allies who have suffered much over many years, even though they had no such ties as his to the house of Priam (413ff.)? Exploiting the stereotype of the drunken Thracian, he accuses Rhesus of having passed his time in uninterrupted drinking and couching (418–19), and we are again reminded of the *Acharnians*, where Dicaeopolis charges Lamachus with having stayed away in Thrace where pay was high and danger far away (*Ach.* 595ff.). The contemporary audience, however, had another point of reference, for romantic stories were told about Rhesus, and in one of these the reason for his absence from Troy was that he was lingering with Arganthonē, the Amazon queen of Ceos, hunting and feasting with her (Parth. *Amat. Narr.* 36).[51]

In his response Rhesus makes excuses, something no tragic hero should do,[52] but he manages to convict himself of greed and vainglory without ever meeting the charges made against him. He was held up, he says, by a Scythian war and by the need to organize conquered territory into a taxpaying realm (435), all of which naturally took time.[53] He tries to claim that he has suffered as much, in his short march down to Troy, as the Phrygians have in the long years of war (having been chilly in frosts and cold winds), but he sensibly abandons this point and turns to the offensive. So he is late! How can worthless armies of Trojans and allies, men who have accomplished nothing in all these years, dare to complain about one who has come to do the job for them in a single day (443ff.)? Even the enthusiastic chorus recognizes the presumption of these words (455–57), but they are convinced for themselves and merely pray that Zeus shall not take offense.

Like Dolon,[54] Rhesus boasts that he will not only fulfill his duty but go much further, for he will not merely win the war, he will kill every man in the opposing host (449) and then invade the Greek mainland and punish the enemy by conquering all of Hellas (468–73). In the same way does Lamachus, when Dicaeopolis accuses him of cowardice, answer with a threat of total war against the Peloponnese (*Ach.* 620–22). What this golden man wants most is visibility, and he dreams of winning the war by single combat,[55] though this is contradictory to his other notion of slaughtering every Achaean,[56] and this inconsistency is typical of his mind. War is not war for him,

but a means of self-aggrandizement: he believes in story-book cam-
paigns and fairy-tale cruelties (his fantasy of spitting the live body of
Odysseus is worthy of the *Arabian Nights*), but he is so ignorant of
the actual battle that he does not even know that Achilles has withdrawn (491). He cries "On to Greece!" and the seasoned Hector has
to remind him that they must first face an actual enemy, tomorrow
on the field before Troy (485; cf. 518).

The prodigiously fulminating Rhesus is soon led away to bed,
and he goes off, as Dolon did, delighting in the ironic fancy of a
bloodied Odysseus (513ff.). His one scene is now finished and his
portrait is complete. The charge of drunkenness and the further reference to Adrasteia, the only divinity that he recognizes (468), have
made him more than ever the caricature of a Thracian. And meanwhile the mixture of apology and grandiloquence in his manner has
rendered him ridiculous and contemptible, just as the plan to invade
Greece turns him into a swaggering pseudo-Xerxes.[57] He is over-
stuffed and offensive, but it is hard to feel that this man is in any
tragic sense ready to be killed, for he has been good so far only for
words (his name puns perfectly with *rhēsis*)[58] and in this, his only
appearance, he has neither done anything himself, nor influenced
anyone else's action. Hector has not been won over, for he had decided to receive the Thracian before he appeared. Nor have the two
leaders quarreled; nor has Rhesus stepped into a trap; nor has he
been tempted into any kind of risk. In fact, the two princes have not
even decided the one question that was before them—the position of
the Thracian forces on the morrow—and we realize with dismay
that the "many . . . many . . . many" newly arrived chariots and men
will not know where to go, when the trumpet sounds at dawn.
Rhesus thus leaves the stage and heads toward his death without
ever having, in any dramaturgical sense, lived.

The offensive self-importance of this useless and tardy ally has
been given a particular resonance by the twice-repeated use of phrases
about victory in "one single day" (443, 455–57). These words remind
us that the semidivine Rhesus of the cletic hymn—the hero whose
parents were Strymon and a Muse—ought to have a day in the field.
He had already appeared in a poem of Pindar's,[59] probably also in
some pre-epic tale that made the Thracian warrior far greater than he
is in the Doloneia,[60] and he had a traditional *aristeia*. The Pindaric
Rhesus fought for one day and in that short time did so much dam-

age that Hera and Athena became concerned for the survival of the Greeks, and consequently inspired Diomedes (or his men) to kill him. There were, in other words, two poetical Rhesuses: the Pindaric semidivine being who performed brilliantly, and the Homeric Thracian who was killed almost accidentally before he could do anything at all. Anyone could see that the first of these was a potential tragic hero and the second was not, yet the *Rhesus* poet chose the second, and having done so, he emphasized the inadequacy of his weaker principal by giving him the other's parentage and also by referring to the "single fateful day" that could reasonably belong only to the creature he was not.

If the poet had granted the lyric single day of action to his Rhesus, he could have dressed his fate in a full and classic solemnity. After such a day the Thracian would have been loved by the entire Trojan host, and the *pothos* of a nation would have followed him, when the Muse bore his body away. And after such a day, too, it would have been clear that this hero had posed a real threat to the Olympian plans for the outcome of the war. As it is, however, the day of glory is signally missing from the *Rhesus*, and with it all of these tragic effects. Not long before he leaves the stage the Thracian makes a plain allusion to this great loss by claiming that "for me, the light of a single sun will suffice, as I storm the walls, fall upon the ships and kill the Achaean host" (446–48). His bravado moves the chorus to an eager interruption, and they cut in with a short strophe that ends, "If only I could see that day, lord, when your spear and your much-bloodied hand bring them punishment!" (464–66.)[61] But they will not see that day because Rhesus will never see another; it is only what-might-have-been, as far as the play is concerned, and the emptiness of the watchmen's hope is given structural expression, for their little strophe is not echoed in the ode that follows Rhesus' exit. It is left unanswered here—a dangling bit of melody that gives an air of incompletion to the central portion of the play—and its responding stanza is heard only when the man who was to have been responsible for so many deaths is lying dead himself. He has no deeds ahead of him and no deeds in his past, and in this staged present all he has done is talk, sleep, and then die between a strophe and its antistrophe. As the messenger soon says of all the Thracians: "They came. They died" (841).

The Messenger

Rhesus has his admirers among critics, and to them his excess and bluster are only the legitimate characteristics of the barbarian, while his failure to perform a single deed is precisely the source of his tragedy. He is the crude man of promise who is killed prematurely, before he has had time to prove himself, and who therefore dies the more poignantly.[62] The idea that stillborn actions may be tragic is more modern than antique, but as *Rhesus* is manifestly not an ordinary classic tragedy, it would be a mistake to assume that the mere absence of deeds proves that this principal is offered as a nontragic or paratragic figure. Ultimately, his tragic quality will derive from his *pathos*, and so we must move on to consider the nature of Rhesus' death before drawing any conclusions. To begin with, there are certain formal details that seem to minimize any possible tragic effect, for this is not a kin-death or one based on misunderstanding, and so it can provide no recognition or peripeteia. It has, moreover, no passion in it, because the reasons for the killing are unemotional. Nevertheless this death does represent the overturn of magnificence and it is reported in a messenger speech, quite as if it were the pathos of an unquestionable tragedy, and therefore we must search that speech for signs of the poet's attitude toward his dubious principal. In it the dramatist might still give his victim some final posture of bravery; he might dress the event in some ennobling suggestions of heavenly design—one thinks, for example, of the tragic effects that are contrived in the report of Neoptolemus' death, in Euripides' *Andromache*.

The epic account had provided an ideal tragic messenger in the person of Hippocoon, a kinsman and perhaps a lover of Rhesus (*Il.* 10.518ff.) whom Apollo roused as soon as the slaughter was done. With this nobleman to report and lament the death of his chief, a poet could easily have magnified the dead Thracian and made him sympathetic, if not glorious, but the *Rhesus* poet refused to introduce Hippocoon. He chose instead to innovate, and into a scene that was already disorderly he brought a moaning, singing, barbarian groom to tell about Rhesus' last moments on earth.[63] The man is undignified and furthermore he is unqualified, for he was not even a witness to the killing; consequently it should not be surprising that he tells the audience nothing at all about how Rhesus died. The mayhem of the Doloneia has presumably occurred just offstage (though not behind the *skēnē*, as it would in vengeance tragedy), but we are given no description of it because the man who comes on as messenger was, like all the other Thracians, fast asleep when the crime was committed! Consequently there can be no last words from Rhesus, no ironic recognition of his assassins, no ultimate *aristeia* of resistance—there is not even a finite, indicative statement in which the end of his life is recorded. The charioteer mentions some incidental groans of dying men, he thinks he felt a shower of blood from his master's corpse,[64] but his business was with horses, not princes, and so this crucial matter is hardly mentioned.

The *Rhesus* messenger fails his tragic function, which is to bring to the play the solemn chill of experienced mortality. Indeed, he degrades the suffering that might have been at least fearsome, for, having himself received a random cut, he howls like Philoctetes in his seizures or Heracles wearing the robe of pain. He is highly excited over his own fate, and there is really only one fact about Rhesus that he manages to make clear. That one, however, is damning, for the man reports that Rhesus did what no responsible commander would do; he went to sleep and let his army sleep around him, without thinking to post sentries or guards of any sort. In coarse military terms, he has earned his end, having let himself be taken by surprise. His death thus marks him not only as a poor general but also as a poor tragic hero, for his overturn has come simply as a result of unsoldierly improvidence. The great Thracian chieftain has fallen, as the charioteer says, senselessly and without glory (*aboulōs kakleōs*, 761), and one might add that he has died without poetry as well, for the phrase is distinctly prosy.

It is Odysseus' theft, not Diomedes' act of killing, that interests this groom, and because of his occupational prejudice horse stealing becomes the central event of this play.[65] Even the theft, however, is not given a direct description, for the poet has borrowed a motif from Book 10 of the *Iliad*, the victim's nightmare, and has given it to his charioteer, making him the one messenger in surviving tragedy who comes on, not to report observed facts, but to recount a dream. He did not see the murder and he does not describe the taking of the horses; instead, he tells us how, in his sleep, he seemed to see two wolves (783) who attacked the Thracian team and then drove it away.[66] By the time he awoke, Rhesus was dead and the animals were gone, and so all this messenger actually brings to his listeners is his own vision of silvery steeds that flew away in the night. The image is poetic, but nevertheless the speech effects the same process of animalization already observed in the Dolon scene and the Rhesus hymn. Dolon was reduced to a wolf; Rhesus was identified with a horse; now Rhesus' death becomes a mere incident in the disappearance of these two prime animals.

This, then, is no ordinary messenger.[67] He minimizes the principal and his pathos, suggesting that the loss of a pair of horses is more important than the loss of princely life. He reports his own experiences instead of those of the victim, and he wails over his own minor cuts as only the mighty may wail, in Attic tragedy, over major disasters. And as if that were not enough, he caps all of these anomalies by a direct outrage upon theatrical convention, for when his "message" is done and he ought to make his exit, this man stays on and attempts a dramatic role. He is convinced that only Hector could have killed his master and so he, a Thracian groom, turns on the Trojan commander with insults, calling him *barbaros* (832) and suggesting that even Paris has a nicer sense of hospitality than a man who would murder an ally (841–42).[68] His words have no practical effect upon the situation, but his ugly suspicion leaves a slight scar upon the final scenes. It also puts the last touch on the play's presentation of its principal, for in the end this slur on Hector's honor is the single sign that Rhesus leaves behind. His coming, and his dying, have marked the Trojan cause only with this bit of passing unpleasantness.[69]

The Intrigue

Clearly there are nontragic, antitragic, even comic elements in the treatment the *Rhesus* gives its hero, but the problem to be solved is whether or not these have been employed with purposeful consistency by the dramatist. The prince himself has been made into a caricature of a Thracian and cheapened with bragging speeches, but he has not been shown as positively base. His pathos has likewise been robbed of both awe and magnificence by the extraordinary messenger, but the event has not in any obvious sense been made humorous. There are moments in which the charioteer must cause a smile, as when, in his heavy Thracian accent, he says, "I don't know what these things are, these 'odysses' you keep talking about" (*ouk oida tous sous hous legeis Odusseas*, 866), playing the boob and sharply reminding us of the Phrygian eunuch in *Orestes* who said, in much the same situation, "I don't know anything about this gorgon-head you mention" (Eur. *Or.* 1521). Nevertheless, he does not openly declare himself as hoping to get a laugh, and so, if this were all, we would still wonder whether the *Rhesus* were ridiculous as a result of carelessness or by the poet's care.

This, however, is not all. The wounded charioteer draws our attention to yet another anomaly by casting an unflattering light upon the chorus of this play. He argues that the killing of Rhesus must have been an inside job because no enemy could have passed into the camp and out again through the Trojan guards. If any enemy had even tried such a thing, some members of the watch would now lie injured from having resisted him. The charioteer's line of thought is perfectly reasonable, and it is wrong only because the Trojan guard— the chorus—behaves throughout with treasonable idiocy. Among the first words of the play are Hector's angry "Why have you left your posts?" (17–18) but these irresponsible men stay on. They never go back to those posts, and in the middle of the play they all drift sleepily off in search of their relief,[70] leaving the camp completely unprotected. Their unsoldierly behavior is shocking, and it is marked as an anomaly by its structural result, an empty stage (564). This phenomenon can of course be paralleled in a few other tragedies, but only here does the withdrawal of a chorus amount to aiding the enemy, and only here is it motivated by sheer fecklessness. The choral departure thus threatens the physical safety of the camp, and also the dramatic seriousness of the entire *praxis*; consequently we must ask what it was the poet gained by making deserters of the Trojan guard.

In a mechanical sense, the chorus goes off in order that the killers of Rhesus may enter. There is, however, no reason why these assassins had to be seen as they made their way toward the hero's tent, and consequently the withdrawal of the chorus shows us first of all just how much the poet wants to bring his Greeks onto the stage. Indeed, once rid of the guard, he does much more, for he mounts a self-contained play-within-the-play, just for Odysseus and Diomedes.[71] This passage of 158 lines extends from 565 to 723, breaking the Trojan sequence just beyond its halfway point, and it opens with a reverse-parodos[72] sung by a chorus that marches in the wrong direction. In this ode the sounds of dawn and the happy suggestion of spring cross with an image of a lamenting nightingale to make a terse emblem for the crossing of comedy with tragedy. The scale is just right to introduce an inner playlet, and an elegant reference to lines from elder poets (554–56; cf. Pind. *Pyth.* 9.23 and Bacchyl. *Pa.* 4.77) lends an air of conscious, playful grace. A sense that something new and perhaps joyful is about to begin is thus created, and it is enhanced when the chorus actually disappears, for events that occur on an unwitnessed stage are no longer certified as public and solemn matters. Such unsanctioned episodes can even be silly or shameful, as Menelaus' arrival in Egypt proves (Eur. *Hel.* 386), and the *Rhesus* poet exploits this opportunity for levity by making a change, precisely here, in his traditional tale.

In the Doloneia, Odysseus and Diomedes came, instructed by Dolon, with the intention of killing Rhesus, but in this staged version they know nothing of the golden Thracian prince. They are not, at this point, the agents of destruction for that hero; their purpose is a wholly different one, one that will be frustrated, and the nontragic hollowness of their intention is made plain in physical action that could be transferred to any comic stage. In spite of the watchmen's premonition of dawn, the night seems to become much darker than before because there can be no torches now, and the two spies feel their way about, trembling with fear (*phobos*, 569, is one of their first words). The killers of the Doloneia were matter-of-fact and effective, the sort that makes use of darkness as an advantage (*Il.* 10.251), but these two are baffled by the night, obstructed by error, and soon acquainted with failure and panic. When they find that they have attacked an empty tent, their "plan of action" becomes a shameful (589) plan to run away.[73]

By bringing his assassins on in this benighted way the poet achieves a number of effects. He makes his Greeks act out their own ignorance and ineffectiveness as they discover the absence of their intended victim, while he yet shows what Dolon's treason might have led to. At the same time he prepares for a comic reversal, since he is now able to change this initial despair and failure into the joy of a final success. In passing, he also erases what would otherwise have been too strong a resemblance between these men and the efficient principals of vengeance drama, while he also keeps their action from being a serious tribute to Rhesus' reputation. All this the poet accomplishes by making fools of his assassins, but there is in addition a final effect that is the most significant of all, for by this same comic means he saddles his interfering Athena with the entire responsibility of the new plan that will now be carried out. She becomes the author of the killing of Rhesus and the theft of the silvery horses. In the Doloneia, the goddess merely heard the prayers of the Greeks (*Il.* 10.295ff.) and lent them strength when they needed it (10.366 and 482; cf. 10.275–76, where she is merely the resolution of problems caused by darkness), but here she comes in person to design every detail of the Greek attack. She claims Odysseus and Diomedes as her agents, forbids them to look further for Hector, and tells them to go instead against Rhesus; he must be killed, for if he survives this night, no Greek will be able to resist him and he will take the Argive ships (600ff.).[74] The goddess insists and she gives the assassins a token—the wonderful pale horses—by which they can recognize the place where the Thracian sleeps.[75] In this way she herself becomes the supernatural agent of death for the barbarian king.

In her interference with the physical action, Athena at first seems to be an extraordinary but not an unparalleled tragic divinity. One thinks of the Iris who gave the action of the *Heracles* a mad new turn, or of the Athena who put an end to that same madness,[76] but there is very little time for comparisons, for Athena soon begins to behave as no other deity has done in preserved Attic tragedy. From her superior position (627; if the *skēnē* represents Hector's tent she must be in the *mēchanē*) she perceives a threat to her expedition in the form of a none-too-bright Paris, come to tell Hector that the camp is in confusion.[77] Before this apprehensive young man can reach the playing area Athena rushes her Greeks off by the opposite parodos, toward the Thracian camp; then she turns, to take care of the inconvenient intruder herself. His coming has been unmotivated, and it will be without consequence; it is also untragical, because it asks only for a little frisson of excitement at the melodramatic notion that the spies might be discovered. From the point of view of the *praxis* it is a useless event, necessary neither to fiction nor structure, for the need to have someone on stage while the killings were going on would be more naturally met by bringing the chorus back a few minutes sooner. All of which makes it perfectly clear that Paris has arrived now because the poet wants to display his goddess in the act of saving her Greeks. And an "act" it certainly is, as the gruff and martial Athena dazzles poor Paris with a brief, bewitching impersonation of the goddess of love.

Suppose we give the stage a moment's thought. Athena is pretending to be Aphrodite, and one's first comparative vision is of Dionysus pretending to be Heracles in the *Frogs*, with a bit of saffron skirt hanging out from under his lion's skin. Along these lines, Gilbert Murray wanted Athena to pull a flower and a dove from some pocket in her cuirass and flaunt them as Aphrodite's attributes,[78] but in theory at least the transformation should not depend upon costume at all, for Athena is invisible to everyone on stage. Probably the player who took the goddess' part did not deny himself a few Aphrodisiac stances for the amusement of the audience, but officially the deception of Paris will have to be strictly vocal. It will depend, as Athena herself says, upon "rotten words" (*sathroi logoi*, 639), using a phrase that describes corrupt speech at *Hecuba* 1190.[79]

Because her means are so limited, they will necessarily be exaggerated, as the goddess changes her voice from its normal mode and delivers her speeches to Paris in an affected version of the Cyprian's traditional honeyed tones and beguiling chatter (cf. *Il.* 14.216–17). Something warmer and more feminine, something almost cooing, will be needed to fool this devotee of Aphrodite's, and whatever Athena's vocal trick is, it manifestly works. She is here, this false Aphrodite says, because she has brought her creature Rhesus (the phrase casts a new light on the Thracian) to aid the Trojan cause, and there is no need for alarm. She lies outright, saying that nothing new has occurred since the guest withdrew (661), and Paris marks his fatuous good faith with a play on her assumed name (*su toi me peitheis*, 663).[80] He is content, but in closing Athena gives a final show of virtuosity just for the pleasure of it. She makes Paris a promise full of irony—"You in particular will learn how much I favor you," she murmurs in the voice of the Cyprian (667)—and then she bawls out the very next line in a full resumption of her true tone, shouting like a top sergeant to the offstage Greeks: "Hey there, you overeager killers—Laertiades!—put your swords away!" (668–69).

A goddess who defends her friends as they harm her enemies is potentially a serious figure, and most critics have tried to take this performance by Athena as a dignified tragic event. The scene is compared to the fooling of Ajax in the Sophoclean play,[81] but the parallel is inoperative because the determining feature of disguise is absent there: Athena can remain herself, because her dupe is mad. She can also evoke a terrified awe from her audience there, because her victim is a great man. Paris, on the contrary, is sane and in no way great, and consequently other critics urge us to respond with tragic emotion, not to him, but to the display of divine "cruelty" that Athena makes.[82] This, however, proves to be impossible, for we see Paris make his exit, feeling petted and secure, and we know that he is not going toward any immediate pain. True, his beguilement occurs simultaneously with the killing of Rhesus, but the result of this timing is not to make the fooling of Paris sinister, but rather to make the killing of the other almost a burlesque—a quick and easy job done during a divine masquerade.

The Athena of this inner playlet does not act in a solemn and godlike fashion, for her means are beneath her. The Athena of *Heracles* tossed an enormous boulder; the Dionysus of the *Bacchae* made the palace tremble; the Poseidon of *Iphigenia among the Taurians* sent an enormous wave against the shores of the Taurians—comparisons such as these show that Athena's trick in the *Rhesus* is petty both in scale and in technique. There is nothing cosmic or even magniloquent here; rather, the goddess uses the same everyday methods that a mortal might have found, speaking in an assumed voice just as village pranksters had done since the invention of speech. Even by the lax standards of epic her trick is small and low, for there, though gods may disguise themselves in order to fool mortals, they never take over one another's voices or forms. The only strong classical parallel to Athena's performance comes from the satyr-play *Cyclops*, when Silenus pretends to be Ganymede (585ff.) and, somewhat like Athena here at Troy, seduces the enemy.[83] As a proper tragic divinity, the *Rhesus* Athena might have transformed nature or herself by a miracle; she might have sent dreams or madness; she might have taken a mortal shape, or she might have appeared blindingly in her own, but she could not have descended to this base mimicry of a sister god.[84]

And mimicry is base, as the *Rhesus* itself has already shown with Dolon and his "four-footed miming" (*mimos tetrapous*, 256). Moreover, Athena has been put into physical contact with Dolon's beastly trick, for the poet, by another innovation, had brought her agent Odysseus into this inner action dressed up as Dolon dressed up as a wolf.[85] His costuming is made clear in a bit of dialogue worthy of Aristophanes, for when, before Athena's coming, Diomedes and Odysseus decide to creep away, Diomedes suggests that it will be shameful to return having done nothing. To this, Odysseus answers sharply, "What do you mean, nothing? Didn't we kill that ship-spy Dolon and capture this very outfit?" (591–93). As he speaks, he must gesture toward his own gear, thus informing us who are merely readers that he wears the wolf-suit throughout the episode.

Athena uses someone else's voice, her agent wears someone else's clothes, and when he reappears (after Athena's "turn") Odysseus' actions live up to his disguise.[86] The action in this brief passage (674–721) is all-out farce and there are questions about its staging that cannot be answered,[87] in part because the poet, creating nonsense, really did not care about verisimilitude. The essentials, however, are perfectly clear, for this is a scene of scuffle in which the assassins of Rhesus are captured and then let go again. Athena has shouted to her men, "What are you waiting for, with the enemy coming down like a thunderbolt? Save yourselves!" (673–74) and then she has disappeared. There is a sudden silence and an empty stage; then muted activity is perceived in both entranceways as from one the chorus enters, while from the other two men (one hairy and one smooth) come sneaking in. All grope quietly in the imaginary dark until the two groups bump into one another; then the chorus, aware of having caught something, lets out a hunting cry. The call is "*balle balle balle balle!*" (675), and hearing it one experiences a ridiculous *déjà entendu*, for this, with consonants switched, is the old *labe labe labe labe* of the doglike Furies of Aeschlyus (*Eum.* 130). Aristophanes parodies the same august scene, or perhaps the present *Rhesus* scene,[88] when his chorus of Acharnians pounces upon Dicaeopolis shouting *balle balle balle balle* (*Ach.* 280; cf. also *Ach.* 282, *paie pas* and *Rhes.* 685, *paie paie paie pas*). There are similar cries and scrums in two Sophoclean satyr-plays, *Inachus* and *Ichneutae*,[89] but there is nothing in all of tragedy like the blind turmoil and the physicality of this *Rhesus* chase, for at this point the drama's latent absurdity and bestiality take over the stage.

One party of chorus members gets hold of Odysseus while another seizes Diomedes, and the first challenge from the capturers is met with childish surliness:

CHO. What's your company? Where are you from?
OD. What's it to you? Harm me and you're dead. (682–83)

The password is demanded, but Odysseus only answers, "Don't get excited"; he seems to have forgotten it, though he was rehearsing it with Diomedes only a few lines ago (573). The two captives are brought together by the two groups of watchmen, who believe that they have caught some local thieves, and everybody begins to strike and poke at the strangers with their lances while Odysseus complains, "Hold it, men, hold it! . . . Don't strike a friend!" (687). Then at last the password comes to him, and when he is challenged a second time he triumphantly answers "Phoebus." The guards put up their spears and in the next instant the two unknowns have disappeared into the gloom, so that the command, "Hold your lances, everybody" (688) is followed immediately by a mystified, "Do you know where those fellows went?" (689; cf. Eur. *Cyc.* 689). The instantaneous disappearance of the self-proclaimed allies proves even to these dull-witted Trojan soldiers that something fishy has been going on, and they begin to rush about in a bootless search, while they sing a little song about Odysseus:

> Who's the man that got away?
> Who's the one who lives to boast
> of slipping through my grip?
> Where's he got to, that——
> what can I say he's like?
> a fellow that comes in the night
> and tiptoes through the lines
> and past this guard
> on feet that aren't afraid! (692–98)

Someone suggests that this must have been the work of Odysseus, and then at last they all understand who it is that they have let go:

> He's the one that came before!
> He had a shifty, bleary eye,
> wrapped in tattered rags he was
> but kept a knife hid in his shirt.
> He whined and scrounged

just like a begging slave,
showed his filthy scaly scalp
and how he lied!—he spat
upon the princely Atreid hearth,
and claimed he was their enemy! (710–19)

Here is a kind of recognition (the only one to occur in the play), but it is without effect. Soon the chase is abandoned, for the guards are paralyzed by fear of Hector's inevitable punishment. There is one man, however, who has never recognized anything, and from time to time his voice is heard asking plaintively out of the darkness, "Who?" "Who are you talking about?" "Who has got past us?" "Why should Hector be angry with us?" (708, 724, 725, 726). His puzzled words act as a stage direction, if any were needed, to tell us how the scene should be played: idiotically.[90]

In the midst of so much imbecility the forgotten password goes almost unnoticed, but it is important as a reminder that everything about this capture and release has been gratuitous. The password is the fruit of the killing of Dolon; it gives its possessors a kind of invulnerability, and the two Greeks have been equipped with it from their first appearance. If they had used it the instant they made contact with the Trojan guard they might have escaped at once, as they do eventually, all of which means that the poet has temporarily driven it from Odysseus' mind for a special purpose. Evidently he wants to gain a few moments in which he can show the wily Odysseus pretending to be a Thracian,[91] and, more important, in which he can produce the spectacle of a creature in a wolf-suit who is baited and beaten with sticks.[92] With such a spectacle he compensates for the lack of any description of Dolon's end, while he also stages the idea that Dolon's animal trickery has reverted destructively upon the Trojan camp. In verbal confirmation of this notion, he will make wolves drive off the horses of the charioteer's dream (785), and he will record that Rhesus died *doliō plēgēi* (748).[93] Because of their own sly wolfishness, the Trojans have lost their great ally, and the near-capture allows them a vicarious punishment of Dolon, as they beat his wolf-suited proxy as if he were a scapegoat.[94] Meanwhile, the near-capture also provides a second moment of divine salvation (one, that is, like Athena's, achieved by pretense and disguise), for when

Odysseus finally pronounces the stolen name "Phoebus" they are set free instantaneously.

One of the reproaches made against the *Rhesus* is the frequency of its reference to this password (12, 501, 572–73, 629, 684f.), which is supposed to betray a fourth-century interest in tactics.[95] Be that as it may, the password certainly announces the dramatist's interest in the god Apollo, for his name cannot have been chosen accidentally. The Trojans have been given "Phoebus" as their shibboleth, presumably because they trust their safety to an Apollo who is, within this play, peculiarly their god (note the choral prayer at the end of the Dolon scene). However, because this password does not ensure Trojan safety (any more than that prayer brought safety to Dolon), and because on the contrary it works the salvation of the enemies of Troy, the play must be telling us that the Trojan trust is misplaced.[96] Either the Trojans were mistaken to begin with, or else Apollo's favor has been withdrawn, and, since tradition made him a god who loved Troy, the second of these suppositions is the natural one. What the play shows, then, though indirectly, is Apollo in the act of turning away from his city. His movement is like that of Poseidon, in the *Troades* prologue, or more distantly like that of the Apollo who opens the *Alcestis*, and his reason is represented quite plainly, for Dolon betrayed not only Hector but also Apollo when he gave up the "Phoebus" password to the enemy. The "Dolonism" of Troy, the debased "temper" that the chorus so proudly claimed for the whole army, has evidently caused Apollo to withdraw his support.[97]

The Chorus

When the Greeks have gone the Trojan guard stands denuded of every tragic pretension. Thanks to their dereliction and their return, the play has been invaded by elements of pure comedy—parody, mimicry, stupidity, farce, and physical hurly-burly. Furthermore, they have been bamboozled into letting the hero's assassins go free. Militarily speaking, this chorus ought to be shot, and that is just what Hector says as soon as he returns. He roars out in martial rage at their shameful and cowardly conduct (808ff.) and he swears that they will know decapitation—or the lash (note the comic collapse in the second alternative, 817), and on this he takes his oath by Zeus. The men answer in a lyric whimper, swearing on their side by Simoïs that they did not fall asleep (which has nothing to do with the case), and also that they are blameless (which is patently untrue). The scene moves on, the charioteer interrupts with his accusations, Hector has no time to answer the men, and the criminal desertion of the watch is finally overlooked. The chorus will escape the punishment that it confessedly deserves (723), and this fact reflects badly upon Hector. In his clemency or his indifference he must, by his own oath, be viewed as a "coward" and a "nobody," for he has sworn to punish this guard or be called by both those names (818–19).

It is true that an evil Aegisthus threatened the old men of Argos and then did nothing to them (Aesch. *Ag.* 1621ff.); it is also true that an angry Pentheus tried and failed to keep the Bacchantes in prison, but in both of those cases the chorus was innocent, and so the dissolution of the threat did not harm the gravity of the situation. Here, on the other hand, the chorus is by our own witness guilty of misdemeanor, and instead of being tragically defiant it lies and squirms when it is accused. The result is that when it gets off scot-free, the spectator concludes that nothing in this camp is to be taken seriously. The unpunished crime and the threat that leads nowhere cannot possibly be looked upon as *pragmata spoudaia*, and so they cannot serve as parts of a genuine tragedy. The chorus has thus betrayed not only Hector and Troy, but the genre of tragedy, and when we see them in their fawning culpability we understand why Hector's opening words to them—"Why this noisy confusion?" (*thorubos*, 15; cf. 45)—echoed Pratinas' famous phrase about an unruly satyr-chorus (1D). By the time the play is finished the bungling *Rhesus* chorus has fallen in with a man in a furry suit and become patsy to a crime of violent thievery. These watchmen have given the satyric cry for help (6ff., 22ff.); they have exhibited the satyric panic (36) and have had to be shushed (17; cf. Eur. *Cyc.* 624ff.); they have boasted groundlessly (e.g. 248ff; cf. Eur. *Cyc.* 596) of bravery and have failed to show it; they have given way to silly irrelevance (note the dochmiac foolishness of 198, "Still, it would be nice to be a tyrant's in-law!" which not only contradicts the sentiment just expressed but would undo the whole of Dolon's choice). They have cringed and contradicted themselves[98] and caused a serious charge to be made against their commander, but after all this they escape without punishment, and it is their impunity, in the end, that leaves them smelling most strongly of goat.[99]

The Exodos

The existence of an epic original of gargantuan violence (as in the *Cyclops*), the presence of an assertive worm like Dolon (a Silenus in wolf's clothing), the escape of thieves in the midst of confusion (compare 689 and 692ff. with Eur. *Cyc.* 689),[100] the destruction of the outlandish barbarian who gives his name to the piece (as do Busiris and Syleus and Sciron to theirs)[101]—each of these constitutive elements reenforces the satyric odor of the chorus and indicates that the *Rhesus* poet was himself engaged in an act of mimicry, dressing up a satyr-drama as if it were a tragedy. The structural anomalies of his piece (its brevity, its short songs, its curious entrances, its oddly shaped episodes, its excessive choral motivation) have all found their best parallels in the satyr-plays, and the uneven verbal style seems to express the satyric impulse toward parody.[102] The central fictional motifs of animality, deception, disguise, thievery, and salvation likewise belong to satyric conventions, and it may be noted that even the inappropriate (but satyric) notion of drunkenness is present in this ostensible tragedy (418–19; 438; cf. 363–64).[103] The *Rhesus* is thus strongly satyric in both matter and manner, but nevertheless when this much has been said a new question at once arises. What, one must ask, is a grieving Muse doing in the final scene of such a play? The satyr-dramas, as far as we know them, humiliated their victims, stole from them, maimed them sometimes, but as a rule they did not kill, and they did not make the victim's suffering the subject of a formal staged lament. Yet here is a Muse, the mother of Rhesus, come to play both the deus ex machina and the mourning relative of high tragedy.

The Muse's function, in Aristotelian terms, would properly be to give the last transcendent shape to our pity and fear, but the problem is that no such emotions have been aroused. She must stand in the same machine that Athena so recently vacated, and that earlier goddess, with her outré impersonation, had confirmed our sense that Rhesus' death was no more awesome than his deeds were glorious. Now this second-comer must step up to the same spot and deliver the kind of speech that Artemis gives over the remains of Hippolytus, that Cadmus gives over Pentheus, or Hecuba over Astyanax. She cannot do it in noble seriousness without discrediting either herself or all that has gone before, and so it comes almost as a relief to find that the poet has not asked her to voice a genuine lament. Her exodos speech is, in fact, almost as odd of its type as was the messenger speech, and its most striking characteristic is the degree to which it does *not* appeal to the listener's tragic emotions.[104]

To begin with, since we have already seen a surrogate victim in the bleeding charioteer, the corpse that the Muse carries in has a diminished sensational effect. The eye of the spectator has lost a bit of its eagerness for gore, and meanwhile his mind has been diverted from the idea of death, because he has watched an action of escape. Thus prepared, he may be able to think about Rhesus, but he cannot feel his destruction as if it foretold his own. The Muse, being a Muse, understands the disengaged mood of the listener, and with her first words she defines the artful, cardboard-theater tone that she has prepared for his ear. Instead of speaking, this mourning mother sings (like the charioteer, but like no other god in the machine), and to mark the oddity of her performance she produces a witty little apology that plays on the fact that she is herself the inventor of song. She seems, indeed, to be the Muse of Preciosity as she dusts off an elegant citation from Bacchylides in her opening line (895; cf. Bacchyl. 2.11).[105] Nevertheless, once her little song is finished, she goes through the work of the deus ex machina in a businesslike way, exonerating Hector, cursing the killers, predicting the death of Achilles, and explaining that Rhesus will after all survive in cult. As a prophet, she is mechanically effective, but she is not nearly so satisfactory as the weeping relative. In praise of her son, she fails to remember his tender regard for his elders, as Cadmus does of Pentheus (Eur. *Bacch.* 1316f.), but mentions instead that he came to grief through disobedience (900–901), and in passing she characterizes the man she mourns as bloodthirsty (932–33).

Looking for a deeper cause for the present state of things, the Muse passes over all that might possibly make Rhesus heroic—his own deeds and heaven's enmity—and unexpectedly hits upon the scene of his conception (917ff.). The image of the august female divinity swirled about by amorous waters has already been presented in a somewhat incongruous context (346ff.), but now the lady herself revives and embellishes it. She tells of the infant's birth and of his nurture, and her entire reminiscence is accompanied by imaginary melodies, because her meeting with Strymon came at a time when the Thracian Thamyris[106] had challenged the Muses for sweetness of song. Other tragic laments touch upon past wedding celebrations as foil for the sorrows of the present (cf. e.g. Admetus at Eur. *Alc.* 914ff.), but this extended birth-tale is without a parallel in any other threnody or exodos. We do not know whether birth motifs were, as Murray and others have supposed, a common element in early satyr-drama, but we do know that they are unheard of in the final tableau of a full-fledged Attic tragedy.

Threats of balancing disasters, on the other hand, do belong to the final passage of a tragedy, and so when the Muse rumbles against Odysseus and predicts the death of Achilles, we think of Artemis in *Hippolytus* and feel that she shows a certain seemliness. Soon, however, the goddess makes a third threat that is in its way far more peculiar than the tale of Rhesus' birth, and one that, like that tale, works against the solemnity of her speech. Identifying the play's Athena with the modern city of Pisistratus and Pericles, she promises to get even with the goddess who has killed her son by taking a special revenge upon Athens. The city is in her debt, she says, for she has given the Athenians Orpheus and his unspeakable mysteries (943);[107] she has also reared Musaeus for them, but the Athenians have repaid her benefactions with the body of her son (948).[108] Her anger is presumably terrible against this ungrateful people, but look at the revenge she threatens in return—she will stop off the supply of mystics that has been coming down from Thrace, and she will not bring another diviner or adept (*sophistēs*, 949) among them![109] From now on Athens will be deprived of oracle-sellers and mystery-men; there will be no more northern sorcerers to bend the will of the gods in support of tyrants (Pl. *Leg.* 10.908d), no more drunken initiations with their scandalous secrets (Eur. *Cyc.* 576ff.; Pl. *Resp.* 2.363c–d), no more incantations to raise the dead (Eur. *Alc.* 966) or shape the passions (Pind. *Pyth.* 4.218; Eur. *Hipp.* 478) or do the work of lazy men (Eur. *Cyc.* 646; cf. Ps.-Orph. *Arg.* 254), no more vegetarians (Eur. *Hipp.* 952), no more false oracles to lead men astray (Hdt. 5.90; 7.6; cf. Ar. *Ran.* 1034; *Av.* 96off.),[110] and no more fear of retribution in the nether world (Pl. *Phd.* 69c)! With punishments like these, who would want a reward?

By bringing about the death of Rhesus, the plot of this play has defeated an influx into Athens of a Thracian religion identified with the oracles of Musaeus, the mysteries of Orpheus, and the worship of Bacchus-Zagreus. This much the Muse makes clear, and in good northern fashion she also reports that her son has not really died,[111] though he will be as if dead to her (962ff.). Like the Thracian Zamolxis (like Lycurgus and like his own legendary self),[112] Rhesus will be hidden away in a cave, but he will "look upon the light" and he will act as prophet for that Bacchus who inhabits the rock of Pangaion and is "an awesome god to his initiates" (970–73).[113] Here again the *Rhesus* poet has reproduced a Thracian actuality, for there was a working oracle on Pangaion. According to Herodotus (7.111) its official spokesmen came from the tribe of the Bessi and its mouthpiece was a woman, but the Muse here teaches us to think of her hero-son as the power behind this exotic oracular voice. The immortal Rhesus will thus be a servant of Zagreus, the god of the Thracian mysteries and the barbarian counterpart of the Hellenic Dionysus.[114] All of which means that the play's assassins, by killing him, have not only supported the Olympian scheme for the war and rescued Greece from a Thracian invasion, they have also repulsed an exotic religion that rivaled accepted Greek beliefs.

The Full Statement

Athens in particular has been saved from foreign rule and from being overrun by the enemies of the true Dionysus,[115] and such an achievement could have lent itself to a fully satyric treatment. The *Rhesus* poet has nevertheless chosen not to pin the tails on openly (except in the case of Odysseus) becuse his poetic intention was not one that could be conveyed by the joyous cruelty or the fantastic quality of the satyr genre. Instead he has made a piece that is neither tragic nor satyresque, one that is cruel without much jollity, but agonizingly real, precisely because of its absurdity. It closes with a scene that by its very form—the flawed lament—signifies the decline of the heroic virtues, and so we end by lamenting the death, not of this dull barbarian principal, but of nobility itself. We are not cleansed, we are simply disillusioned, and our last glimpse of Hector fixes this hollow condition upon us. Ridiculous as it was, the adventure of Odysseus and Diomedes has promised that Troy will fall, and so when a tired, belittled Trojan prince marches out with his incompetent men toward another day of futile war,[116] we feel pity for him, but also scorn, and these emotions become agonizing because they spread to cover all of humanity. Hector thinks he marches toward victory while in fact he moves toward defeat, but it is not his simple error that evokes our response, it is the dissolution of the Homeric ideals. Victory, in this play, has been figured as a dream of snow-white horses—horses that disappear in the night—while war has been shown to be a time of darkness, confusion, trickery, bestiality, and shameful behavior on the part of all: Trojan, barbarian, Greek, and god.

These revelations are not fearsome and beautiful, like those of tragedy, nor are they primitive and apotropaic, like the statements of a satyr-play. Instead, they are mean and ugly, as Dolon is, and so we have been asked to smile wherever we could, so long as our smiles were bitter grimaces of self-recognition. The Muse, after all, has cursed not just Odysseus and Diomedes, but Helen too, and the whole complicated war (910ff.), and following this generalizing imprecation we mourn, in the end, not Rhesus or Hector but all barbarians, all Trojans, all Greeks, and all mankind as well, for being caught up in such bloody foolishness.

Authorship

If the *Rhesus* is the sort of play I have just described, does this make any difference to the question of its authenticity? I think it does. In the first place, the Muse's emphatic refusal to let her son be buried at Troy (962) ought to mean that the play was produced before the oracle about Rhesus' bones was given to Hagnon in 437, because after that time all Athenians knew that the relics had lain at Troy until they were dug up.[117] The fact that the Lamachus of the *Acharnians* seems to be derived in part from the Rhesus of this play supports a date before 425 B.C., and so do the intellectual tendencies of the play itself. Its anti-Thracian stance and its identification of Rhesus with Xerxes are well suited to an early period when Thracian cooperation with Persians (Hdt. 7.115 and 106; Plut. *Cim.* 14) and Thracian slaughter of Athenians (at Amphipolis in 465/4, Thuc. 4.102; Hdt. 9.75; Diod. 11.70) were still lively memories. The play's view of religious matters is likewise easy to reconcile with mid-fifth-century composition, for it treats Orphism and the worship of Zagreus as foreign cults that have begun to insinuate themselves into Athens, but whose influence can still be arrested.

Rhesus thus takes on the appearance of a play from the forties or the fifties of the fifth century, and if this is its period then it must be given to Euripides. It will be the earliest play of his that we have, just as the ancients thought, and it is easy to accept as such, for parody is usually a young man's art. The poet of *Rhesus* has a knowledge of the tragic manner equal to that of Aristophanes, but he seems to be restless under the weight of great predecessors and without reverence for his rivals. He has not yet found his own mode; he loves but distrusts the conventional forms, and so he raids and ridicules the work of others without a qualm. In *Rhesus* he writes a play against war, but he makes it also an attack on the traditions of tragedy by systematically reducing his familiar structures and materials to the level of the absurd.

Seen in this way, the *Rhesus* is proof against the objections that have been made to its authenticity, for these have been based on deviations from what were presumably the norms of Euripidean tragic practice. The lack of pathos and the deflation of ethos that would be faults in a tragedy can now be recognized as successful expressions of a parodic purpose, and the same is true of the overblown greeting to Rhesus, the unusually realistic chorus, and the touches of egregious comedy. The mosaic technique of combining snatches of tragic phrasing[118] no longer betrays a tasteless archaizer, but speaks instead of a ruthlessly clever young scoffer. Even specific anomalies like the unusual number of non-Attic words and the frequency of repetition can be explained as part of the play's intentionally "literary" sound.[119] Line by line the *Rhesus* does not strike the later Euripidean note: verbal wit, delight in paradox, lyric luxuriance, and subtle refinements of meaning are for the most part missing here. Nevertheless, there is a structural wit to be observed, and also a knowing experimentation with dramatic forms, and these are qualities that are found elsewhere only in the mature plays of Euripides. The interest in exotic religion, and the balancing dry, demythologized, but serious glance given to the Hellenic gods, are exactly what we should expect from the poet of *Helen, Iphigenia among the Taurians,* and the *Bacchae.* And as for the play's scornful pity for men, its delight in their imperfections, its disgust at their acts of war—all these are effects made familiar by the authenticated works of Euripides.

The Power of Aphrodite: Eros and the Boundaries of the Self in the *Hippolytus*

FROMA I. ZEITLIN

For Charles Segal
φανερωτάτῳ ἀστέρι

The Second Phaedra

The *Hippolytus* of Euripides may be unique in the history of the Greek tragic theater as an example of a second treatment by the same poet of a myth he had earlier represented on stage. The first *Hippolytus* has not survived except for a few suggestive fragments of the text and in the traces it has probably left behind in later works.[1] But our evidence seems to agree that the play outraged its audience by the shamelessness of its Phaedra who openly declared her guilty passion to Hippolytus, and when rebuffed, just as brazenly confronted her husband face-to-face and herself accused Hippolytus of sexual assault.[2]

The second *Hippolytus*, according to the hypothesis of the play, corrected the indecencies and improprieties of the first (*to . . . aprepes kai katēgorias axion . . . diōrthōtai*). The changes were not in the terms of the myth itself but in the depiction of the principal female character. The new Phaedra is now the opposite, we might say, of her former self. She is the unwitting victim, the respectable woman whom Aphrodite, as the goddess tells us herself in the prologue, has coldly chosen as her instrument in order to avenge herself upon Hippolytus, who has scorned her worship (47–48).

This Phaedra is now the paragon of female virtue, embodying the ideals of *aidōs*, *sōphrosunē*, and *eukleia*—the *aidōs* of shame and modesty, the *sōphrosunē* of wifely chastity, and the *eukleia* of her good reputation. Instead of a well-born Phaedra who asserted her sexual desire and therefore dangerously subverted the norms of feminine behavior in an affront to all respectable women, as Aristophanic comedy several times reminds us,[3] there is a Phaedra who knows all too well the conventions of Greek social life that relegate the woman to a silence that would be her glory.[4] The new Phaedra knows full well that women are vulnerable to blame, to the charge of being a hateful thing to all (misēma, 406–7), and reserves her personal hatred (misō, 413) for the type of disgraceful wife the earlier Phaedra had exemplified, as if she were responding directly to and identifying with the audience's reaction to the previous play.

Unlike the first Phaedra, this Phaedra will not seek to justify her love for Hippolytus, nor will she scheme with drugs and potions to bring about its fulfillment. Rather, she seeks desperately to repress her desire. She certainly will not address herself directly to Hippolytus, whose name she cannot even mention (352). It must therefore fall to an other, the devoted nurse, to adopt all these positions in her pragmatic concern to save the life of the sick and suffering woman she loves as her child. And it follows that this Phaedra would never confront her husband face-to-face, once the nurse has extracted her guilty secret and betrayed it to Hippolytus, and Phaedra has overheard her stepson's outraged reaction. Phaedra would rather die from shame, and die she does, at her own hand, before the return of Theseus. She thus concludes the resolve upon which she had determined at the beginning of the play to save the honor by which she defines herself in her own eyes and in the eyes of others. Deeming that honor more precious than life—both her own life and that of Hippolytus (721)—and responding now to the tragic impasse of a self caught hopelessly between innocence and guilt, "desire and honor, conscience and reputation,"[5] inner self and external image,[6] she too, like her wicked counterpart, lays a false charge against Hippolytus. But now she chooses the indirect form of a letter which together with her lifeless body will serve as silent and concrete testimony to her accusation.

In the end, the honorable Phaedra only seems to corroborate the supposition of woman's essentially duplicitous nature, and her defeat therefore seems even more explicitly to support the accusations flung at the entire female sex by Hippolytus in his memorable outburst against that "counterfeit evil" we call women (616). Yet if the virtuous woman is ruined, the scandal of the first play is averted, and above all, the myth is saved. Hippolytus must meet his fate in order to confirm again the truth of the cultural dictum that no one may with impunity refuse the power of Aphrodite, not even the Amazon's child and the worshiper of Artemis. Phaedra's reversion to the role the traditional story (and the earlier play) had assigned to her only reinforces the lesson that the power of Aphrodite is indeed irresistible and justifies Aphrodite's confidence in the prologue (40–41) that the queen, as Pasiphae's daughter (as perhaps any woman), will eventually become her ally as well as her victim, if she, like the goddess before her, is scorned by the other. But in the process—because of the process—the innovations of the plot necessitated by the new Phaedra deepen the import of the myth as the play shifts its focus to consider the discrepancy in the self between character and role, between, we might say, the second and first Phaedras.[7] Through the twists and turns the drama now must take, it must also reach a level of unparalleled complexity and it is this complexity, I will argue, that is essential in itself for our understanding of Aphrodite and the correspondingly more complex part she is seen as playing in the theater and the world.

Thus we should consider the significant elements of the new plot for their intrinsic as well as their practical value in the structuring of the story. It matters, for example, that where there were shameless declarations in the earlier play, there are now only lacunae in the text, communications never made public but only judged from the reactions of those who hear (Hippolytus) or overhear (Phaedra) or read them (Theseus). The ruling theme of eros is expanded if instead of the outrageous confrontations between male and female of the first play (Phaedra and Hippolytus, Phaedra and Theseus), the burden of the plot is now carried by parallel encounters between female and female (Phaedra and nurse) and male and male (Theseus and Hippolytus). Finally, we should observe that to overcome the initial reticence, the aidōs that threatens to block the plot devised by the goddess, the play is obliged to find oblique strategies by which to seduce Phaedra into playing her part so that Hippolytus may be seduced into playing his. As a result, the most striking feature of our drama is that it reaches its expected conclusion only through deviation and detour, and above all, through the acting of each character for an other.

For one critic, who is concerned only with ends not means, the play demonstrates that Euripides has here turned the tables on his "philistine" audience to suggest that the *aidōs* of the new Phaedra might be as much or more a source of evil and moral disorder as the shamelessness (*anaischuntia*) of the first.[8] But one could equally argue that the scandal caused by the first play verifies the concern that Phaedra feels for the demands of a society that will judge her solely by its conventions. The "palinode" therefore incorporates and turns to its own purposes the external social reality that marked the actual relationship between the first play and its spectators.

Furthermore, the conventions which the Phaedra of the second play seems to respect too much and which now will determine the course of her actions have more ambiguous and more suggestive implications in the larger world that the action of the play aims to represent. Conformity to social rules is always open to criticism insofar as it gives public image precedence over other, more valued, considerations of inner integrity. But on another level, respect for convention acknowledges the realities of social relations in which the self must also be responsible for the image it presents to others, an inevitable fact of life which is as true for Phaedra as she (and the structure and events of the play) will prove it to be for Hippolytus.

For the first Phaedra, who would contrive to satisfy her passion, Eros is the *didaskalos*, as she declares, the teacher of boldness and daring (*tolma, thrasos*), the god who is most resourceful (*euporōtatos*) to find a way where there is no way (*en amēchanois*, 430 N[2]). This is the first time, as far as we know, that Eros has earned the title of "didaskalos."[9] The novelty of this term is matched by another novelty on stage, namely, the woman who coined it, who, daring to use Eros as the teacher for her own ends, indirectly teaches others in turn by her bad example. Thus in Aristophanes' *Frogs*, Aeschylus can reproach Euripides for having put debased women such as Phaedra on stage, claiming that "the poet (like Phaedra, it would seem) ought to conceal (*kruptein*) what is wicked and not produce or teach (*didaskein*) such things" (*Frogs*, 1049–56).

For the second Phaedra, however, who would contrive with all her power to conceal (*kruptein*) what is wicked, notions of teaching and learning recur in the theatrical context but now with different and still more novel connotations. Phaedra means to teach Hippolytus, as she says enigmatically in her last statement before she leaves the scene to write the fateful letter and to take her own life. "He will share in my disease (*koinēi metaschōn*) and he will learn (*mathēsetai*) to practice *sōphrosunē*" (730–31), the quality of modesty/temperance/chastity, which both have claimed and which paradoxically belongs to the domain of Artemis rather than to that of Aphrodite. Hippolytus has already spoken of a virtue that cannot be taught (79–80 but cf. 667)[10] and his father will later take up the theme of education in his angry speech against Hippolytus (916–20).

Phaedra, we may recall, whether as victim or agent, is only a means to another end. The true objective of the play (and Aphrodite) might be called the education of Hippolytus. This is the moment for the young man to complete the initiatory scenario that would make him pass from the yoking of horses to the yoking of maidens, from the hunting of game to the hunting of a wife.[11] Phaedra may incriminate Hippolytus to save her own honor (716–21) while Aphrodite intends, like all divinities, to safeguard hers, and perhaps these are lessons enough about the nature of the adult world. But in the question of passage from one state to another in which eros is culturally programmed to play an essential part, the second Phaedra has much herself to learn and in turn to teach Hippolytus in the larger scheme of things beyond the traditional functions of Aphrodite, which the play must over and over again celebrate,[12] and beyond the stereotyped interplay between the lustful woman and the chaste young man, which emphasizes the dangers female sexuality is thought to pose to the social system. These lessons the characters need not and ought not express directly because they underlie the surface operations of the plot and are conveyed by the structures and details of the play itself.

For broadly speaking, Hippolytus' refusal of eros can be summarized as the self's radical refusal of the Other. Eros is the most dangerous of all these relations: while answering most deeply to human needs of dependency, reciprocity, and empathy, it is also perceived to threaten most seriously the boundaries of the autonomous self and under the magnetic pull of desire to put the self in the power of an other. At the same time, its exercise acknowledges the force of the animal nature within us. But it is also needed, as we will see, for constructing an adequate model of that self and for defining it socially in a network of proper relations.

Hence to meet Hippolytus' challenge, the entire dramatic structure, as I hope to show, enacts through the development of its actions, gestures, and language the irresistible power of Aphrodite as it acts upon the structure of the self and puts it, even and especially against its will, into relations with others. And we will discover that the self must learn to play its theatrical role in the complex—knotted and reknotted—plot of life itself; that is, it must enter into the necessary but inevitably ambiguous exchanges between self and other, exchanges now confused and distorted to a maximum degree by reason of that refusal to worship the goddess.[13]

Thus although Phaedra's prophetic statement about Hippolytus (723–31, cited earlier) looks to the future events of the drama, the process of education has effectively begun long before this midpoint of the play is reached. In fact, from the moment Aphrodite determines to avenge herself upon Hippolytus, not directly but through an other (Phaedra) who will act for the goddess in the human domain and yet will, through her own language, gestures, and actions, prefigure and determine the experience of the other (Hippolytus), the goddess activates a plot remarkable in its construction in that, unlike that of any other extant play, it binds all the characters together in an "inextricable nexus of interdependence."[14]

The last part of this essay will call the role of Aphrodite into question. It will suggest that Aphrodite's revenge upon Hippolytus through the displacing of desire only on to an innocent other (Phaedra) runs contrary to her typical mode of intervention in human affairs. As a result, there is a latent tension between the familiar narrative patterns to which the story of Phaedra and Hippolytus belongs and the mythic patterns usually associated with Aphrodite and the motif of her wrath. But before we can come to understand just how well this initial deviation also works in the service of Aphrodite's plan, we must follow out the intricate and various ways by which the goddess operates, especially through the images of the knot and the mirror. We must examine why she uses the woman as her instrument and agent on the stage and deploys all the theatrical means at her disposal in order to demonstrate the fullness of her power over the self. Without resorting here to a detailed summary in advance, let me simply propose that at its most inclusive level, that power will prove to be consonant with the power of the theater itself—as regards, for example, the structure and functions of plot; the representation of the body and its sensory faculties; relations between inside and outside, between seen and unseen; types and modes of communication; role playing and reversal of roles; actors and spectators, as well as the general mimetic properties of dramatic art. As a way then of entering into Aphrodite's world (and that of the theater), let us begin by taking the measure of that phrase, "the inextricable nexus of interdependence," that was used in order to characterize the plot of the play.

The Plot: To Bind and Unbind

In exploring the complex dynamics of the play in which Aphrodite rules, I want first to demonstrate the workings of this nexus or knot, which is actually a leading image, both literal and metaphorical, of the drama. Through the idiom of binding and unbinding/loosening (and related terms), the nexus operates on a number of different levels and embraces a wide variety of references, all organized around Phaedra's despairing cry at the turning point of the drama after the betrayal of her secret to Hippolytus: "What devices (*technai*) or words (*logoi*) do I have, now that I have been tripped up, to loosen/ unbind (*luein*) the knot, the *kathamma*, of the *logos*?" (670–71).[15]

The knot of the *logos* that implicates Phaeda—the *logos* that includes the speech of the nurse to Hippolytus and his response overheard by the queen—can only be undone with the fastening of another knot. This knot is first the noose Phaedra binds around her neck (770–71) and from which she will be loosened once she is dead (781, 783). It is also the knot of the new *logos* she fabricates for Hippolytus and suspends from her suspended body (*ērtemenē*, 779, 866). That action finds its first echo in Hippolytus' own gesture when he suspends (*artēsas*) his body back upon the thongs of his reins (1222), as he strives to steer the stampeding horses who no longer turn in obedience to his guiding hand, nor to their own binding harness (*hippodesmōn*, 1225), nor to the compact structure of the chariot. But the knot of the new *logos* will in fact eventually entangle Hippolytus in the reins (*emplakeis*, 1235) and will bind him in a bond that is impossible to unravel (*desmon dusexelikton . . . detheis*, 1237). This binding results directly from the tablet Phaedra has wrapped around with cords to seal it and which Theseus must unravel (*exelixas*) in order to read its message. These bonds of Hippolytus, as those of Phaedra, will only be loosened (*ek desmōn lutheis*, 1244) at the cost of loosening his limbs from the bonds of life (cf. Eur. *IT* 692, Bacchyl. 1.43, Soph. *OC* 1720). This sequence of events which brings death to Hippolytus fulfills perhaps the ominous etymology of his name as he shifts from the "one who binds (or yokes, 111, 1183) and loosens horses" to one who is truly Hippolytus, that is, "loosened by horses," thereby perfectly adjusting the tragic action to the name.[16]

But the action corresponds, in turn, to the condition of Phaedra at the beginning of the play. There her soul is bound fast (dedetai) to her sickbed (160) while at the same time, the "fastenings" of her limbs are loosened by the afflictions of her disease—eros: (lelummai meleōn sundesma, 199). Eros, according to his traditional epithet, is the lusimelēs, the one who loosens the limbs, an epithet he shares with both sleep and death[17] and from which Phaedra can liberate herself only by the fastening of the tightly drawn rope around her neck (769–75).

Binding and loosening, then, both work their destructive effects on the body itself, but the correspondences between the conditions of Phaedra and Hippolytus can only come about through the irreversible movement of the dramatic action itself. The repetition or re-enactment by one character of the experience of the other is already conveyed by the chorus in the second stasimon immediately before the peripeteia of the drama and just after Phaedra's last exit from the scene (752–63). There the chorus recalls the ship that brought Phaedra from Crete to Athens long ago when she was a bride, and they describe the woven ends of the mooring cables which were bound to dry land (ekdēsanto, 761–63). But the word archai which here means "ends" in the sense of "extremities" more usually, of course, signifies "beginnings." The end point of the past journey that began the story of Phaedra long before the opening of the play is recollected at the moment when her story is to end. In turn, it inaugurates the beginning of the future journey for the other which is to lead him as an exile away from the house of his father to the shores of the sea— neither as a bridegroom on his nuptial procession nor as the young hero following in the footsteps of his own father along a road that had brought Theseus successfully from Troezen to Athens (977–80; cf. 1208–9) to claim his rightful identity. Instead, Hippolytus will take the road to destruction, determined for him in the play from the moment when Phaedra succumbs to the nurse's entreaty to "loosen" the "silent road of her thought" (gnōmē) (290, 391).

At the critical moment of reversal, recorded in the second stasimon, the interlinking of destinies by which the unbinding of one becomes the binding of the other, corresponds quite literally to Aristotle's notion of the basic structures of plot. "Every tragedy," he declares, "has a *desis* and *lusis*. . . . I call the *desis*, the knot, the binding, the tragedy from its beginning (*archē*) up to that part which is the last (*eschaton*), from which the change of fortune proceeds, and the *lusis*, the dénouement, from the beginning of this reversal until the end (*telos*)" (*Poet.* 1455b). This *desis* Aristotle also calls a *plokē*, a weaving, and this image too has its literal counterparts in the play. The woven (*plekton*) garland Hippolytus plaits for the goddess (73) (the *anadēma*, 83) finds its doublet in the woven garland (807) Theseus casts down from his own head in response to the twisted cords of Phaedra's noose (783), and leads to the last interweaving, that of Hippolytus entangled (*emplakeis*, 1236) in the reins of his horses. But how might one describe a plot that continuously and variously interweaves the two actions of *desis* and *lusis* themselves? These terms shift back and forth from one signifying level to another, from one referent to another, and persist until the end, implicating not only Phaedra and Hippolytus, but also Theseus, the third one, in a bond that must be unbound.

For Theseus the process of binding begins once he orders the bolts of the doors to be loosened (*eklueth' harmous*, 809; cf. 808) and is completed when, for the second time, he curses his son who, in keeping the oath by which he is bound, does not "loosen" his mouth to tell his father what he knows (*luō*, 1060). Theseus is bound by his own *hamartia*, his error, which causes the death of Hippolytus but from which Artemis can "loosen" (*ekluei*, 1335) him because of his ignorance. Yet at the resolution of the drama, it is Hippolytus, bound and in turn unbound, who has the power to "loosen" or "dissolve" (*luō*, 1442) the quarrel between himself and his father and to free (*eleutherō*, 1449, 1450) Theseus from the guilty pollution of his son's approaching death. In absolving Theseus, however, Hippolytus can be said to have fastened at last a durable social bond, now acknowledged by his nobility (*gennaios*) as the legitimate (*gnēsios*) son of his father (1452, 1455; cf. 309).[18]

And the cause of it all is Aphrodite. In general, Dionysus is the lord of the theater, who regulates the formal symmetries, reenactments, and reversals of tragic plots. Dionysus Lusios, we might say, is the god who presides over the tragic patterns of binding and loosening which reciprocally operate in the service of necessity, entailing constraint (*desis*) on the one hand, and dissolution and death (*lusis*) on the other.[19] Yet this play specifies that all these operations belong to Aphrodite, for whom eros both loosens the limbs and fashions the bonds that bind the self in the nets of desire.[20] Thus in demonstrating the ineluctable necessities that Aphrodite controls, all the mechanisms of the play—structure, action, gesture, and language— enact in their tragic and negative version the terms that are fully consonant with her sphere of power.

Aphrodite, like Dionysus in the *Bacchae*, demands recognition as a divinity. She too insists that mortals recognize the alien power of passionate forces in the world as also intrinsically one's own. But Dionysus' mode of expression is collective: the *thiasos* and initiation into cultic mysteries bind worshipers to each other and to their god and loosen them from the ordinary restrictions of daily life. Aphrodite's desire is directed rather to the mysteries of sexuality and marriage whereby one self is bound to an other and the bride first binds on and then unbinds the girdle of her virginity.[21] More generally, however, her effects extend to the wider network of interdependence and interconnection for which eros provides the patterns.[22]

The intricate network of *desis* and *lusis* not only replicates the abstract notion of plot, it also serves as the particular structuring device linking the sequence of events and binding them (and the characters) into a series of reciprocal and parallel actions, as if the play were demonstrating its own premises and reproducing its message of intersubjectivity in its own composition. Still further, the range of its uses suggests that the nexus reproduces the broader principle of structure itself, whether it regulates the structure of the body in its bounded form or that of the social relations between self and other.

To refuse the bonds of eros, then, means that binding will operate upon the self as a sign of intolerable emotional and physical pressures—as external contacts made upon the body (noose, reins) and as internal constraints upon speech and action—so that unbinding, when it comes, will bring disaster to the self (and the other) but joy to the offended Aphrodite (725–29). The nurse provides the norm, when she warns in reference to her own attachment to Phaedra: "the loves of the heart (*stergēthra phrenōn*) should be easily loosened (*euluta*), both to thrust away and to draw in tight" (256–57; cf. 340 N²). Her gnomic wisdom will apply in more concrete (but still figurative) fashion to the noose Phaedra puts around her neck. But the metaphor of horse racing, of course, will find its literal enactment for Hippolytus, who, refusing the yoke of marriage, must find himself yoked instead to destruction (1389).[23]

To refuse the bonds of eros also means to refuse the bonds of dependence, to attempt to remain alone and aloof from an other—an asyndeton, we might say, in the grammar of life. Once again the play acts out these notions in literal gestures and language. Phaedra can resist the pressure to reveal her secret (thus activating the plot of Aphrodite) until the nurse grasps her and de-pends (*exartōmenē*, 325) from her hand. But after this human contact has worked its purpose, dependency turns back upon the single self, finding a negative echo in the isolated inanimate *deltos* that conceals the secret and de-pends (*ērtēmenē*, 857) from the same hand of Phaedra, now dead. And we recognize the import for Hippolytus in his relation to the structure of chariot and horses by which he defines himself and from whose harness he finally de-pends (*artēsas*, 1222) as he leans his body back upon the reins.

These last two instances show yet another kind of reversion to the isolated self, in which the term *harmozō*, which can designate the "fitting together of a man and a woman in wedlock," is now applied to the one who fits the noose to her neck (*katharmozousa*, 771) and to the other who fits his feet in the footstalls of his chariot (*harmosas*, 1189).[24]

At the end Artemis, the other goddess, is on stage, but Aphrodite, long vanished, is also there. She had presided at a distance over the main event that unleashed the demonic and destructive energies of eros which were manifested in the interaction between the bull from the sea and the horses of Hippolytus.[25] We also find her in Hippolytus' reunion with his father at the end. His last act, which absolves the other, is demanded by Artemis and granted by Hippolytus in obedience to his goddess' commands (1435, 1442–43). But as it now brings together those who had been divided from each other, it is likewise an act behind which Aphrodite and the complex structure of the play stand.[26] For the direct aim of eros, ambiguously concealed behind the nurse's delicate suggestion of a love charm to cure her ailing mistress (508–10), is, of course, sexual, that is, physically to "join together (*sunapsai*) one *charis* from two" (515). We can say, however, that the two principal encounters in the play (between the nurse and Phaedra and between Theseus and Hippolytus)

also show Aphrodite at work. Love for Phaedra is the primary assumption behind both encounters, as it motivates all the nurse's actions and leads Theseus in turn to condemn his son without a second thought.[27] Yet beyond this simple fact, the contents of these two
interchanges imply that Aphrodite rules over other forms of face-to-
face intimacy along the spectrum from *erōs* to *philia*, where reciprocity and exchange are involved and where seduction/persuasion
take place. The goddess, to be sure, shows a different side in each
case; appropriately enough, the nurse's persuasion of Phaedra succeeds while Hippolytus' appeals to his father are dismissed as shameless hypocrisy.[28]

In the woman's world, the nurse functions as a maternal figure to
Phaedra in a relation corresponding in the man's world to that between father and son, for all of whom the linking power of Aphrodite
invokes the more diffused and more ambivalent side of eros. When
the nurse complains how "grievous a burden it is that one soul suffer
pain on behalf of two" (258–60), the self and the other, she is referring, of course, to herself and Phaedra. But in her homely complaint,
she can speak for the other characters in the play who will each have
experienced this necessity.

At the end, it is the goddess Aphrodite, the one (*mia*) who has
brought not two, but three together—the son, the father, and his
mate (*sunēoron*) out of their isolation into the commonality of their
ruin (1403), as a belated family reunion.[29] More specifically, the one
who had refused contact with others and had abhorred the touch of
another's hand (606, 1086), preferring his association with the goddess Artemis which necessarily excluded both sight and touch, finds
at the end an embrace in his father's arms (1431–32, 1445).[30]

Having refused to cross the boundary between child and adult,
thereby also transgressing the boundary between human and divine,
the self experiences the transgression of its own boundaries in the
plot that entangles Hippolytus in the complexities of human life.[31]
Subject to the constraining bonds placed on the untouched and un-
touching body, first in speech and then in action, he will be released
only for death. The operations of binding and loosening enacted
along the seashore transform the workings of eros—the rhythms of
tension and relaxation—into those of death. At the same time, it delivers him from one state to another in the modality of birth by
which bonds are also loosened.[32] The child comes forth in death, on

the one hand, in filiation, on the other. And this filiation is none other than the birth into a fuller selfhood, not only socially as the legitimate son of his father, but cognitively in the experience of a tragic consciousness. This experience, in tracing its signs on and within the body, has now defined the proper boundaries of the self in the world, a self who has moved from the territory of the untouched meadow from which he had culled the flowers of Artemis' woven garland (73), her binding crown (anadēma, 83), to the place on the shore where land and sea define each other's boundaries.[33]

The Plot: Time, Story, and the Self

The untouched meadow, as many have observed, is the spatial analogue of Hippolytus, who, in identifying himself with the meadow and its immortal mistress, defines himself as an unworked territory—all surface and no depth, outside of time that marks the seasonal activities of human culture and the cycle of human generation.[34] Always (aei), alone (monos), and all (panta) (80, 84), define the self in regard to this Edenic enclosure whose perfect circles of time and space exclude the temporal and linear narrative of a human life. "May I turn around the telos, the goalpost of life, exactly as I began it" is the fervent wish that concludes Hippolytus' prayer to Artemis (87).

Hippolytus will indeed realize that telos in the action of his horses and chariot, which will bind his life to the destiny, the moira, appointed for it by Aphrodite (894, 1436). But, in truth, Hippolytus' wish is not granted as he would like. How can it be granted when the end is separated from the beginning by the entire chain of narrative events in the play? Hippolytus does, in fact, fall into time—not an eternity, but its diametrical opposite, the split second in which he condemned an other (Phaedra) and then was condemned in turn, when his father would not wait for time to reveal the necessary proofs of his innocence (1052–53, 1322). As a result, Hippolytus falls into narrative. And as a result, he becomes at the end the subject of a story for maidens always to tell (1428). For now the love Phaedra bore for him will be made public in a recital whose cultic repetition relegates it appropriately to the permanence of abiding time (di' aiōnos makrou, 1426).

Hippolytus is to be bound, not without irony, to Aphrodite and Phaedra forever, in the cult of the nubile maidens.[35] Yet given this future commemoration of his story, the mechanics of the new plot which the goddess has furnished for the new Phaedra assumes a richer significance. Without Phaedra, we might say, Hippolytus cannot be an actor in the drama of life, which the text imitates in all its baffling complexities. Alone in a perpetual cycle of ludic repetition, he can have no story, no *muthos*. The *agones* of athletic competition (1016) promise him a life without the risks (1019) which the Greeks deemed essential in the achievement of the heroic (i.e., manly) self (cf. Eur. 1052 N²). Hippolytus' activities only keep him from action, the serious *praxis* of life which, as Aristotle tells us, drama imitates (*Poet.* 1450a.12).

Hippolytus' story comes into being because the lying message Phaedra leaves behind on the writing tablet in effect reverses subject and object (I desire him/he desires me). By making him "share in her disease" (730–31), Phaedra will now have transferred her story to him so as to make him the unwitting double of herself. Accused of a deed he did not commit, he now will imitate her *praxis*, so to speak, in an *agōn* for his life and honor, as she had struggled for hers, on the level of both language and action.[36] More precisely, she has required him to stand in the place of the other, to be identified with her, to hear from the other, his father, what she, the other, had heard from him, Hippolytus. In short, he will have to live through her experience in every respect, sharing the symptoms of her "disease" in the eyes of the world until the condition of his sick and suffering body as seen at the end of the play symmetrically matches her state at the beginning. Perhaps most important of all, by playing the role Phaedra has assigned to him, Hippolytus will be required to be an other in relation to himself and, as we shall see, to suffer the consequences of his own alterity in the adult social system that requires one to verify the self through the perception of an other.

This means that, on the level of the action, the entire chain of communication in its deviations and detours, whereby everything passes indirectly through the intermediary of an other, can be understood as bringing into focus the implications of Hippolytus' having refused to allow the presence of an other to intrude upon his visual and tactile space. It means too, as far as language is concerned, that the typical proleptic techniques of tragedy, by which the first part of a play prepares for the second and can only be fully comprehended in the light of its sequel, now have a double duty to perform in forecasting through its images the fates of not just one but also the other. The new plot finally insists that this principle of alterity be permanently installed in cult in that the male's story will later and for all time serve as the model for the female. Yet this outcome is preceded by its exact reverse: the female and her story will serve throughout the play as the model for the male.

The Feminine Body: Virgin

In the exchanging of roles, the play is, in a sense, simply acting out what Hippolytus' claim to the status of *parthenos* (1106, 1302) implies and therefore arranges his initiation into the world as one resembling the experience of the female body.[37] After all, the image of the *parthenos* plucking flowers in the inviolate meadow (73–80) already invokes its paradigmatic antecedent—the Kore figure for whom the doors of Hades will gape open just as Aphrodite predicts for Hippolytus in the prologue (56–57) and Hippolytus himself echoes at the end (1447).

Hippolytus' virginity in the service of the goddess Artemis seems to tell us that the untouched body can only be imagined as feminine, but it also suggests that untouchability bears a metaphysical charge transcending the laws of nature and even of gender. Hippolytus sacralizes virginity and the terms on which he worships the goddess to the exclusion of all others suggest the cultural values that virginity can always entail. For the self to be alone with the goddess in the pure space of the meadow implies that virginity can be interpreted as a quality that represents the self as "an image of an original identity: that is, what is objectively untouched symbolizes what is subjectively contained."[38] Yet Kore's experience reminds us that the *parthenos* cannot linger forever in the meadow, content to embody a static symbol of external and private wholeness. Rather, the mythic associations of flower, meadow, and maiden align the human maturational cycle with that of the seasons so that the *parthenos* above all is the one who is poised precisely at the place and moment of passage. The virgin must enter into the temporal flow of life, which is represented by the progress of the drama itself and recollected within it as the retrospective experience of Phaedra, who, after all, was once a *parthenos* (429) but now is a woman.

The drama is built, to be sure, on the erotic tensions between male and female and on the contrasts between the genders, so that when Hippolytus reenacts and imitates the words, gestures, and actions of the other, we recognize the workings of the dramatic rule of reversal into the opposite which defines a tragic peripeteia. Yet Hippolytus' identity as the *parthenos* figure suggests that this *kouros*, this young man, may well be the potential bride as well as the bridegroom, and this role then logically leads him into the wider sphere of feminine experience which his secret double, Phaedra, exemplifies. In other words, the quality of "subjective containment" that the male as virgin (*parthenos*) embodies also automatically entails an intersubjective relation with the woman (*gunē*), the no-longer *parthenos*, who is Phaedra, so that these same devices of imitation and reenactment also attest to the hidden affinities between them.

This relation between the two selves is marked exactly at the turning point of the action just before Phaedra's posthumous message will ensure that Hippolytus will be called upon to play her part. There in the second stasimon, to which I have earlier referred, those *archai*, the ends and beginnings of the ropes that bound Phaedra's nuptial ship to the shore when she came to Athens as a bride, signify the end for one (Phaedra) and the beginning of the story for the other (Hippolytus) (762–63). Lamenting Phaedra's fate, the chorus starts its song with reference to the maidens who "drip their radiant tears into the purple deep" in mourning for Phaethon (735–41), who plunged to his death when he lost control of the fiery steeds of his father, the sun-god. Phaethon, as has been observed, is the male doublet of Hippolytus, as both a driver of chariots and a failed bridegroom, while the maidens' lament reflects the grief of the chorus for Phaedra and also is already foretelling the place in the cult for virginal brides that Hippolytus will receive.[39] But Phaethon, the "shining" one, who shares his fate with Hippolytus but his name and etymology with Phaedra,[40] is also the figure who mediates this intersubjective relation between the two selves. Phaethon is the mythic Other through whom the identities of the two characters are momentarily confounded just at the moment of crossing when their paths are to take linked but separate directions to their respective deaths.[41]

The Feminine Body: Woman, House, World

Eros provides the focus for confronting the more general experience of relations between two subjects because rather than effacing all differences, eros calls for a complementary opposition between one self and an other. In dramatizing the implications of Hippolytus' resistance to eros which extend outward to encompass all the relations between one self and an other, the play appropriately develops and enlarges this "intersubjective" experience in ways that involve not only himself and Phaedra, but all the characters, including the nurse, Theseus, and even Aphrodite and Artemis. One critic defines this distinctive characteristic of the play as a *discordia concors*. By this term he means that "while each character stands alone as a unique individual, he/she still shares in and mirrors qualities of his/her opposite."[42] Strangely enough, this critic's formulation has a Greek equivalent located in the text itself: its specific referent is none other than the body of the woman.

As the first choral lyric tells us, "woman's nature is a *dustropos harmonia*, a discordant harmony (or *discordia concors*), and there is wont to cohabit with it (*philei . . . sunoikein*) an ill, unhappy helplessness (*amēchania*) that goes with travail (*odinōn*) and unreasoning thoughts (*aphrosunē*)" (161–64). Through the natural processes of the body, the woman experiences herself as a diversity in unity. Biological constraints subject her to flux and change and put her at odds with herself, creating an internal *dustropos harmonia*, an ill-tuned harmony: in short, a "natural" oxymoron of conflict and ambiguity.

Woman herself can therefore be construed as a self-reflexive microcosm of the differential relations between the various characters in the play, herself included, and more generically, between one self and an other. Still further, she is, in a sense, the topocosm of the world of the here and now upon which can be mapped life's conflicts and ambiguities. Because the play locates these specifically in the area of sexuality, the "natural" construct of the woman's body serves as the proper and literal terrain for the work of Aphrodite. At the same time, this feminine body supplies the objective correlative to the broader questions of intersubjective relations explored in the play.

Woman is a character in the drama, acting and acted upon; she struggles, in truth, against the facts and desires of the body, but she is also a sign. An enigmatic sign like the world itself in which she lives, she is difficult to interpret, requiring the services of a *mantis*, as the nurse and chorus say in the face of her stubborn refusal to speak (236, 269–70, 346; cf. 873, 729, 858). The conjectures made in the first choral lyric about the etiology of her disease are instructive beyond their interest for Greek medical ideas, as they indicate what general influences impinge upon the representative figure that is woman. The symptoms Phaedra presents are overdetermined; they can be interpreted indifferently according to each of the three cardinal zones of relations in which the self is involved: the divine domain where she might be one who is possessed by a god (141–50); the personal domain of relations within the family, either husband or parents (151–60); and, as we have seen, the body in its conflictual relation with itself (161–69) as the appropriate model for all relations. In other words, this complex organism that is her body supplies the symbolic locus for organizing the entire cultural system— physical, psychological, social, metaphysical, epistemological, and ethical—of which Aphrodite is the cosmic emblem and Phaedra her human instrument and tragic paradigm.

Yet it is significant that the chorus at this moment calls not upon Aphrodite but upon Artemis, who guards women in childbirth (166–69). It has often been noted that the women's invocation demonstrates how insufficient is Hippolytus' view of the goddess both in his exclusive claim to her and in his denial of natural procreation through the female body.[43] But I want to emphasize further why Artemis properly belongs in the world of women, whether presiding over their integral state as untouched virgins or over the moment when that "breeze" (*aura*), as the chorus refers to labor pangs, "darts through the womb" (165–66).[44] There is no contradiction in the fact that she protects the female body, whether closed or open. In her links both with virginity and childbirth, Artemis' intervention tells us that for the married woman, society insists that maternity be separated from sexuality and rejoined with chastity, closing and enclosing the body in the inner spaces of the house. This then is that other *dustropos harmonia*, the social rather than physiological fact in woman's life, namely, the cultural oxymoron of the chaste wife. Aphrodite, in truth, has no continuing visible place in married life once the bridal period is over, and appropriately in her Homeric Hymn she leaves the scene forever after she has borne the child she now gives to others to rear. In some contexts, childbirth and sexuality overlap, both attesting to the permeability of the body's boundaries, and are often in fact conflated in image and metaphor (e.g., Archilochus, 104D), but at the same time they are antitheses, as opposed to each other as Artemis is to Aphrodite.

In defining the inner conflict of Phaedra as one between Artemis and Aphrodite within our frame of self and other, one can further justify the role Phaedra plays as model for Hippolytus, not only in formal but also in thematic terms. After all, the other is no longer truly an other. The Phaedra of this play, as many have shown, shares many traits with Hippolytus. Despite their contrasting genealogies which might polarize the sexual attitudes into two representative extremes—the child of the Cretan mother (Phaedra) and the child of the Amazon (Hippolytus)—temperamentally they are not incompatible. Both are concerned with purity of body and soul, both would maintain the integrity of their inner selves, and both display an aristocratic idealism. It is precisely Phaedra's refusal to abandon these "Artemisian" values, in fact, that leads her to engineer Aphrodite's revenge, and it is the power of Aphrodite, above all, that defines the Artemisian by situating it in a differential relationship with what she herself represents so as to make all confront the "*dustropos harmonia*" of the world in which everyone must live. Thus Phaedra's affinities with Hippolytus are indispensable to the workings of the plot. Moreover, they are indispensable because they tell us (and Hippolytus) that the simple dichotomies of Hippolytus' existence will not be able to withstand the complexities of Phaedra herself.[45]

This last observation, in the most general terms, constitutes the drama's fundamental lesson common to the experience of all tragedy: Only in discovering that the universe is one of conflict, and that words, values, and man himself are ambiguous, can one accept a problematic vision of the world and acquire a tragic consciousness.[46] Tragic man, like Oedipus, is a riddle to be solved, and Hippolytus, in his anomalous state between beasts and gods, male and female, child and adult, is yet another distinctive example of this configuration.[47] But Greek thought also tells us that the very source and origin of ambiguity and conflict that is the essence of the human condition is none other than woman herself, who steals from man the simple integrity of his original state. Defined in her nature by the mode of her creation, Hesiod's Zeus introduces her into the world to redefine its topography, which henceforth will be modeled on that of the female body: a dichotomy between outside and inside, seen and unseen. Hippolytus, in his tirade against Phaedra, will reinvoke the canonical Hesiodic characterization of this first woman, Pandora, both the lovely useless *agalma* that husbands will ruin their houses to adorn, and the deceitful conniving bitch, the counterfeit evil, in whom Aphrodite brings mischief to birth (616–18, 630–33, 642–44).[48]

One might say that Hippolytus' replication of the Hesiodic discourse at the heart of the drama defines him as the nostalgic standard-bearer of the Golden Age.[49] Even more, his fall into the human condition is none other than the experience of its deceptions and falsehoods, stereotypically contrived through the agency of a woman. The drama indeed builds on the Hesiodic foundations of human culture, which are based on the imperatives of marriage, procreation, and agriculture, and whose rules Hippolytus by his mode of life transgresses. But it also transcends these, as it must on the tragic stage, to attain its proper objective—the fashioning of a tragic consciousness, experience of which is essential to the construction of the self which is otherwise imprisoned and isolated in its world of single meanings.

The woman, as the other, is the object who embodies for men the external realities of the world. She therefore constrains and defeats the boundless desire of the male self to escape these unwelcome necessities. But, as a speaking subject, woman also embodies the prerequisites for that fuller consciousness to develop in herself. Given the social constraints under which she must live and the strains of the multiple roles and identities assigned to her, she is best constructed to experience this tragic "double bind." Breaking the silence that propriety demands from her, she necessarily transgresses in turn the social rules which would repress and deny, if they could, the best-kept secret of cultural ideology, that is, the reality of the sexual, even adulterous wife.[50] Aphrodite therefore plays a critical role. In entering into the woman and into the house as the agent of illegal and unspeakable desire, she transforms the "natural" dissonant unity of the woman's body in pregnancy and childbirth into a cognitive dissonance within the self. That self, now in struggling to harmonize its disparate aspects, experiences subjectively her own ambiguities and through them is led to an epistemological inquiry into the world whose structures she also objectively represents (374ff.).

There is a paradox here. Woman as body may be relegated in the eyes of society to the corporeal side of human existence. But her physical structure which stresses her interior space already predisposes her to a self-consciousness that replaces the virginal quality of "self-containment" with a mature subjectivity capable of furnishing a more adequate model of the self. This self must now confront that interiority, which is made problematic as the subjective container of the secret that must be hidden within. The text even distinguishes between these physical and cognitive dissonances. To the *dustropos harmonia* of the woman's body, the birth pangs (*ōdinai*) she suffers, she replies with a passive *aphrosunē*, an *anoia* (164, 398), the surrender of mental faculties in the face of biological pressures. But the other dissonance, the anguish of her desire, demands rather the exercise of *sōphrosunē*, an active attempt of the intellect to constrain the irresistible forces of instinct and desire (399), and it evokes from Phaedra the cry of pain (*odunāi*, 247) for the effort to set her mind aright.[51]

Without Aphrodite, the ambiguities of women's lives pass unnoticed as they freely come and go in widening circles from the house to the outside spaces that the women describe in the parodos and which they leave behind offstage. The idyllic vignette of women washing clothes in the water's dews of the river's stream (124–30) contrasts both with its preceding counterpart in which Hippolytus defines his meadow (which *aidōs* metaphorically tends with its river dews, 78) and with Phaedra's subsequent imaginings (which simultaneously overlay longings for purity with erotic desire, 209–11).[52] In the women's scene, the dripping water is said to issue from Oceanus, that is, it is fed subterraneously from the primordial source, and sends forth a running stream. Here all is flow and flux, surface and depth, as the women dip their pitchers into the water and wet the crimson cloaks to cleanse them, laying them to dry upon the back of the sunny rock. Purity is not original or constant, but in the cycle of household tasks, it can be restored in the washing of clothes that having touched the body were subjected to the ordinary pollutions of daily life. But with Aphrodite, purity and pollution split into irreconcilable opposites. And with the revelation of Phaedra's secret, the simple details of women's work will reveal their deeper affinities with the tragic situation which is foretold by that split.

The women's contact with the clothing, described as *teggousa*, wetting, will find its analogue in the tears that will wet their flooding eyes in grief over the misfortunes of the house and the bereaved husband (128, 854). But this contact implied by *teggousa* is earlier invoked by the nurse who, reproaching Phaedra's silence, laments that her mistress is not at all softened or persuaded by her words (303).[53] Women are expected to mourn for the sorrows of others and, like the clothes they soften in the water, to be pliant and permeable themselves. *Teggousa* already intimates the potential dangers to come, but there are other signs more ambiguous still. The water that drips from the rock will echo in the desire that drips by the agency of eros from the eyes (121, 526). And the benign heat of the sun (128–29) both suggests the passions of eros itself (cf. 530) and is later recalled in the invocation of another spring, the mouth of Dirce at Thebes, which sets the stage for the erotic encounter where "Aphrodite gave Semele as a bride to the flame-girt thunder" when she was pregnant with Dionysus (554–55).[54]

In the second stasimon sung by the chorus at the midpoint of the drama (mentioned earlier) the language of the parodos reappears. Fiery sun and water are now transformed into the amber-gleaming radiance of the tears (*dakruōn tas elektrophaeis augas*, 740–41) which the mortal maidens let fall in grief for Phaethon as objectified tokens of their subjective emotions.[55] And the ambrosial springs that pour forth unhindered (748) are meant now only for the erotic paradise of the Hesperides where the bed of immortal Zeus and Hera is, a land that offers no road to sailors at the boundaries of the world, beyond mortal limits where heaven and earth meet.[56] This is the point that returns us to the very context of the parodos and the implicit contrast between purity and pollution. There the chorus shifts immediately from the description of their outside scene to think upon Phaedra, who lies sick within the house from that as yet unknown disease, eros. The robes the women have exposed upon the sunny rock (126) give way to the robe with which Phaedra shades her face to hide the secret shame that pollutes her (131–32).

Now the women will leave the stage no more and Phaedra, except in her fantasy, will make only the briefest journeys from and to the house. The world narrows down to the space of the stage and what lies behind it as she oscillates between secrecy and revelation in the conflict she experiences between the virtuous wife and the desiring subject. These spaces are therefore intensified, as it is that oscillation that exerts pressures on the normal unquestioned relations between inside and outside, bringing these tensions and ambiguities into play to recode into complex psychological enclosures the private areas that are the woman's body and the isotopic house she inhabits.

INSIDE AND OUTSIDE   The drama exploits to the fullest the symbolic potentials of Greek scenic conventions, which in setting the actions on stage before the facade of the house arrange a dialectic of space between outside and inside, seen and unseen, open and closed, exposed and hidden. In one respect, the secret finds appropriate shelter in the inmost recesses of the house (as it does within the deepest marrow of the soul, 255), the place that harbors other undisclosed secrets of women's lives that modesty protects. In another respect, of course, this secret of adulterous desire is incompatible with the house and the social values it objectifies, so that woman is no longer "at home" with herself or in the space that is commensurate with her own anatomy. Rather, the secret, confined and repressed, confines her to her bed, and blocks all the normal forms of domestic exchanges and those of the body itself in that food can neither enter in nor can the secret issue forth.[57]

The door is the significant boundary between the two zones. Once Phaedra has crossed its threshold from interior to exterior, her dramatic action already informs us that the secret, if not yet revealed, is at least now out-of-doors. Only outside can she find her voice and begin to speak. And what she says in riddling terms, as she recodes her erotic passion into passionate longing for the Artemisian spaces of remoter regions (208–38), demonstrates how far from domestic territory is the site assigned to female desire. Phaedra's exit indicates in advance the homology, which the text will later make specific, between the door and the mouth as apertures to the interior which can either be opened or closed. In the idiom of the play, these operations are principally those of *desis* and *lusis*, binding and loosening,[58] which are to prove the determining factors of the plot. Indeed, only through the first *lusis*, that is, the exit of Phaedra from the house and the ensuing "exit" of the secret from her mouth, can the true *desis*, the binding of the plot, begin and the door become the pivotal point of passage and exchange. This is the same door, let us recall, at which Aphrodite had stood in the prologue, unrecognized and unaddressed by Hippolytus (100–101), and this is a stance that Phaedra will herself exactly repeat (cf. 575).

Phaedra leaves the house at the beginning and enters it again permanently as the place of her death. Hippolytus, on the other hand, enters the house upon his arrival on stage and leaves it in indignation at the nurse's proposal communicated to him within. He is never to enter it again. Once his father has discovered the secret, Hippolytus is banished not only from the precinct of the house but from that of the land itself, all because three times Theseus performs a significant act of opening: the doors of the house (*chalate kleithra . . . pulōmatōn/eklueth' harmous*, 808–9); the unwrapping of the *deltos*, the tablet (864–65); and the utterance he can no longer contain within the "doors of his mouth" (*stomatos en pulais*, 882).[59]

For both Phaedra and Hippolytus, the house has become the purveyor of death. The house reclaims one of them literally for its own and expels the other beyond its limits, until he is brought back at the end, when on his deathbed he beholds, as he says, the "doors of the region below" (*nerterōn . . . pulas*, 1445–46; cf. 895). Aphrodite's ominous statement closing the prologue, "he does not know that the doors of Hades are gaping open for him" (56–57), corresponds, as noted earlier, to Hippolytus' dying utterance. But Hippolytus' passage from the beginning of the text to its end has indeed taken him through the doors of the house itself, whose interior secret spaces anticipate its sinister analogue—the house of Hades.

This relation between inside and outside which correlates the self and the house is continued through an important gesture shared by Phaedra at the beginning of the play and Hippolytus toward the end, namely the covering of the head. In social life, the woman ordinarily veils her head as a distinctive mark of feminine *aidōs*, modesty. But the context of the play deepens the traditional meanings associated with this sign of social invisibility. Before her entrance on stage, the chorus had described the queen on her sickbed, who, shading her head with fine garments, was doubly enclosed in her resignation to silence and death in the interior of the house (131–40). Once outside, however, Phaedra alternatively removes her headdress to

speak and then covers her face with her cloak to hide her shame
(243–44, 250), suggesting as Artemidorus later confirms,[60] that there
is an analogy between the house and the cloak as coverings for the
self, both connoting a spatial relationship between inside and outside. Hippolytus, as has been observed, repeats her gesture at the end
when he calls for Theseus to cover his face with his robe (*pepla*,
1458), not only showing that, as Phaedra predicted, he shares in her
disease,[61] but also making the appropriate sign to greet approaching
death, which will indeed cover over the body.[62] From this perspective,
one could say that Hippolytus' final physical gesture at last, even if
only for a moment, creates on the open stage an interior dimension
for the body that by now has experienced for itself the boundary between inside and outside.[63]

What in fact determines this conclusion is the other enclosure,
the miniature *deltos* which, like a pair of doors, must be opened and
which, in both content and form, mediates the analogy between the
body of the woman and the house. The *deltos* is an inanimate object.
Like the house, it cannot actually voice an utterance. But when it is
opened, like woman, it can, in its message of erotic violence, speak
the language of the intimate body. Even closed, the *deltos*, allied to
the triangular *delta*, can be identified as the external sign of the
woman's inward parts, exposed yet still concealed.[64] Artemidorus'
observation is particularly relevant here: to dream of a *deltos* is to
dream of a woman because all sorts of imprints, *tupoi*, are left in
her.[65] Phaedra has effectively bound herself again to the interior of
the house in the noose she attaches to its rafters. And she completes
the image of the chaste wife, not only in the *tupoi* that presumably
are the *grammata* inside the *deltos*, but also through external signs.
For Theseus explicitly refers first to the imprint, the *tupoi*, of her
signet ring on the outside (862) and second, to the encircling embrace of the seals (*peribolas sphragismatōn*) by which she has re-
fastened the tablet. As keeper of her husband's house (cf. 787), the
woman keeps safe and sealed for him both the treasures of the house
and herself to which he alone has private access.[66] It is therefore entirely proper that Theseus first imagines her message will implore
him not to allow another woman into his house and bed (860–61). It
is equally fitting that he open the doors of the house and then the
deltos as well as open his mouth to utter the curses against the male
he believes has trespassed upon his domestic space.

On the level of the action, the *deltos*, which constitutes Phaedra's plot to cover up her shame, plays a pivotal role in the plot as a whole. It is also the nodal point investing all the other acts of opening and closing in the play with their wider associations. Mouth and genitals, speech and sexuality, exterior and interior, exposed and hidden—all these converge in this metonymic condensation of the feminine that is displaced onto the inscribed object. The *deltos* therefore is the most concrete sign of the pervasive conflict between inside and outside which the woman resolves only through death— for herself and for the other.

For this other, Hippolytus who is now barred from the house, her message will bring about a new relation between inner and outer space to be projected on a vast cosmic scale, in effect converting the entire landscape into an enclosure. For the messenger describes how first the giant wave that was to bring forth the bull from the sea towered up to heaven so as to obscure the sight of the Scironian shore and to hide the Isthmus and Asclepian rock (1207–9), and he ends his recital with the words: "the horses and the terrible prodigy of the bull were hidden somewhere, he knew not where, on earth" (1247–48).

Between the two moments, the first, when the engulfing wave has confounded the boundary of land and sea, and the last, when Hippolytus covers his head as he approaches the boundary of Hades whose doors he now sees before him, Hippolytus comes to an experience of the body which replicates that of the sick and suffering Phaedra seen at the beginning. Her prediction that he would "share in her disease" comes to a violent physical fulfillment here when the combined action of the bull from the sea and the stampede of his own horses have subjected his body to what might be called a demonic parody of eros. The congruence is even more striking as Hippolytus goes out to meet his fate in terms that recall precisely those used to describe the body of his secret double, the woman.

That *dustropos harmonia*, the "*ill-turned fitting together*" with which the woman is wont to *dwell* (*sunoikein*, 161–63), supplies the model of a conflicted self, a condition Hippolytus imitates literally in two ways: first, in his relation to the ensemble of chariot and horses which represents the spatial extension of the self; and second, in the experience of the body itself. Hippolytus first *fits* (*harmosas*) his feet into the matching footspaces in the chariot (1189),[67] fusing himself, as it were, with the object representing his own integral structure (cf. *kollētōn*, 1225), while it is with the ways of horses that he is said to *dwell* (*sunoikōn*, 1220). With the advent of the bull, the horses do not *turn* with (*metastrephousai*, 1226) the bindings of their harness or with the compact structure of the chariot, but are *turned* back (*anastrephein*) by the bull until the disaster ensues.[68] Then once Hippolytus is separated from the entangling reins (1244), the chariot and horses are separated. The chariot is broken, like the body of Hippolytus (1239), and the horses disappear together with the bull (1247–48).

Brought back on stage in a pitiful state, pain brings him to a direct experience of a physical interiority, and he expresses himself through language that imitates the symptoms of such a *dustropos harmonia*. He cries out that pangs dart through his head (1351) as they were said to dart through the belly of the woman in travail (164–66) and that a spasm leaps up in his brain (1352); a little later, he voices his desire (*eramai*) for a two-edged sword to divide his body in two and "put his life to bed" (1375–77). In conflating the language of childbirth and sexuality,[69] Hippolytus has come to mime these two aspects of female experience. As a result, he is compelled to acknowledge the permeable boundaries of the physical self, both those of the head and of the body. We recognize here the power of Aphrodite which, when refused, converts rapture to pain and eros to death. But we know too that this physical experience is the culmination of the longer and more significant process by which her power affects the self in mind as in body, mind through body, as a more complex perception of interior space.

The body Artemis will bid Theseus to take into his arms (1431–32). At this moment, however, when the physical and mental are still unified in a living organism, she has already distinguished between the effects of eros on body and mind. For she identifies the passions of Aphrodite (*Kupridos ek prothumias orgai*) which have violently invaded the body (*demas*) (1417–18), but in predicting the prenuptial rites of Aphrodite in which Hippolytus will have a future share, Artemis gives him the spiritual recompense for that somatic suffering which his good *phrēn*, his mind, has earned (1419).

The text has earlier suggested how extensive are the ways by which Aphrodite works in a remarkable phrase uttered by the chorus just after Hippolytus has left the stage to begin his last journey. This phrase significantly reorganizes those topological spaces with which Hippolytus had identified himself—the woods and the meadow. In the prologue, Aphrodite had spoken of Hippolytus who consorts always with the *parthenos* (Artemis) in the verdant wood (*chlōran d'an hulēn*) and we recall too the garland whose flowers Hippolytus says he had culled from the virgin meadow (*plekton stephanon ex akēratou leimōnos*, 73–74). Now the chorus, lamenting Hippolytus' irrevocable departure from these Artemisian spaces, combines the two previous allusions by referring to the "deep verdure," the *batheian . . . chloēn* of the resting places of the maiden of Leto (i.e., Artemis) which no longer will receive their customary garlands (*astephanoi de koras anapaulai/Latous*) (1137–38). This is the only instance in the entire play of the word *bathus*, "deep," and at this critical moment in the text it is a subtle but significant clue that a corresponding shift from surface to depth has taken place in Hippolytus himself.

The context of the phrase is still more suggestive, because the chorus follows this leave-taking from Artemis with their regret that, by his exile, the maidens have lost their bridal rivalry for Hippolytus' bed (*numphidia . . . hamilla*) (1142–43). In this erotic setting of what we might call an "anti-epithalamium" (since the chorus of Hippolytus' agemates divides into male and female parts)[70] the phrase "the deep wood" may already foreshadow the sexual connotations of what will happen to Hippolytus by the shores of the sea through the bestial violence of the bull and the horses.[71]

Yet through the language it uses in the preceding stanzas, the ode integrates more fully these overlapping levels of mind and body. The chorus reflects on what has earlier transpired for Hippolytus to bring him to this moment of leave-taking and they translate his experience into the expression of their own subjective feelings. Here at the moment of Hippolytus' own peripeteia, the chorus is moved to ponder the general peripeteias of the world (1104–10). They allude to their own interior perceptions, their *phrenes* (1104), and they speak of a consciousness (*sunesin*) which they hide (*keuthōn*) in their hopes within the self (1105). Praying for a spirit (*thumon*) that is untouched (*akēraton*) by pain (1114), they find, when reviewing Hippolytus' story, that their own *phrēn*, their mind, is no longer pure (*katharan*) (1120), and like him, that their innocence is forever polluted.[72]

The Secret and the Construct of Self

The depth, therefore, by which the chorus qualifies the wood and the meadow must surely recall the preceding initiation of Hippolytus into this interior life, which began at the moment Phaedra's secret was transmitted to him. Then, through its violation of his sensibilities, he feels the first penetration of the self, and under the secret's burden, he begins to develop a consciousness (*sunesis*) that must properly be hidden within the self.[73]

The point of entry is the orifice of the ear, whose pollution he would cleanse with purifying streams of water (653–54). But the wounding effects of the knowledge the *logos* imparts cannot be undone. Having heard these words, as he declares at the end of his long speech, he seems no longer pure to himself (654–55). Henceforth he is conscious of a frontier between being and seeming; he is aware of the body's surface as a boundary between outside and inside. As a result, the Edenic harmony the body had enjoyed with its natural territory in a relationship of unquestioned identity is forever disrupted.

By its very nature, a secret alienates the self from its exterior space and divides the self into two. For in disjoining that which can be said from that which cannot, the action of the secret creates a distinction between public and private, self and other. It therefore brings into being an interior space to contain what must be hidden within. This space, coextensive with the organic interior of the body, is henceforth also a "cognitive mental region" dividing inner thought from outer expression.[74]

In Hippolytus' case, Phaedra's secret is doubly divisive because it reorients the image of the body in more specific ways. The secret enters the self as an alien intrusion from an other, which, bearing a message of illegal desire, is utterly antithetical to its new owner. Its effects therefore pollute the self at its deepest level, alienating the self from what it perceives as its true essence and mobilizing its defenses for resistance.

Still, *despite* his resistance, Hippolytus has already become a sharer in the disturbing circuit of communication by which he now possesses the secret of an other, which had been betrayed to him by yet another. Like its original owner (Phaedra), Hippolytus also must oscillate between the necessity of retaining the secret within and the desire to betray it too to still another. But *because* of that resistance, we perceive the first sign of the duality of the self in Hippolytus' famous cry: my tongue (*glōssa*) has sworn, but my mind (*phrēn*) has not (612). A gap has now opened up between inside and outside, inversely matching the earlier confession of Phaedra: my hands are clean (*hagnai*) but my mind (*phrēn*) is polluted (*miasma*) (317).

There are formal resemblances between the two statements, but the paradox of Hippolytus' words is more profound. In confronting the differential between the absolute speech form (the oath) and its context (the secret), he momentarily repudiates the oath to protect the integrity of the self. At the same time, he is betraying that integrity because an oath guarantees at all times that the self is forever bound to its word. Moreover, an oath in itself can be viewed as an autonomous self-validating act, as fidelity to its terms in the human domain is an obligation of the inner self. Its public pronouncement must be matched by an internal determination to remain true to what it has sworn. Hence, although it is the nurse who has required his pledge of silence, oath taking is an act entirely appropriate to Hippolytus. For it is commensurate with that autonomous "subjective containment" that virginity can represent, and the virtue of keeping that oath in the moral sphere finds its logical equivalent in the virtue of keeping the physical body pure.

His moment of hesitation, however, is irrevocable; his story has now begun. There is a brief period between his lapse and recovery during which he castigates the duplicity of the other. He reasserts the external dichotomy in the world, as he had done before (80–81), between those who are good and those who are wicked. This time, however, he defines the latter pole as exclusively female (616, 629, 632, 642, 649, 651). In this interval, before the tongue that has sworn accepts the limits that the barrier of the oath has imposed upon its freedom to speak, a torrent of language spills forth from within. Here Hippolytus defines the self at the furthest remove from the other, denying, if he could, the right of speech to the other (645–48), as he strives to heal the cleavage he now feels in his being. Yet at the same time, he has, in effect, left open for the overhearer a potential space in himself where he too might "hide one thing in his heart and say another" (*Il.* 9.312–13) and where his unswerving attitude might yield to change and reversal (cf. also 1109–10, 1115–17).[75]

As the objective interpreter of the secret, Hippolytus confirms for Phaedra what she already knows. The world will judge her as it does all women, reading her divisions not as a conflictual ambiguity between self and role but only as a generic duplicity. When Hippolytus reiterates that Hesiodic position, he prompts her to close up this enigmatic space between self and role. Her aim is to defeat the image of the counterfeit woman he had assigned to her but she ends in fact by sustaining it. To resolve the "knot of the *logos*," her "double bind" has indeed turned into double dealing. In acceding to the stereotype of feminine nature, the woman reduces complex duality to simple reversal from inside to outside and plots a revenge that comes as close as it can to the general definition of all revenge: that is, "to repeat what was done to you but reversing it on to the other."[76] Because both women and the young occupy spaces on the margins of male society, they are also deemed more marginal to its dominant standards. Their ambiguities therefore leave them both more open to suspicion of their actions and motives. In the case of Hippolytus, the correspondence between them is even closer as the counterfeit charge against Phaedra finds its direct equivalent in his social status as bastard, *nothos* (309, 962, 1083).[77] Phaedra's lying message can therefore persuade Theseus of its veracity because it substitutes one stereotype (adolescent) for the other (woman) and in the process subjects Hippolytus to those same conflicting pressures from inside and outside to which she herself had succumbed.

Thus in the open space on the stage before the oath secures the secret within the self, Hippolytus has unknowingly already included himself as a sharer in Phaedra's scheme. Rejecting complicity with the other (Phaedra), he has, in fact, collaborated in the broader scheme of Aphrodite which, when eros is denied, aims to confound the identity of one with the other by replacing radical separation with hidden identification. When he who has judged is judged in turn on the same terms and then discovers the misfit of inside and outside, only then does he subjectively experience the same cognitive dissonance and acknowledge it too for the other.

The sign of that cognitive dissonance Hippolytus shares with the other is precise and formal, indicated as a purely semantic shift and appropriately placed at the end of his long speech before his father:

ἐσωφρόνησε δ'οὐκ ἔχουσα σωφρονεῖν
ἡμεῖς δ'ἔχοντες οὐ καλῶς ἐχρώμεθα

She practiced virtue (*sōphrosunē*) not being able to be virtuous, while we, having the capacity for *sōphrosunē*, did not use it well. (1034–35)

In the light of Phaedra's own closing words, "he will share in my disease and will learn to *sōphronein*" (730–31), Hippolytus' statement seems to fulfill her prediction *to* the letter, and *in* the letter. Indeed his words seem to distill the issues of the play into a semiotic lesson on the potential of the signifier to include more than one signified and that of the speaker to distinguish between competence in the abstract rule (*langue*) and individual performance in the speech act (*parole*). This lesson is nevertheless far from elementary considering the general relationship between language, thought, and consciousness, and the particular relationship language has, as a mode of communication between self and other, with the problems and plot of the drama.

The syntactical relations of Hippolytus' two verses are therefore especially illuminating. The structure divides (or doubles) for each the concept of *sōphrosunē* and then through chiasmus makes one the inverted double of the other. As the grammatical near-asyndeton between the two tells us, they are not interlinked but are rather situated together in a relation of identity in difference. In one sense, we can say that Hippolytus now shares with Phaedra a recognition of verbal paradox that for her revolved around the allied concept of *aidōs* (shame), which although bearing two different and opposing meanings, as she lamented, is nevertheless composed of the same letters (385–87).[78] Hippolytus' statement advances still further. The play on a single word extends from a single observation on the experience of one character (*aidōs* for Phaedra) to a relational term, that of the differential experience of two (*sōphrosunē* for Phaedra and Hippolytus). And in so doing, his statement also recasts as a phenomenon of language (the oxymoron) the psychic phenomenon of a divided self which each had expressed earlier in separate but parallel terms (my hands are pure, my mind is not [Phaedra]; my tongue has sworn, my mind has not [Hippolytus]).

This recognition is critical for acquiring that tragic consciousness which the action of the drama achieves, compelling the self to relinquish the dream of a pure and univocal language. Such a language would correlate the speakable with the true and would eliminate any semantic confusion between signifier and signified that might make interpretation problematic, subject to the charge of being *asēmos* (nonsignifying, 269, 369) or *parasēmos* (falsely signifying, 1115). Human nature aspires to live in this utopia of signs, either to be reserved as the private property of a single individual and a single point of view or, according to Theseus' dream of two voices (one true, one speaking anything else, 928–29), to serve as a communication to an other whose relation to its speaker would be immediately transparent.

The lessons of language may be viewed as a gain when we consider that "if everything we know is viewed as a transition from something else, every experience must have two sides; and either every name must have a double meaning, or else for every meaning there must be two names."[79] Phaedra is therefore essential to Hippolytus, we might say, for only through the exchange of roles with her does he come to acknowledge that *sōphrosunē* indeed has a double meaning—for himself and for her—and that for this expanded definition, there are indeed two names, Hippolytus and Phaedra, who are entitled to share it.[80] On the other hand, there is loss, if ambiguity can be said to contaminate this ideal of a pure and innocent language and to violate unity of word and meaning either with confusing admixtures or, alternatively, through fragmentation and dispersal of its "original" signification. In this sense, our drama amplifies the tragic lesson by choosing for word play the specific terms for purity (both *aidōs* and *sōphrosunē*) and adjusting that game to the demands of Aphrodite in the links it makes between speech and sexuality.

The secret—the knowledge of adulterous desire—which both now share and both would deny, would seem to be the route in this play to articulating a language and hence a consciousness more adequate to the complex geography of body and world than the shallow surfaces of the untested meadow and the unchallenged language of the self would allow. Double speaking is inevitable in the face of adulterous desire, which indeed contaminates social meanings and confuses interpretation of social roles. It is unspeakable for Phaedra in terms of the proprieties of the social code which calls it *aischrologia* (shameful talk). It is unspeakable now for Hippolytus through the oath that constrains his speech. Hence language is thickened through the riddling ambiguities to which he must resort and opens plain speaking to the charge of duplicity. And there is no way in this system of controlling language (or eros), least of all another oath, which as a transaction between self and the world beyond (because gods, not mortals, punish perjurers) has no human context to support it.

Double speaking is perhaps a disease that the bewildered Hippolytus suspects is being attributed to him (933) when Theseus himself first enigmatically utters his wish for the two voices that would distinguish in the self the true from the false word (927–29). But it is an inevitable disease, inflicted first on Phaedra as the secret of Aphrodite, which in arousing simultaneous desire for its fulfillment and its repression, necessarily recodes language into the double entendre. And, as Aphrodite's secret of desire, owned or disowned (by both Phaedra and Hippolytus), it, like desire itself, cannot be contained but instead finds devious paths of language in order to entice the one who has refused Aphrodite into the mysteries of worldly communication.

Hippolytus had been privy to the sacred mysteries of Demeter, as the text tells us when it arranges Phaedra's first glimpse of him at the moment when he came to Athens for initiation (25), thereby directing our attention to the potential parallel between sacred and profane secrets, both of which are *aporrhēta*, unspeakable in their respective milieux.[81] That mystery of Aphrodite will eventually reveal itself as the supernatural epiphany which the goddess shares with Poseidon and which initiates the body of Hippolytus into a demonic version of eros. But the initiation had begun far earlier with the "mystery" at Troezen: that is, the secret desire of the silent Phaedra, which organizes the entire play around the notions of hiding and revealing, speech and silence, because "the *muthos* is not *koinos* (shared) in any way" (609; cf. especially 293–96) and Phaedra is ruined once she has revealed her woes to the light (368). The nurse says enigmatically that she will speak only "to those within" (524), a mystic formula that conceals her plan to address Hippolytus in the secret interior of the house, while the chorus, hearing Phaedra's report of the muffled words of Hippolytus (which are uttered still inside), responds with the pronouncement: he has revealed the secret, that is, has shown forth the hidden things (*ta krupt' ekpephēne*,

594). Theseus continues the theme of unspeakability in another way when he responds with horror to the sight of his dead wife (*ou rhēton*, 846) and once he has read the message of the *deltos* (*ou lekton*, 875 [pace Barrett]). But it is Hippolytus, bound by his oath of silence, who must play the initiate, because in confronting his father he may not reveal what is forbidden (*ou themis*) to tell to those who do not know (1033).[82]

At the beginning of the play, the servant had inquired of Hippolytus: do you know what *nomos*, what rule is established for mortals in regard to social relations? and Hippolytus had replied: "I do not know" (*ouk oida*, 90–91). But when all his words have failed and he leaves the stage, he goes as the true initiate, that is, one who knows but cannot speak. Now his last despairing cry, "I know this but I don't know *how* to declare it" (*oida d'ouch hopōs phrasō*, 1091), suggests that with her mysteries Aphrodite has also revealed how his refusal of eros has affected his general status as a speaking subject in his society.

Eros and Logos

From this perspective let us reexamine the judgment, shared by many critics, that language in the play operates in a "pessimistic and regressive frame as an instrument of seduction and entrapment, of compromise and theft, or as an impotent means and a dismal failure" in human relations.[83] It is true, of course, that the play offers a wide spectrum of different forms of communication, all of which end in what might be called a "failure" of *logos*. But such an assessment perhaps states the problem in reverse, in that it does not consider relations of cause and effect: that is, the failure of *logos* is directly related to and determined by the prior "failure" of eros. In order to understand what happens in the domain of the *logos*, it is the extent and significance of this first failure that we must rather measure.

Eros itself is the representative form of communication, of reciprocity and exchange in the world. Physical in nature, it is culturally regulated as a communication between the proper partners in the social system of marriage. That system, like a system of language, articulates its own proper grammatical rules and in the social differentiations it enforces, it is designed to produce unambiguous meanings. In this system, "women, like words, are signs to be communicated and exchanged among men," but "women too, as persons, are generators of signs. . . . In the matrimonial dialogue of men, woman is never purely what is spoken about; for if women in general represent a certain category of signs, destined to a certain kind of communication, each woman preserves a particular value arising from her talent, before and after marriage, for taking her part in a duet. In contrast to words, which have become wholly signs, woman has remained at once a sign and a value."[84]

In refusing eros, then, Hippolytus has refused to enter into that other system of communication in which the self in all its senses might be integrated. Instead, with the horses whose ways he shares (1219–20), whom he can both see and touch, he may speak perhaps but they cannot reply in kind. On the other hand, he reserves his language (and only his language) for the ears of the goddess whom, according to the rules that govern relations between mortals and immortals, he cannot see and cannot touch. In that virginal enclosure of the meadow (or mountains or shore), he is still outside human communication with others not exactly like himself, and more particularly, outside contact with that other goddess, who, as the servant reminds Hippolytus at the beginning of the play, wishes, like all mortals and all gods, to be addressed by an other (*en d'euprosēgoroisin*, 95). To honor the goddess here means to address her image that stands at the doors of his house (99) because, as the servant says, she is *semnē* (august) and *episēmos*—that is, significant—bearing the mark of a sign, like a device on a coin. But Hippolytus has no words for her except to wish her a long goodbye (113).

This modest dialogue is worth recalling when, after the nurse has revealed the secret to him, Hippolytus utters his long denunciation of all women. Just before he expresses the wish to cleanse his ears with pure running streams, he utters another more dramatic wish: no servant should be able to come near a woman. Rather women should dwell together (*sugkatoikizein*) with savage beasts who have no voice. In this way, he would never have to address (*prosphōnein*) any one of them nor receive in return from them any voiced utterance (645–48). The reason is specific: "But as things are," he says, "the women sit *within* and in their wickedness contrive wild schemes and these their servants bear to the world *outside*" (649–50). His indictment is also generic. Hippolytus, we might say, desires to repress all the "speaking signs" that are women. While reserving the right of speech for himself, he forbids women to communicate in any system of exchange and reciprocity. The earlier part of his long diatribe supports this interpretation: there he reveals how intimately this desire for linguistic univocality and control is linked to his repression of eros.

Woman indeed is a sign for Hippolytus, but a counterfeit sign and therefore an unworthy source from which to beget children. Rather he proposes that "mortals deposit in the temples of the gods either bronze or iron or gold in order to buy the seed of children, each man according to the amount appropriate to his assessment. Then one could live in houses that are forever free of the female" (616–24).

In purchasing children in the temples, Hippolytus bypasses that shadowy ambiguous interior of the woman and the house in favor of the domain of the sacred. And he bypasses that ambiguous realm of social relations in favor of a direct and unerring judgment of the gods on a man's value. Instead of matrimonial exchange and reciprocity, he prefers the commercial exchange of coinage—palpable tokens of the self's worth. He thus indicates his desire for a world without dissonance and without dialogue, refusing any resignation to ambiguous mixtures which the Hesiodic view accepts as the human condition once men have been separated from the gods. Like Hesiod, Hippolytus describes woman in terms that recall the creation of Pandora—a beautiful form, an *agalma*, like a statue that one must adorn (631), but a counterfeit evil within (616). In the Hesiodic economy, however, man cannot dispense with that beautiful evil with which he must dwell. Although she sits within the house and drains his resources, she is nonetheless essential precisely because of her reproductive function by which a man continues the paternal line. Hesiod accepts the compromise that requires a man to accept an other into his house, and through the contract of marriage to bear legitimate children he can claim as his own. But Hippolytus rejects this solution, which only fictively fulfills the "dream of a purely paternal heredity that continually haunts the Greek imagination."[85] This counterfeit woman cannot bear true children, that is, true to the autonomous masculine self whom they cannot perfectly reproduce. Instead, Hippolytus fashions another fiction that would guarantee progeny as continuing signs of the self. As objects exchanged for true and durable coins, they would then forever bear the stamp of a single original identity which can never be lost.

In Hippolytus' world, then, woman is truly the other with whom dialogue is refused. Alone in this world, he is free to speak as he is free to roam in those external spaces where Phaedra's verbal imaginings also wander in order to escape from the imprisoning word of the secret. But in the social system of communication, it is Hippolytus, in truth, who is the other. He is the one who in essence is not a "speaking sign"; figuratively, as I have indicated, because in maintaining his virginal status he has excluded himself from the system, and literally in the fact, as he will later acknowledge, that he is unaccustomed to speak before those who are not identical to himself (986–87). The unspeakable secret is alien to him. Yet paradoxically, the silence its repression requires better exemplifies the permanent aspect of "nonspeaking" that his virginal condition of "subjective containment" implies. In addition, the oath demanded by the nurse, which formally restrains his speech, corresponds in its inhibiting effect on verbal expression to the condition of physical restraint that the denial of eros imposes. This oath of silence to the nurse serves the more direct needs of the plot, but the second one, volunteered by Hippolytus in his own defense, shows in yet another way why an oath in itself is appropriately now his only verbal recourse. For in general, an oath, construed as a speech act, is an isolating form of utterance as it breaks with dialogic exchange and its value to the other depends wholly on the representation of the speaker who swears it. How could its use not then only condemn Hippolytus further in his father's eyes? (1025–40; 1054–57; cf. 960–61).

The oath, apart from a context in which the self is known to its society, might be termed a disembodied voice. It corresponds on a symbolic level to the strategies of the plot, which works its baneful effects through speech detached from the physical presence of its original speaker and destined to circulate without that face-to-face contact which might guarantee its trustworthiness. The text explicitly formulates this principle in Phaedra's statement that applies to her, but still more to Hippolytus: "For there is nothing trustworthy (*piston*) in the tongue, which knows how to admonish the thoughts of someone else but which itself by itself (*autē d'huph' hautēs*), wins a multitude of troubles" (395–97).

Those critics who study the status of language in the play, focusing either on the abstract dialectic between speech and silence or taking inventory of the varied and intricate forms of communication which the drama employs, have much to teach us about Euripidean attitudes and techniques.[86] But to grasp more fully why and how communication operates in the *Hippolytus* as it does, we need to look to the larger questions involving the plot—how does it operate and what purposes does it serve? In this perspective, Hippolytus himself is the determining factor, who, as the precision of tragic justice requires, needs (and receives) a plot made expressly for him. That is, the plot must reply to his first refusal to address the statue of Aphrodite on stage, which he will only greet from afar (102), and to the nature of his relation with Artemis, whose voice (*audē*) he hears but whose eye (*omma*) he cannot see (86). Hippolytus will feel, as we know, a rift between the tongue and the *phrēn*, but the more fundamental cleavage in his system is that between the tongue (or the ear) and the eye.

The Tongue, the Ear, and the Eye

Hippolytus fetishizes the ear, as it were, first, as we have seen, through his anguish at its penetration by the secret and then again when he enquires of Theseus whether one of his friends has slandered him (*dieballe*) "into" his father's ear (932–33). And it is no coincidence that the first sign of the demonic epiphany is that terrible chthonic echo, that deep-booming roar, terrifying to hear, to which the first response is that of the horses, who prick up their ears and raise their heads to heaven (1201–4). In the first part of the play, all long to hear the secret (270, 344), and in the revelation of the fateful name, Hippolytus' words about Artemis—*kluōn audēs*—recur exactly when the nurse asks: do you speak of (*audāis*) Hippolytus? and Phaedra replies: you hear it (*klueis*) from yourself, not from me (352–53). The chorus immediately responds in the same acoustical code: you have heard (*aies*), you have heard (*eklues*) of the sufferings of our mistress which are unhearable (*anēkousta*), unfit to hear (362–63).

But Hippolytus will indeed hear these things inside and his voice will in turn be overheard by the other, first from within, when she eavesdrops at the door of the house, and then when she remains unperceived on stage while he speaks outside. The scene at the door is a remarkable coup de théâtre between the chorus and Phaedra which, let us note, focuses on the voice which can be heard but whose author cannot be seen.[87]

Phaedra hears the voice first, indistinct, and then identifies it as that of Hippolytus, who "is speaking terrible evils," while the chorus, further away, now hears the voice, although not clearly. They perceive only the cry coming through the doors until Phaedra finally repeats the message she hears, as he speaks forth (*exaudei*, 590).[88] These painstaking details serve more than a purely theatrical function. Indeed, we will not overlook their significance if we recall that the tragedy now fully begins with the voice of Hippolytus himself. For he has come out upon the stage where he and Phaedra are both present for the first time—but not to each other—so that she *hears* every terrible word he utters but he does not at all *see* her eye. We understand therefore why these earlier fateful lines must echo again at the end, when the chariot overturns and Hippolytus' head is crushed against the rocks. Now one last time he will speak forth in the same way (*exaudei*), uttering terrible things to hear (*kluein*, 1239).

Consider too that before this, Hippolytus will have come again having *heard* the shout of his father, and *not knowing* the news, he will, just like the nurse with Phaedra, wish to *hear* it from the other (904; cf. 344). Theseus, on the other hand, his patience exhausted, will cry out to his servants: Won't you drag him away? Have you not *heard* me now for a long time addressing (*prounneponta*) him for banishment (1085)? almost exactly repeating the servant's admonishment of Hippolytus to address (*prosennepeis*) the figure of Aphrodite (99).

Hippolytus will wish at the moment of direst need that the house could utter a voice and bear witness for him, but it would be a voiceless witness, as his father reminds him, because it is the deed itself that speaks (1077).[89] What he requires, most of all, is an eyewitness since Phaedra no longer lives, no longer "sees the light" (1023). It is worth observing that not any witness will do, because what he wants most of all is not an other who is truly an other but a carbon copy, one, he says, "just like himself" (1022). By contrast, the nurse can call upon the chorus to witness her zeal in her mistress' misfortunes (287), as the women are present face-to-face with her upon the stage. And the chorus, in turn, assumes that Theseus, were he at home, could judge the nature of Phaedra's symptoms by looking at her face (280). But now that Phaedra herself is a witness (the clearest witness of all because she is a corpse) present on stage before his eyes (972), Theseus must wish that there would be some clear token of proof (*tekmērion*) for mortals of their friends and some means of distinguishing their minds (*diagnōsin phrenōn*, 925–26). "What oaths," after all, Hippolytus' father had said, "what words would be more powerful proof than this body?" (960). Conversely, Hippolytus realizes that if he indeed "loosens his mouth" (*luō stoma*, 1060) to break the oath he had made to the nurse, he could still never persuade the other, his father, of the truth.

Here in this juridical procedure, when Hippolytus must present his face to his father, the split he has made in his life between voice (*audē*) and sight (*omma*) assumes its fullest implications. At one end of the visual spectrum is eros, which drips desire from the eyes (525–26) in accordance with Greek psychological notions that persistently associate eros with the eye of the other. Phaedra had been possessed in her heart of a terrible eros when she saw Hippolytus at Athens and dedicated a temple to her passion on the rock of the Acropolis which stands as a silent lookout (*katopsion*) of her love, gazing now over the gulf to Troezen (26–34). Not to see or be seen then means not to love but rather to stand outside the range in which the attractive magnet of desire works its effects. In the general sphere of social relations, however, not to see or be seen also means to have no reciprocity of regard by which one can accurately judge when looking at the face of the other and conversely, by which one can find an other, an eyewitness, to verify the self, whether to judge—or to pity and mourn.

Without that other, one might wish that the house whose facade is visible on stage could take voice and speak as a witness (1074–75). Or one might long for the impossible—to divide oneself into two: "Would that I were able to stand opposite and look at myself (*prosblepein*), so that I could weep for myself at the woes I am suffering" (1078–79).[90]

Let us clarify this problem of sight and the eye. It is not, of course, that Hippolytus does not see. Rather, it is the mode of his seeing that counts. His own words give us the clues: "I do not know the *praxis* of eros, except having heard of it by speech (*kluōn logōi*) and seeing (*leussōn*) it in painting (*graphēi*). For I am not eager to look upon (*skopein*) these things, having a maiden soul (*parthenon psychēn*," 1004–6).

His is an observing and distanced view of life; he sees objects rather than subjects—an appropriate mode for one who greets Aphrodite from afar. Hippolytus knows the body of the other as a sculpted form, as an *agalma*, like the statue of Artemis which stands in for the goddess, and he is guardian, in fact, of all her images (*phulax agalmatōn*, 1399). For him the woman is also an *agalma* which her husband adorns as Hippolytus had adorned the statue of Artemis with the garland of flowers. As a passive object endowed with little sense, this type of woman is little less repugnant to him than the other kind—the intelligent woman (*phronousa*) who, in his view, will use her wits only for contriving evil (641–44).

It is in Phaedra's interest, of course, to leave behind these "clearest proofs" (972), the visible evidence of the body and the objectified speech of the *deltos*. But Hippolytus too, in his plans for acquiring children, expressed his wish for a clear proof of identity, the material substance of coinage which answers to an external standard of value. Even more, Phaedra's action returns against him a caricature of his image of the feminine: an *agalma* that is the lifeless body and the *deltos* which conceals its duplicity. Now, as a "dead letter," she can truly be only a "speaking sign" (cf. 857). It is appropriate too that this tableau of sculpture and inscription will prove to destroy him, because his view of the world allows him to see only secondhand, through pictures and books.[91] But we are in the theater now where the spectator too may see from afar. Let us turn then to the "viewing place," the *theatron*, to take the measure of its potential lessons for the self.

The Theater, Identity, and the Self

The spectacle Phaedra arranges as her last appearance on stage is well devised as an act of theater—her body as a bitter spectacle, a bitter *théa* (809). Theseus is the first to behold the sight (the *théa*) when he has the doors opened in order to view it. He has just returned from a mission as a sacred observer, a *theōros* (792), but now discarding the woven garland that was the sign of his happy errand, he can only declare himself an unfortunate *theōros* (806–7). Hippolytus is the next to view this *théa*. Having left her, as he says, still "looking at the light," he regards her face-to-face for the first time now that she is dead and expresses amazement, the *thauma* that all spectacles arouse in the beholder (905–8).

Reference to theatrical spectacle will recur in a cognate word at the end of the text when the epiphany of divine power is truly revealed, as it brings together those two sensory affects of sight and sound which Hippolytus had earlier sundered. First, sound alone: then sight and sound together. At the first subterranean roar, the wave rose up to heaven "so that my eye," says the messenger, "was deprived of seeing the shores of Sciron" (1207–8). But what follows next, once the wave has cast up the bull from the sea, is another terrible sound, which fills up the whole earth; and for those who were looking, there appeared a spectacle (*theama*), too great to behold, which terrified the horses into their mad stampede (1215–18). The bull keeps appearing before them (*prouphaineto*, 1228), but now as a silent vision it redirects the horses and chariot to ruin until in the manner of epiphanies it finally disappears with the horses, who vanish too.

For the messenger, the apparition had provided a great and terrible spectacle, which he viewed from afar in company with the other onlookers and which he can carry back as an eyewitness report to share with those other spectators on stage. But for Hippolytus, it provided the most dramatic moment of his life, when he acted and was acted upon in confrontation with the forces of beasts and gods.

Aphrodite and Poseidon, it is true, arranged this remarkable ordeal for Hippolytus. Theseus was its more immediate cause, but Phaedra, of course, was its true agent. Thus to grasp the import of this epiphany within the visual code we have been following, let us look back to an earlier moment in the text for another word from the theatrical lexicon, a word, in fact, among the last that Hippolytus utters in his long speech against women. "I will go away and keep silent, but when my father returns, so will I, and I will be a spectator (*theasomai*), looking at the way that you will look at (*prosopsēi*) him" (661–63).[92]

What happens is that she will be the *théa*, the spectacle, that all will behold and it is Hippolytus who will be obliged to present his *prosōpon* before his father (947; cf. 1458). Now he has been assigned the leading part in the drama. Accused of committing an act he did not commit, he becomes an actor in both senses of the word—as one who puts on a *prosōpon* to assume the identity of an other (Phaedra) and as one who must now enter into dialogue with an other (Theseus) which will lead to the final action of the play. Scheduled to play a role that the other had transferred to him, he will find himself accused of only playing a role, showing a *prosōpon* that will be viewed merely as a mask, offering a false mirror of the self in the eyes of the other.

The wish cited above, "would that I could stand opposite and look at myself so that I could weep for my sufferings" (1078), can never be fulfilled except with the experience of the mirror, which teaches the self the first lesson of perspective on its own alterity. For in viewing oneself in a mirror, one sees oneself both as a subject seeing and as an object being seen. Through it therefore one takes the first step toward recognizing that the identity of the self must always include "the representation of its subjectivity in relation to an other."[93] "The mirror," as Vernant remarks, "is the means to know oneself, to lose oneself, to refind oneself, but on condition of separating oneself, dividing oneself, posing oneself at a distance from oneself, as self to other, in order to attain an objective figure of the subject."[94]

Narcissus finds a mirror in which he misrecognizes the self for the other. But Hippolytus, when others misrecognize the self, discovers for the first time the need for a mirror to return to him an objective acknowledgment of the self's experience. Yet Narcissus and Hippolytus meet at the same point: in the absence of the other, the self can only divide (or double) and can only hopelessly yearn to play both parts of self and other. Narcissus wastes away, caught in the specular fascination of impossible desire, doomed only to gaze at the surface of the water but never to experience its depths. Hippolytus, however, as he mounts the chariot and takes up the reins of the horses who will lead him to disaster, goes on to act out the consequences of having refused to meet the eye (or touch) of the other in human contact, and he does so, as we have already seen, through an active reprise of those terms belonging to his secret double, the woman—terms that exemplify the culture's perception of her body: that *dustropos harmonia*, that divided self, which suffers in eros and childbirth.

The horses with whom he identified himself indeed prove to be the other—creatures alien to the self—though, as he reproaches them, they were his own, reared and nurtured by his own hand (1240, 1356). And in the same breath (1242) he now calls for an other—a man—who would be beside him to save him. But the others, his companions, are left far behind (1243–44), no longer even able to witness the final spectacle of his ruin.

Upon his return to the stage after the disaster, Artemis is waiting there, having already bidden Theseus to *hear* the story she will recount (1283, 1296, 1314), and the last implications of "hearing her voice, but not seeing her eye" are revealed. We note that now when she addresses Hippolytus, he no longer responds to her presence by referring to the voice he is used to hearing. Rather, he acknowledges her proximity by alluding to the perfume of her divine emanation (*osmēs pneuma*, 1391–92), and his stress now falls on the aspect of sight. Although the rules had precluded his sight of her, the converse need not, of course, apply to the goddess. Now Hippolytus insists that he be seen by an other: first, Zeus (1363), whose eye Theseus had accused him of dishonoring (886), and then Artemis herself: "Do you *see* me, miserable in the state that I am?" (1395). What he demands from her is that she play the role he could not accomplish by himself—to be the other who stands opposite and looks at him so as to weep for his sufferings (1078–79). "I *see*," she says, but according to the same rules, "it is not *themis* for a goddess to shed tears from her eyes," still less permitted to pollute the immortal eye with the sight of the dying (1396, 1437–38). Such are the restraints in the system, then, that necessarily limit the value of a divine regard in the human world.

Hippolytus will obtain, however, a version of that earlier wish. Continuing to weep for himself, he goes forth with his comrades to meet his ruin (1178).[95] But once he no longer "looks upon the light," there will be others to weep for him. The chorus in their closing lines will refer to the common grief (*koinon achos*) that all the citizens share and to the tears that will follow hereafter (1462–64). In the cult that is founded for him for the future, the *muthos* has indeed become *koinos* (cf. 609); it is the one, however, he has shared with Phaedra (cf. *koinēi metaschōn*, 731). The others, the maidens, will forever mourn for him as the other, mourning in truth for themselves.[96]

Once the drama, the spectacle, is over and the body has gone to the "hiding places of dark earth into the house of Hades, the unseen," (Theog. 243), then and only then will hearing and the voice by itself come into their own. In his second oath sworn before his father, Hippolytus had prayed that if he proved a base man, he should perish *aklees* (without *kleos*, renown) and *anōnumos*, without a name (1028, 1031). The oath did not save him from destruction, but Artemis' prophecy, by answering the terms it proposed, saves the power which the oath must have to guarantee the truth. For as she says, "there will always be a concern for making song (*mousopoios . . . merimna*) for you on the part of the maidens, and not without a name (*anōnumos*) will the eros of Phaedra for you be kept silent" (1428–30).

After death, only the name and the story remain: in short, a *kleos*—for others to tell and for others to hear (*kluō*)— in the long span of time—the *muthos* of himself and of Phaedra whose own longing for *eukleia*[97] brought all the events to pass.[98] By these terms, Hippolytus achieves the immortal status he had longed for, given to him as a gift by the one whose voice he had heard but whose eye he did not see. And the process has already begun in the grief we witness on stage; it extends into the future through Theseus' last words, those he addresses to Aphrodite: I will remember (*mnēsomai*) the evils you wrought (1461).

Theseus' promise provides the transition from personal experience to collective commemoration in the name of Aphrodite and fittingly closes this last scene in which Hippolytus, in his last mortal moments, repairs his relationship with the other, his father. That is, he now reverses the otherness his father had assigned to him: first, as bastard, and more recently as a *xenos* (stranger/exile), the status that marks the extreme limit of alienation in social relations (1085).

The previous dialogue with his father showed at the end what it meant to have no other—as witness or mourner. But the exchange of roles that Phaedra brought about introduces Hippolytus to the principle of reciprocity. When required for the first time to stand in the place of the other (Phaedra), he is also required, for purposes of persuasion, to invoke a rhetorical identification with the other (Theseus). Hence he must reverse the roles between speaker and hearer in order to share the perspective of the other. "If I were the father and you were the son . . ." (1042), he says. The technique does not succeed, but it does prepare him for the future when, in their shared suffering, he and his father exchange sentiments of mutual pity. Thus to Hippolytus' statement, "I grieve for you more than for myself," his father replies, "If only I could be the corpse in place of you" (1409–10). And on these same terms, the son can forgive his father, for "to forgive" in Greek is *suggignoskein*, "to know something with" someone else, and through the consciousness of that shared knowledge, to forgive. In return then for the curses, whose verbal power Theseus has released (*ephiēmi*, 1324) to destroy his son, Hippolytus now grants him release (*aphiēmi*, 1450) from blood guilt, sealing his word with Artemis as his witness (*marturomai*, 1451). Before he could only release (*aphiēmi*) his tongue to speak through necessity in his own defense (991), a tongue constrained by the oath he had sworn to the nurse. But now he validates at last the power of his own *logos* through his shared experience with the other.

This scene also repairs that other sensory defect to which his relation with Artemis had consigned him, that is, of touch. For having refused the touch of the other, he could not himself be touched until he had lived through the sequence of events that followed from seeming to have "touched" what he was forbidden to touch (652, 885, 1002, 1044, 1086). Given the premises of his existence, his earlier *logos* can only fail, for the one who is not open to eros is also not open to persuasion, and on that same principle he will also have no convincing means by which to persuade the other. Instead, when he tries to exercise *peithō* (persuasion), the other judges his words as deceptive seduction and false rhetoric.[99]

By the same logic, the one who is open to contact with others is also open to eros, and open finally too to persuasion. As a result, the entire chain was set into motion by the touch of another's hand, when the nurse supplicated Phaedra. She held fast to her hand, vowing never to let go (326; cf. 335), demanding that the queen *look* at her (300) and *touching* her first with the simple mention of Hippolytus' name (310). Yet the chain also depended on the one from whose eyes tears were able to fall and who would turn her own eye away in shame (245–46). So to protect herself lest she be seen among the wicked among mortals (428, 430), Phaedra became, in turn, an evil to him (729). Accusing him of "dishonoring the majestic eye of Zeus" (886), she gave him that *prosōpon* that mirrored her own.

Time, the Mirror, and the Virgin

The mirror effect is the operative term in the drama that will finally prove to govern the more general patterns of imitation. I invoked it just now metaphorically so as to bring us back to the text itself. We have already seen the import of Hippolytus' impossible wish "to stand opposite and look at himself" (1078–79) and how it can be read with reference to a mirror. But in view of an earlier direct mention of a mirror (*katoptron*), his turn of phrase gains in significance as an oblique reminder to us of that first allusion and its context. Phaedra is the speaker and the statement that closes her great speech on the mysteries of life is strangely enigmatic: "Only this, they say, competes in life, a good and upright judgment (*gnōmē*) for the one who has it, but the wicked among men time shows forth, when it happens to, when before them as before a young virgin, time sets up its mirror. Among these may I never be seen" (426–30).

The mirror, as Barrett remarks, is both self-revealing where one sees oneself, or other-revealing, where one is seen, revealing it to another.[100] But the notion of the mirror is far more extensive, since it applies not to one character but to two, and the image that links together time, the mirror, and the virgin concentrates in its optic all the significant problems of the drama. It holds the key to its structures and to its underlying mythic patterns, as we will see, making use of all the dazzling complexities that a play of mirrors affords. Unlike Hippolytus, Phaedra as a woman indeed has knowledge of the mirror in all of its meanings—for herself and for the other, most especially in its capacity to double the self in its reflected image. The drama is built on the contrast in access to modes of vision, perception, and knowledge as it counters Hippolytus' preference for the ear over the eye with Phaedra's heightened awareness of the uses of seeing and being seen, exemplified in the contradictory, even antithetical qualities associated with the mirror.

A brief inventory of these will suggest why Phaedra's curious remarks merit closer inspection and why, at this late stage in our study, it is worth looking over the ensemble of the drama from the perspective afforded by the key symbol of the play that is the mirror. The mirror is that which reveals the true and yet offers a deceptive illusion. It reflects back the image of feminine vanity, but it offers too the means for deep introspection. It poses at its most problematic conjunction the division between being and seeming, between seeing oneself for oneself and how one is seen by others.[101] In embracing the whole of the phenomenal world, *ta phainomena*, the mirror encompasses the spectrum of that which one sees with the eye of eros and the eye of knowledge. Thus it includes in its purview the illusion of appearances with their refractions and distortions of the real, but it also shows us what is revealed outside, what is brought to light in the spectacle of divine epiphany and its aftermath.

Phaedra's struggle is between that interior self and her external image in the eyes of society, and she chooses finally to dishonor herself by honoring the conventions that regulate her life. At stake, let us not forget, are her children, who require their parents' *eukleia*, good name, in order to speak freely in the world (421–25). At stake too is the self that will feel radically dishonored by the words of an other. But in its new representation of Phaedra, the play can probe the dialectic of reality and appearance, of being and seeming,[102] and can through the mirror that belongs to Aphrodite pose the fundamental epistemological questions of human life.

Let me clarify what we might infer from the mirror of Aphrodite by contrasting it with another mode of knowing, one more typical for tragedy, namely, that of Apollo. In Aeschylus' *Seven Against Thebes*, we meet the sixth combatant, Amphiaraus, the seer who alone among all the warriors carries a blank shield, without a visible sign to the outside world, because he would rather *be aristos*, than *seem* so, "reaping the deep furrow through his mind (*phrēn*) from which trustworthy counsels burgeon forth" (*Sept.* 591–94). In the eyes of the Theban Eteocles, he is acknowledged as possessing the four essential virtues. He is *dikaios* (just), *agathos* (brave/good), *eusebēs* (righteous), and above all, *sōphrōn* (prudent, 610), because he knows how to speak the appropriate words, *legein ta kairia*, 619, having the stability of an interior self that knows what to bring forth from his mouth and what to keep hidden within. But he is also the great prophet of Apollo, who mediates between divine and human worlds. As seer, he has a synoptic vision of past, present, and future. He knows his mortal limits—knows them too well—for he prophesies the very day of his death. But he knows too the cult that awaits him when he will be buried in the earth of the other city that is

Thebes (*Sept.* 587–88). Thus to speak *ta kairia* means that he controls for himself the polysemy of language but also that he has the capacity to speak the ambiguous language of oracles to an other (Eteocles) whose fate will validate the veridical Apollonian word which comes forth from Delphi.[103]

In Aphrodite's play, Eros takes the place of Apollo (and Zeus), as the chorus seems to tell us after the nurse has taken Phaedra's secret inside the house and they begin a great hymn to this god who "drips desire from the eyes" (525). In vain, they say, we offer sacrifice by the Alpheius (Olympia) and at Delphi, but Eros, the tyrant of men, we do not worship. Rather than to the inmost shrine at Delphi from which prophecy issues forth, one must give reverence to the keeper of the keys of the inmost chambers of love (*philtatōn thalamōn kleidouchon*, 540) where the *logos* has no *mantis* (seer), the *kairos* (the opportune time/place) is not clear, and no one knows how to read the signs without error (269, 346, 386, 585).[104]

The seer, as the bearer of Apollo's word, needs no other and can see without being seen (the blank shield). The woman, however, as the agent of Aphrodite, is at the opposite end of the spectrum; she needs the polished surface of the mirror because society requires, above all, that she see herself through others' eyes. But the language of furrow and field as well as the seer's contact with time and process are borrowed from the agricultural world where the feminine earth sown and reaped by man now supplies the metaphorical field he finds within himself, a process that the Greek idiom more typically exemplifies through the career of the *parthenos*. Like the meadow, she must not lie unworked for too long, but must be transformed from its flowering surface to a deep furrow. The woman, like Amphiaraus, has a *sōphrosunē*, but, as the chorus says immediately after Phaedra's allusion to the mirror, its function is to reap noble *doxa* (glory/reputation, 431–32), a trait that includes the visible phenomena of the social domain.

In Aphrodite's world, the woman has insight drawn from her experience of the social and physical body, because time has taught her much from which she can take her counsels (375–76) and has given her a mirror as an instrument of double vision:[105] first, as the truth and the semblance of the true, and second, as the eye of the self and the eye of the other. Time will indeed reveal her to herself. Yet because self and other coincide in the image of the *parthenos*, reminiscent of an anterior state in her life but corresponding to the present moment of his, Phaedra possesses the only means by which Hippolytus can, as the *parthenos*, see the self, particularly in a perspective of time.[106]

REVERSING THE IMAGE   That medium is the mirror and we can only grasp the full extent of its power in the play if we recall the simple fact that the mirror not only reflects but that what it reflects must also be a *reversed* image which is returned to the one who gazes in it (cf. e.g., Pl. *Ti.* 46a–b). In invoking the image of the mirror and linking it to time, Phaedra has indeed activated the dynamic mechanism of the plot, which works precisely by reversing the image of one for the other and by playing out in the dramatic sequence of events the interrelations of being and seeming to which the mirror naturally lends itself. In the vision of the reversed image that governs the play, what is the peripeteia here, that formal reversal of one state into its opposite, if not a turnabout that reverses the image of the self and projects it onto the other? And what is the message on the *deltos* ("he desires me" versus "I desire him"), if not a species of reversal we might call "mirror writing"? And the rhetorical play with *sōphrosunē*, which I earlier called a chiasmus, might well be recoded in visual terms to suggest that the first sentence is but the mirror image of the second.[107]

Better yet are the words of the servant in the prologue addressed to the statue of Aphrodite once Hippolytus has left the stage, asking her to pardon (*suggnomēn echein*) the foolishness of the young man, for "one must not imitate or play the part (*ou mimeteon*) of the young who think in this fashion" (117, 114). Rather, he implores her to be *wiser than mortals* and "to *seem* not to *hear* him" (*mē dokēi toutou kluein*, 119). Aphrodite does not reply but Phaedra, her substitute, does as the one who will play the goddess' role in the human domain. For the servant's plea proves to be an exact reversal of what will actually occur in the dramatic structure of the play. Phaedra must *seem* to Hippolytus not to have heard the words he speaks at the door although, of course, that is just what she does. And the result is that she will arrange for the young now to imitate the adult, by giving him the role that the reversal of *prosōpa* will require him to play.

Why should this be so? Because Phaedra rejects the nurse's practical morality which names those as *wise among mortals* who overlook those things that are not *kala* (465–66). After all, says the nurse, "how many do you suppose of those who have good sense, when they see adulterous affairs (*nosounta lektra*), *seem* not to *see?*" (*mē dokein horan*, 463). But among these Phaedra will emphatically refuse to be seen (or to seem to be). That is, she refuses to be an actor—masking the self through playing another's part (413–18). She refuses too to imitate the gods by using as models their mythological amours which the nurse's sophistic rhetoric would have her believe it would be hubristic to reject (474–75). But with the mirror as her instrument, Phaedra does in fact become the *pikra thea*, not only the bitter *spectacle* (*théa*) but paronomastically, the *pikra theá*, the bitter *goddess* (cf. 727), who can make one the unhappy mimetic double of the other, when like the goddess before her she feels Hippolytus' scorn. Phaedra may discover that her own image rejoins the reflection of that other self, her double in the first play, which she had been determined to resist. But through her inversion of the mirror's image, Hippolytus will discover, as we have seen, what it means to have no mirror of the self and an other.

What Phaedra brings about in the play through her concern for the mirror would seem to provide a premature and ironic commentary on a famous text of Plato in which Eros is shown to provide the route to that knowledge of the self through the metaphor of the mirror. As Socrates observes, "the face (*prosōpon*) of the person who looks into another's eyes (*theōmenos*) is shown forth in the optic confronting him as in a mirror, and this we call the *korē* (pupil), for it is the *eidolon* or image of the person. . . . Then an eye viewing another eye and looking at its most perfect part (the *korē*) wherewith it sees, it will thus see itself" (*Alc.* 1.132e–33a).[108]

Phaedra, who brings together time, the virgin, and the mirror, would seem indeed to be the first *korē*, the *parthenos* of the past, who sailed from Crete to Athens for her nuptials with Theseus. And she provides the *prosōpon* for the other *korē*, the *parthenos* Hippolytus, who will pass through the identity of the first one as through a mirror—of illusion and not of truth. Time at the end will show her forth, as she says, a *kakon* to him, and her prediction will also turn out to include Theseus, as the third, in the same charge.[109] But in the temporal span of the drama, when time *seems* to show Hippolytus forth as wicked, the mirror of Phaedra suggests that confronting the interplay of truth and illusion is an essential phase of development that teaches to all the critical lessons of perspective and configures the self as an entity with both internal and external dimensions. Such an interplay continually subtends the dynamics of daily life in the encounters and exchanges between one self and an other. It also lies at the heart of the experience of the theater as it involves the relations between actors and uses the resources of the stage as well as that of the curious status of theater itself as the frontier between the fictional and the real, the perceived and the true.

The theatrical process opens the way for Hippolytus to achieve an objective status as a subject in the world where Aphrodite, as the play says, rules alone (*mona kratuneis*, 1281), a world of realities that would otherwise lie beyond his ken. The ending of the play with Hippolytus restored to his father and his honor vindicated on stage by the goddess Artemis along with the promise of his cult for the future suggests the validity and necessity of the workings of the plot. The experience is required, it would seem, for authenticating a filial self whose bastard status would have forever cast a long shadow in the social domain on his claims to nobility. More broadly, his implication in the demands of this world also provides the opportune occasion for resisting them, and in so doing, to prove the valor of remaining steadfast to the ideal of a self he continues to cherish. Only by these actions can his life take on meaning as he makes the transition, once his span of time on earth is ended, from a mortal youth doomed in the here and now to the role of perennial cult hero. His experience of pain will provide the symbolic model for the physical experience of the others, the nubile maidens on the eve of their weddings. But weeping for him, as they retell his story of eros refused, they are acknowledging at the same time that his story is one they themselves must not literally imitate.

If the world of Aphrodite replicates, often with startling fidelity, a version of the real world in all its confusions and contradictions, it would also seem to be equivalent to the theater itself, whose play with realities offers the ideal medium for such an initiation. Illusion is what the theatrical effect aims to achieve through its mimetic conventions in order to deceive the audience with its visual representations of the real. That is its formal function. But in cognitive terms, the question of illusion goes still deeper into the content of this drama, where in the binding/unbinding of its plot, it must stage a two-leveled "imitation of an action" in order finally to bring to light what lies behind the facade of the visual spectacle. Only then is the anagnorisis complete and does ignorance give way to knowledge and illusion to truth.

Yet what is that knowledge and what is that truth if not the acknowledgment that illusion and deception are necessary components of reality for the self in the world, without which that self cannot be constituted?[110] Hippolytus had been tripped up when his chariot overturned through the action of the bull from the sea (1232). But this event comes to pass because, as Theseus says to his son at the end, "I was tripped by an illusion, a *doxa*, that emanated from a divine source" (1414).[111]

The true anagnorisis is, of course, that Aphrodite was the agent, a fact revealed to the audience in the prologue but imparted to Hippolytus only at the very end as the last of all the characters to know. "*Phronō*," I understand, he says, "the divinity who destroyed me" (1401), thereby acknowledging at last, if only for an instant, the power the goddess has had, even over himself. Anagnorisis comes late and hard and finally only through another goddess, Artemis, who will reveal the truth first to Theseus and then to Hippolytus. Without her there would be no full anagnorisis because the characters in the drama could never attain the requisite knowledge from their own participation in the events of the play.

The obstacle, of course, is Phaedra herself, whose desire to repress and deny her secret ultimately leads her to install the fundamental mis-anagnorisis at the heart of the play when she reverses the terms of the message on the tablet and disappears forever from the scene. But the real obstacle, I suggest, lies even deeper in the very structure of the play, which is organized from the outset around a more fundamental reversal, one that the chorus signals to us in the parodos.

There in their conjectures on the possible causes of Phaedra's disease, the women pose a set of questions which are early exemplars of the reversing mirror effect that will regulate the drama. They query whether her husband tends a secret love in the house (151–54), when we know the proper subject is Phaedra herself. Or perhaps some news from faraway Crete (155–159), they suggest, when the cause of her woe, Hippolytus, has just been present on the stage. But it is the preceding strophe that furnishes the essential clue, where the chorus logically begins its enquiry by speculating on a divine cause for the queen's illness. There are two possibilities. Is she in fact *entheos*, possessed by a god, whether Pan or Hecate or the Corybantes or the Mountain Mother (141–44)—all apposite choices as they are supernatural agents often presumed responsible for erratic behavior. Or, they enquire, is the cause an offense against Dictynna, the Cretan Artemis, for a fault committed in the neglect of her worship? (145–47). This last query, let us note, doubles the mirror effect, offering not one but two pivots of reversal. The goddess in question is, of course, Aphrodite and not Artemis, her polar opposite (and the Artemis of our play, we might even add, is not Cretan but in Troezen). An even more critical point is that it is not Phaedra but Hippolytus who has neglected the worship of a divinity. The nurse, upon discovering the nature of the queen's secret, reads the situation as anyone might expect: "the wrath of the goddess has swooped down upon Phaedra" (438; cf. 476). But, as Aphrodite informs us in the prologue, her wrath has Hippolytus as its target and it (her *orgai*) is to rush down upon his body (1418), as Artemis describes his pitiable physical condition at the end.

The new Phaedra is remarkable, as I have emphasized throughout, in that she resists the dictates of desire and therefore those of the myth itself. Because of that resistance, she obscures the truth that she knows, the secret of the love she bears within her heart. But how could Phaedra know the full truth—that is, the reason this passion afflicts her? How in fact could anyone else on stage know, as the plot Aphrodite has devised reverses the usual mode of her intervention in human affairs?

The Wrath of Aphrodite

According to the inexorable law of the talion that regulates the logic of Greek myth, one extreme attitude or form of behavior is countered exactly by its equally unacceptable reverse, and the offender is punished exactly according to the nature of the offense. Thus the one who refuses eros or scorns Aphrodite is typically smitten in turn with an immoderate eros—transgressive, illicit, or impossible to fulfill.[112] The retaliation may take the form of a simple reversal, as when Atalanta and Melanion, both of whom had resisted marriage, consummate a passionate and sacrilegious union in the temple of the goddess herself.[113] The madness that afflicts the daughters of

Proetus and sends them running wildly to the mountains is erotic in its nature and results directly from divine punishment, this time by Hera (or Dionysus), for an offense that suggests they have been loath to marry.[114] The emphasis in other cases may fall on a disastrous choice of love object, the theme that directly concerns us here. Polyphontes, for example, is struck by an outrageous passion for a bear.[115] But more subtly and more faithful to our own understanding of psychological dynamics, the refusal to desire an other will mean that desire, when it comes, will turn not outward but rather within—to the self as an unattainable object of love like Narcissus, or to those intimately connected with the self in the interior of the house. Myrrha falls in love with her father, Leucippus with his sister, *kata mēnin Aphroditēs*,[116] and by this logic, we might expect Hippolytus to long passionately for his father's wife. Indeed, to the best of my knowledge, nowhere else except in this play, the second *Hippolytus*, does Aphrodite punish the one who has rejected desire by inspiring an illicit passion only in an innocent other.[117]

The particular manner in which Hippolytus meets his end, as a driver of horses done to death by his own mares, is a retribution quite appropriate for one who, in refusing the yoke of marriage, finds himself instead bound to the yoke of destruction, thereby reconfirming the familiar Greek associations between sexuality and horse taming. The myth of Glaucus Potnieus, who was devoured by his own horses, supplies a significant parallel as the tradition reports that he too had offended Aphrodite.[118] Let us remember, however, that although Hippolytus fulfills his appointed destiny through Phaedra and Theseus as human actors in the drama, it is achieved at the end through the direct agency of another deity, appropriately enough, Poseidon in his role as Taraxippos, the frightener of horses.[119]

Scholars have long pondered the peculiar anomalies of this story of Hippolytus in which several different motifs oddly converge. The familiar theme of Potiphar's wife, which occurs in Near Eastern sources and elsewhere in Greek myth; the relations of the pre-Greek mother goddess with a young consort; and the combined effect of the bull from the sea and the stampeding horses. Little of the tradition, however, is known before Euripides, although the cult of Hippolytus at Troezen is attested from other sources (e.g., Paus. 2.32.1–3). Such research is valuable for the general study of how mythic traditions develop historically and how the variants of a given myth as well as the motifs shared by figures of other myths can be integrated into a larger signifying system.[120] My interest here, however, lies in the implications we can draw from the completed ensemble that Euripides presents to us and in how it addresses the particular questions with which tragedy as a genre is concerned. To this end, I want to make problematic the direct intervention of Aphrodite herself as a character in the drama and the fact that the motif of her wrath is explicitly invoked. Given what we know about the earlier version, this motif would not have been at all necessary to the first play. Quite the contrary. Phaedra there, as the "bad woman," is determined to satisfy her desire for Hippolytus at any cost. In this earlier drama, it is generally agreed that Phaedra and the nurse exchanged roles so that, like the nurse in our play, it is Phaedra who would have invoked Aphrodite with sophistic arguments to justify her outrageous actions.[121]

But in the light of the new Phaedra, Aphrodite's appearance in the prologue becomes indispensable for our plot. Practically speaking, we need her to reveal to us the simple fact that Phaedra would not reveal—that is, her love-sickness. For the broader dramatic point, it is essential that Aphrodite reveal herself as the cause of Phaedra's affliction and that it be declared an affliction the queen has done nothing to deserve. Without the framing device of the goddesses whose omniscience situates them outside the domain of human action, the play, as has often been observed, makes ample psychological sense in its treatment of the false accusation as the revenge of the woman scorned and love turned to hate. This story pattern of Potiphar's wife contains all the ingredients necessary for a suspenseful and engrossing tale, pitting lust against virtue and falsehood against truth in ways that explain in part its continuing popularity as an episode in later Greek romances.[122] Moreover, the flirtation with Oedipal themes involving an older woman, a young man, and an angry paternal figure also assures its perennial appeal. But I would argue that the wrath of Aphrodite, which obeys the logic of its own rules, works as a significant countercurrent against the predictable structure of the Potiphar's wife story so that the drama may exploit for its own purposes the interplay of these two levels.

On the one hand, the structure of the drama reveals with unblinking clarity the tragic gulf between human and divine domains, and Aphrodite's careless dismissal of the plight of her innocent intermediary has been construed, not without justice, as evidence of Euripides' typical critique of traditional Olympian theology. In formal terms, however, what the wrath of Aphrodite means is that Phaedra's accusation of Hippolytus, *if taken at its face value*, strictly fulfills the terms of Aphrodite's typical mode of intervention. That is, Hippolytus' refusal to assume the proper role of *erastēs* is reversed into its logical opposite—or rather, the *semblance* of that opposite—when he is compelled to play the role in the theater of the *erastēs* who has acted out an illicit and "unjust" passion.[123] In this way, he can end with the punishment that fits his original offense against Aphrodite through the action of the horses and the torment of the body that has refused union with an other.

The mirror of illusion Phaedra provides for the male *parthenos* is therefore, according to the latent mythic pattern, the proper optical medium through which to view the entire network of associations clustering around the organ of sight in its social, sexual, and cognitive domains. Hippolytus must *seem* to have committed the offense of "dishonoring the eye of Zeus" and of witnessing the feminine mysteries which are unlawful (*ou themis*) to view. Pentheus' secret wish that Dionysus brings out of hiding in the *Bacchae*, when the god touches his adversary with the power of his divine madness, is none other than the desire to see the other, and Pentheus goes off, literally dressed in the costume of the female other—to play the voyeur at the secret rites. More generally still for Hippolytus, the typical transgression of the hunter who remains in the entourage of Artemis is to come upon the naked goddess bathing and to suffer the consequences of his illicit viewing. Actaeon, Pentheus' mythic counterpart, invoked as a paradigm in the *Bacchae* (230, 336–40, 1227, 1291), is punished by Artemis herself, who turns his hounds against their master to destroy him, a fate not unlike that of Hippolytus himself.[124] But the nature of Hippolytus' relation with Artemis (i.e., not seeing her eye) precludes him from replicating Actaeon's (or other hunters') offense, as a result of which Artemis, we might say, would be compelled to join forces with Aphrodite.[125] The spectator, as we have described Hippolytus, is no voyeur of the other and hence is unable on his own to initiate the sequence that leads from sight to desire and from desire to contact with the other. Hence the indispensable role of Phaedra. From the perspective of the mythic pattern we have been exploring, she therefore might be viewed (in yet another turn of the mirror) as the one conscripted into playing the part that should rightfully be his, which she is, in this sense, justified in returning to him.

We may assess this whirl of mimetic reflections by examining one last instance of mimesis, which occurs in the beginning of the play, when in the dramatic sequence of events it is Phaedra who follows *after* Hippolytus, who has preceded her appearance on stage. Does she not then express her desire to imitate Hippolytus? That is, to recline on the grassy slope and drink the pure water of the spring, to follow the hunt and the hounds, with spear and javelin in hand, and finally, to race the horses in Artemis' territory, taming the Venetian mares (208–11, 215–22, 228–31)? But as spoken by Phaedra this text, needless to say, surpasses any simple or single mimetic identification. In its impossible ambiguities, it demonstrates the confusions introduced into the system when the *kouros* appropriates the role of the *parthenos* and, through Aphrodite, attracts the eye of the *gunē* (woman). Hippolytus has, in fact, reversed the typical courting pattern, so that when he at last leaves the stage, the chorus of maidens lament that they will no longer be able to compete for his hand in marriage (114–41). Phaedra's fantasies express the mixture of masculine and feminine, active and passive, subject and object, (even mortal and immortal), as well as the fundamental overlapping of the chaste and the erotic. Who does she want to be? In desiring and desiring to be desired in turn, and also desiring not to desire, she plays all the roles—herself (now woman, once virgin), Aphrodite, Hippolytus, and Artemis, the eternal *parthenos*.

But such a mimetism lies only in the theater of the imagination as projections of the mind's eye. Thus while she sets the stage for those far-off places where she desires to cast the javelin (*eramai . . . rhipsai*, 220), the nurse recodes her image as text, interpreting the *epos* that Phaedra has "cast" (*erripsas*, 232) as evidence only of her wandering wits (*paraphrōn*) until the actions of the nurse herself lead her to reinterpret, to find new *logoi* in order to unbind the knot of a still more complex *logos*. This Phaedra accomplishes by resorting to the devices of theater to stage for the other a plot—an "imitation of an action" none other than the drama itself whose events we witness through eye and ear. In this she proves indeed to be the *didaskalos*—the teacher *and* the producer—who binds Hippolytus into his *muthos*, and who, through her insistence that he share in her disease, reminds us of the fundamental role mimesis plays in the making of the self, which, as Aristotle tells us, is the source of the first learning for all (*tas matheseis . . . prōtas*, *Poet.* 4.1448b).

Concepts of Demoralization in the *Hecuba*
KENNETH J. RECKFORD

Dans la domaine de la souffrance, le malheur est une chose à part, spe-
cifique, irreductible. Il est tout autre chose que la simple souffrance.
Il s'empare de l'âme et la marque, jusqu'au fond, d'une marque qui
n'appartient qu'à lui, la marque de l'esclavage.—Simone Weil, *Attente
de Dieu*

One of the most comforting things about a gathering of sophists is
that we share several assumptions. At least, I think we do. I think we
have all formed the habit of reading Euripides with attention and
tact: with attention, that is, to image and metaphor, sound and
sense, irony, ambiguity, foreshadowing and recall, characterization
and plot development; and with that tact which listens to Euripides,
which respects the multiple contexts of his verses, and which refuses to excise simple messages or simple morals from the living
tissue of his plays. May I ask whether we are not further agreed that
attention and tact, while clearly desirable, are somehow not enough:
that we must look beyond—to comparative literature, or the study of
myth and ritual, or psychology, or anthropology, or linguistics, or
some combination of these—if we are to bring fresh insight or a
fresh response to any given play?

There is, of course, some faddishness in all this. Not that anyone
here will listen to the siren song of fashion and be shipwrecked on
the rocks of the avant-garde. But I *do* think there is a clear and
present danger of our taking an overly intellectual approach to tragedy. *To sophon d'ou sophia.* Are we so involved in constructing patterns to catch literary meanings that we fail to bring receptive minds
and hearts to tragedy? As critics we are so busy. As readers we are so
calm. How often we ignore the power of a dramatic moment, a song,
a scene. How often, too, we fail to do justice to such obvious reali-

ties as grief, anguish, and death. Do we really respond to the pain of tragedy? Or to the joy, remembered or imagined, that so often lies behind it?

Please realize that I intend these warnings largely for myself, because I am about to analyze speeches from the *Hecuba* and to read extensively between the lines. Please realize, too, how very grateful I am that we *do* share certain basic assumptions about Euripides' handling of ideas. One is that most speeches in Euripides' plays reveal more than the speaker intends to say or even happens to know. Another is that every speech must be interpreted within its full dramatic context (which, of course, is why it is so idiotic to use fragments of lost tragedies to prop up hypothetical developments in the history of ideas). Our third assumption is that *dianoia*, the expression and formulation of ideas, is always subordinated by Euripides (as by Aeschylus and Sophocles) to the larger, more basic elements of characterization and plot: or, to put it differently, that we are rightly interested in Euripides' thought, but that Euripides' thought cannot be identified with anything less than each entire play with its total intellectual and emotional impact. As scholars, we are naturally interested in ideas. As Euripidean critics, we are dealing with a theater of ideas. That is well and good: only I must insist (still speaking mainly to myself) that the analysis of ideas should always *bring us back* in the end: back to Hecuba, back to the horrid shore of Thrace, and back to those basic human feelings and concerns which are (intellectuals, critics, and classical scholars not exempted) our necessary lot.

In this essay I shall analyze first Hecuba's remarks on human nobility and then a group of related passages from her plea to Agamemnon. Both times, Euripides draws on contemporary ideas; both times, he uses these for tragic point, not casual philosophizing. Let us follow his lead and not be distracted by nondramatic concerns. The meditation on Polyxena's nobility catches Hecuba in a moment of poise before drastic change. It conveys her inner tension, her growing uncertainty of mind, and it looks forward ironically to her deterioration under pressure of suffering. For Hecuba's own fate illustrates exactly what she denies for Polyxena: namely, the power of time and chance to alter the nobility of the soul. My later passages give evidence both of Hecuba's deterioration and (the two are connected) of a perceptible breaking up of the moral universe. They alert us by their peculiar language to a gap between the moral and religious beliefs to which Hecuba nominally appeals and the new, radically skeptical view of the gods, morality, and human existence to which circumstances have brought her. Hecuba's pleas serve the clear purpose of enlisting Agamemnon's help in her revenge. She bends her every capability of mind and will to serve that one purpose of revenge. But her remarks on law, morality, persuasion, and freedom carry a deeper meaning that goes well beyond persuading the weak Agamemnon. They show us that Hecuba is pursuing her private and primitive vengeance not just because she has suffered so much and lost so much, but because she is now living in a demoralized world: a world without justice, without grace, without pity, even without meaning. All that remains, all that can remain in the rubble of lost civilization, is the simple wish to get your enemy's head on a platter—or, in this case, to put out your enemy's eyes and kill his children. For Hecuba, nothing else matters, because nothing else of Hecuba is left.

Critics have written eloquently and with feeling about Hecuba's downfall. Whether they find the play's center in her suffering, in her movement from suffering to active revenge, in the contrast between her fate and her daughter Polyxena's, or in the idea of the more general human grief and woe that Hecuba symbolizes, people seem pretty well agreed about Hecuba's fall from nobility and decency, and about the reasons for that fall.[1] They also seem agreed in their compassionate response to Hecuba's fate. What I think they have missed—what I think scholars in general tend to miss—is the sense of *terror* in this play: not just the more obvious terror of Hecuba's vengeance, of Polymestor's emergence from the tent as a wounded, raging, and appallingly helpless animal—not just this, but the more hidden terror of a meaningless universe that emerges from Hecuba's words. I do not think we can claim to have understood Euripides' play until we have responded to it with a release of the appropriate emotions, of pity and terror: the one being for Hecuba, mother of sorrows, the other being for ourselves and for the broken world in which we live.[2]

I

When Hecuba hears the report of Polyxena's death, she comes near the limit of tolerable suffering. She has experienced the death of many children, the death of Priam, the fall of Troy. From a great queen she has become a slave. She and the other captives are moving into exile. Just now, Achilles' ghost has required the sacrifice of Polyxena, her daughter and sole comfort. She appealed for help, to Odysseus; she invoked the old-time values of gratitude, justice, pity, and human decency; and Odysseus, by rejecting these appeals, taught her in effect that her religious and moral values were no longer current. What is real but for the stronger to impose their will and the weaker to endure it? Polyxena grasped the situation in a personal, intuitive way. It is better, she argued, to die freely than to bear the yoke of necessity and live on ignobly. Polyxena departed; the chorus sang poignantly of exile and slavery, of small hope and great pain; and then came Talthybius' report of Polyxena's death. It was sad yet splendid. We respond with mixed feelings, and so does Hecuba. She begins by speaking of her grief, which cannot be forgotten; but she goes on to say that Polyxena's nobility, the honor and decency of her dying, take away that excessiveness of grief that would be "too much." This alleviates her distress; it gives her consolation. It keeps her anguish on this side of the border of human tolerance.

Next comes her statement about nobility:[3]

> οὔκουν δεινόν, εἰ γῆ μὲν κακὴ
> τυχοῦσα καιροῦ θεόθεν εὖ στάχυν φέρει,
> χρηστὴ δ᾽ ἁμαρτοῦσ᾽ ὧν χρεὼν αὐτὴν τυχεῖν
> κακὸν δίδωσι καρπόν, ἀνθρώποις δ᾽ ἀεὶ
> ὁ μὲν πονηρὸς οὐδὲν ἄλλο πλὴν κακός,
> ὁ δ᾽ ἐσθλὸς ἐσθλός, οὐδὲ συμφορᾶς ὕπο
> φύσιν διέφθειρ᾽, ἀλλὰ χρηστός ἐστ᾽ ἀεί;
> ἆρ᾽ οἱ τεκόντες διαφέρουσιν ἢ τροφαί;
> ἔχει γε μέντοι καὶ τὸ θρεφθῆναι καλῶς
> δίδαξιν ἐσθλοῦ· τοῦτο δ᾽ ἤν τις εὖ μάθῃ,
> οἶδεν τό γ᾽ αἰσχρόν, κανόνι τοῦ καλοῦ μαθών.

How strange it is: that with soil, if it is bad but gets a god-sent opportunity, it bears good fruit, and if it is good but fails to get the nurture it requires, it bears bad fruit; and yet, with human beings, a villain is never anything other than base, nor a noble man anything but noble: he does not change his nature under pressure of misfortune, but is always good.

What counts for more, then: parents or upbringing? One must admit that to have been brought up well implies instruction in nobility. And if a person learns this lesson well, then he also knows what is ugly-and-shameful, once he grasps this by the canon of what is beautiful-and-fine. (592–602)

Hecuba's language is tense and compact. It shows a powerful mind wrestling both with inner uncertainty and with the complexity of human life and human destiny. She believes, or wishes to believe, in the permanence of nobility. Instinctively, she regards it in the old aristocratic way, as inborn nature (*phua* or *phusis*). By this view, nobility is of the blood; it is born with you and it dies with you—and not before. Polyxena's noble death seems to confirm this article of faith. Yet Hecuba's analogy turns in her hand. A positive comparison between the effects of education and those of horticulture would have been more natural, as well as more familiar to Euripides' contemporaries. Instead, Hecuba sets human nobility *against* organic process. Just as she says, good soil cannot guarantee good growth. Plants depend for their nourishment and growth on many external factors, such as moisture and light and care—what Hecuba calls "opportunity" (*kairos*). Is it not remarkable, then—we might say, *would it not be remarkable*—that human nobility should remain ever constant, unaffected by the contingencies that so obviously control the life of the soil for good or bad?

Yet Hecuba's next question almost gives the game away. "What counts for more, then—parents or upbringing?" This suggests the question, contemporary for Euripides, of whether *aretē* could be taught, and if so, how. Hecuba still insists on the paramount importance of inborn *phusis*, yet she feels compelled to grant some virtue to *trophē*. Pindar himself would have done no less. She concedes that good education "can bring instruction in nobility," and she tries to answer the related question: how can one know what is ugly and shameful without direct experience of it? Her answer sounds Socratic. One opposite implies, hence teaches you about the other. Yet the wording and structure of Hecuba's reflections imply something more: for all her effort of intelligence, she cannot grasp the situation she is struggling to understand. As she says herself, "the mind shot forth these arrows in vain" (603). So she returns to her earlier feelings of grief and helplessness, and also to the immediate need of seeing to Polyxena's burial.

What does Hecuba mean by "in vain"? And what does Euripides mean by it? In one sense, speculation is irrelevant because it is too general, too far removed from Hecuba's present situation and the things needing to be done. In another sense, her words suggest that we cannot grasp our situation, far less control it, through even the best efforts of the reasoning intelligence. Phaedra comes to much the same intuitive realization in her great speech about how people strive to live well but fail. In both instances, Euripides shows a powerful mind trying, and almost (but not quite) succeeding in grasping its own inherent limitations.[4] Both Phaedra and Hecuba understand what virtue is; both have a sinking awareness of lacking the power to maintain it. Of course, Phaedra is already generalizing from her own passion, while Hecuba's reflections stem from her most recent experience of Polyxena's death. Yet the abstract considerations point as strongly to Hecuba's tragedy as they do to Phaedra's. On the one hand, rational analysis is simply not commensurate with the irrational reality of human experience and suffering. We cannot grasp, control, or improve our situation by thinking about it. And yet: Phaedra was on the right track when she discussed the ways in which human resolution is weakened, and so is Hecuba when she speaks of the contingency to which most natural growth is subject—and why not nobility too? "Is it not strange" that human nobility can thrive independently of outside factors? Yes, it *is* strange. In fact, it is quite impossible; and that is the lesson (if you can call it a lesson) that the *Hecuba* teaches. To put it simply, as Euripides never would: the soul, like the body, is corruptible.

This realization is connected ironically with sophistic ideas about the power of education; for like all forms of persuasion, education depends on a malleability of the soul. The teacher reshapes the soul through music and discourse much as the athletic trainer molds the body through diet and exercise. But the shadow side of education is propaganda. Euripides and Aristophanes, Gorgias and

Thucydides, and later Plato, have much to say about the power of propaganda. The good teacher's Socratic dream of improving human nature through cultivation of the mind is therefore shadowed by the equal and opposite nightmare that virtue can be *un-taught*, good character corrupted, nobility destroyed. So Euripides' play demonstrates. As she speaks, Hecuba stands dangerously near to the limit of human endurance; yet suffering grows. The final shock comes presently (it was heralded earlier) as she sees the mutilated corpse of the boy Polydorus. This, precisely, is her "too much." Nothing is left for her except revenge. She goes after that revenge, as Medea did, with demonic concentration. Euripides knew, I think, that his audience would take satisfaction in that revenge; that they (may I say, we?) would be pleased as well as horrified when Hecuba tricks Polymestor, takes him prisoner, blinds him, kills his children, and reduces him from a human being to an impotent four-footed beast. We cannot help conniving at this victory. It is (let us admit it) exhilarating as well as horrifying. Yet it is also a terrible defeat for Hecuba, and for nobility. Her intellect remains strong, but only to abet her vengeance. Helpless to do good, powerless to improve her own situation or anyone else's, she can only imitate her tormentors, most notably Odysseus, and inflict suffering like her own upon her enemies. In so doing, she loses precisely the freedom of soul that Polyxena carried to her death. She accepts permanent slavery, provided she can get revenge. She forfeits every shred of decency. And she loses her grip on humanity itself; for her eventual transformation into a howling bitch, prophesied by the suddenly lucid Polymestor, is only the outward realization of that inward "reeling back into the beast" that Hecuba has already suffered.

Looking back now to Hecuba's speech on nobility (as the Athenian audience could hardly do), we can see that it is, in two ways, a funeral oration. Obviously, it is a eulogy for Polyxena. She died, she was permitted to die, a free and beautiful death. In her, nobility found such lasting expression as art confers on human beauty: thus she was compared to an *agalma*, a lovely image dedicated to a god. At the same time, Hecuba is delivering her *own* funeral oration. She is eulogizing the nobility that she herself must lose while still living. Polyxena was her *parapsuchē*: not only her comfort but her "better self." As Euripides indicates again and again through conventional phrases of mourning, Hecuba has outlived herself, she "is no more."[5] And that is the heart of the matter. We weep for Polyxena, but like Hecuba, we can be consoled for her death. We weep also for the little murdered boy; but the death of Polydorus is pathetic, not tragic. What is really tragic is the inner death of the being who was called Hecuba. She suffers what Polyxena escaped, a kind of rape.[6] Her central speech on nobility points to what few of us would like to think about, far less admit: a contingency in things which, if we think about it feelingly, must strike us not just with pity for human weakness, but with—sheer terror.

II

My shorter passages from Hecuba's plea to Agamemnon can be read in several ways.[7] On the surface, they are normal appeals for support. By helping Hecuba, Agamemnon will be upholding justice, law, and decency. The case sounds good. Agamemnon allows himself to be persuaded. He is glad to do the right thing, glad also to help Cassandra's mother—provided, of course, that he will not suffer any inconvenience or embarrassment. Yet as we listen to Hecuba's pleading, we should realize that she is using moral terms as counters of persuasion. She works on Agamemnon's pity and on his rather dim sense of decency to get what she wants from him: connivance in her plot. Not only that: but throughout Hecuba's speech, oddities of language continually suggest that none of the traditional concepts to which Hecuba appeals is real to her: not pity, or gratitude, or respect for the suppliant, or human rights, or good custom, or the gods themselves. All are mere counters. Hecuba has, as Odysseus would say, "been instructed." From her suffering, from her powerlessness, and from instructors such as Odysseus she has learned that there is no real force behind decency and morality. If she wants justice, she will have to make her own. Accordingly, she plays the suppliant's part; she hammers with words on Agamemnon's mind. The ambiguity of her language indicates her hypocrisy, her double-mindedness. What is more important, it speaks to us over Agamemnon's head about the demoralized world in which Hecuba now pictures herself as existing. Let us look at the separate fragments, then at the picture as a whole.

It may be—I grant it—that we are slaves and lacking in power. But the gods have power, and *Nomos* [custom-and-law] their ruler has power, for it is by *nomos* that we believe in the gods and we distinguish right from wrong in the lives we lead. It comes back to you, Agamemnon. If *Nomos* is destroyed, if murderers of their guest-friends, if sacrilegious men are not to pay the penalty for their crimes, then no principle of fairness, no principle of equality is left in the world of men. (798–805)

The overt appeal is clear. Agamemnon should cooperate with a moral order backed by gods. This plea is traditional enough: but what do Hecuba's words mean if we take them literally? Taking *nomos* as "custom," not as eternal "law," they imply that religion and morality are human inventions: good ones, perhaps, but hardly rooted in heaven. The final appeal to Agamemnon is impressive. We might be reminded of the passionate appeal of the chorus in *Oedipus* who ask to see justice clearly and visibly demonstrated, or else there is moral chaos and religion falls away: *errei de ta theia*. The difference is that Hecuba accepts chaos. For her, the gods never listen, they never enforce morality. Justice only exists insofar as it is upheld, or made, by human beings. And if Agamemnon and Odysseus will not uphold it, then who can or will? Only Hecuba herself.

These lines carry the story a step further:

Why then do we struggle so much, we mortals, and bother with other kinds of instruction, when it is Persuasion who is Queen over people's lives? Why don't we strive all the more, paying our fees, to learn that art of persuasion thoroughly, so that, in the very action of persuading, we could obtain whatever we desired? Could one expect to do well by any other means? (814–20)

Here Hecuba exerts pressure by awakening pity for her helplessness. "I wish," she says, "I had the power of persuasion." She has it, of course. An Athenian audience would get that point quickly. They might also catch the reference to contemporary teachers of rhetoric who could be hired for money. Yet Hecuba's question is dangerous, not just playfully anachronistic. "Why do we toil over other kinds of learning but not persuasion, who alone holds sway over men?" Here persuasion is more than a university course. She is a new *turannos*, the only one that counts. Persuade and you will obtain. There is no other way for events to come out well.

Now let me combine these two passages. Whether justice is carried out and morality reaffirmed, comes down to Agamemnon; but Agamemnon in turn can be persuaded, and the art of persuasion can be taught. Pay your money and get what you want. Become like a god.

Hecuba's persuasion in fact works: partly by sheer will; partly by the force of traditional if empty appeals; and most of all, by working on Agamemnon's lust for his mistress Cassandra. "It may be idle to speak of Kypris," says Hecuba; "still, I shall try." Perhaps she is thinking that gods are usually mentioned in vain. Yet Agamemnon is moved, predictably, by Hecuba's plea that he show gratitude now for the times he has lain by Cassandra's side, for the dear nights they have shared, for their embraces in the darkness. It is all terribly indecent. Nothing could contrast more pointedly with Polyxena's free virgin death. But it works. Agamemnon gives in. He will stand by Hecuba and help her, tacitly—so long as this does not get him in trouble with the army.

Hecuba responds with a third, climactic passage of general reflection:

> Alas. There is no mortal who is truly free. They are all slaves, of money, or of chance, or else the mass of voters, or the laws set down on stone, keep them from doing what their mind desires. (866–69)

Her meaning seems obvious. "If even *you* are afraid—afraid of being slandered to your troops, though you are the high commander—then nobody is truly free. All are enslaved to something or other, be it wealth or fortune, politics or law.[8] But really, you need not be afraid. You need not help me act. Just connive with me (*sunisthi*) and quiet any tumult that may arise when I treat Polymestor—as I shall treat him!" Agamemnon assents, and Hecuba goes into action, giving orders like a general. Agamemnon is to give her messenger safe conduct; the servant is to bring a deceiving message to Polymestor; Agamemnon is to delay Polyxena's burial until Polydorus can be buried with her. And again, Agamemnon agrees. He could not grant all this if the winds were blowing, but since they are not, he can afford to wait: and, oh yes, how nice it is for everybody when the bad man is punished and the good man prospers!

So Hecuba takes her revenge. But let us not be swept along like Agamemnon. Let us listen again to what Hecuba is saying. Superficially, she is voicing a truism. We are all slaves to something or other, to wealth, say, or to chance. This was, or at least became, a philosophical commonplace, culminating in the Stoic paradox, "Every fool a slave." The point is usually that a man gains true freedom only by controlling his passions and making himself independent of material possessions and hence of fortune's rule. Yet for an Athenian in the 420s lines 866 and 867 would have a different meaning. They voice a protest against any and all restrictions. They could be the cry of a person who feels that laws and customs shackle his natural instincts, his desires, his real freedom. We find this view spelled out in many places, and for many purposes. It appears in the Old Oligarch's account of how the democratic majority, the *plēthos*, imposes its tyrannical will upon the reluctant minority of good and intelligent people; or in the radical analysis by Antiphon the Sophist of all the real harm done to people by social forms and legal institutions; or better still, in the naked self-assertion of Plato's Callicles, who is eager to break through social and moral restraints and achieve that tyranny over others which is, for him, the height of freedom, offering every exercise of power and pleasure, every kind and degree of self-gratification. All these are analogies. But they bear witness, I think, to a pervasive restlessness, an impatience with constraints, that some members of Euripides' audience may have proclaimed and many others must have resented and feared. The cry that comes through Hecuba's words is very powerful: "Man is born free, but everywhere he is in chains."

Hecuba has come, I think, to grasp a paradox: at a certain point the extremes of slavery and freedom coincide. Her suffering has taught her, even as it compelled her, to be a slave. Not only has she fallen from queen of Troy to a Greek war-captive and slave, but she has learned to see all people in the mirror of her own suffering as slaves to blind chance, *tuchē*, and to recognize *tuchē* as the ultimate ruler of the universe.[9] But still, in this same vacuum of meaning, where "the center cannot hold" and "mere anarchy is loosed upon the world," Hecuba discovers, from out the midst of slavery, a marvelous resurgence of freedom and power.[10] And this is the paradox. If there is really no law, and no order, then a person can do what she really wants: and what Hecuba wants is vengeance now. Nothing can stop her. And nothing does. Yet her triumph coincides with her full acceptance of slavery. All through this play, Euripides has been showing us the degradation of slavery, but when Agamemnon asks Hecuba, in an offhand, patronizing way,

> What do you want to gain? To live in freedom? That is easy for you to have.

Hecuba replies:

> Not so. I would get vengeance on the wicked, and getting it, then be a slave for all the time to come! (754–57)

She gets what she asks for. Polymestor is blinded, his sons are killed. But the cost to Hecuba is greater still. She has found and used the freedom of a despairing slave. Soon she will sink still lower toward the beast. The strange demonic force that has been gathering in her must at last make its epiphany in the fiery-eyed, howling bitch of Cynossema. What is the point, then? We are not free, it seems, to do good to ourselves or to others; the yoke of necessity is too strong for that. Yet in the dark chaos of a godless universe we may somehow be granted the freedom to carry out the destruction of other people, and still more, the destruction of ourselves.

III

Now someone may object that I have been reading too much into these lines. The real problem, of course, is that I have been *reading* the play at all, and rereading it, instead of receiving its impact in the theater of Dionysus among an Athenian audience. I have substituted a modern "we" for the ancient audience. It is hard to reconstruct the stage business for *Hecuba*, harder still to imagine those details of voice, gesture, and stage movement on which the effect of Euripides' verses must largely have depended. And yet: because Euripides the playwright was also Euripides the director, we may assume that what happened on stage was consonant with at least the broader implications of the text we have before us. And we can say with assurance that Euripides' audience were used to irony, suspense, and sudden dramatic reversals, that they did not take every remark or speech at face value. Listening to Hecuba's speech on nobility, they must have remembered Polydorus' ghost at least dimly and had a sense of worse things to come. Later, when Hecuba appeals to Agamemnon, the audience must have realized that Hecuba is *on the move*, that she is gathering strength, that she is working on Agamemnon by force of persuasion, much as Medea (in that play) manipulates Creon and Aegeus and Jason. Euripides' desperate women are so much brighter than his selfish men! Surely the Agamemnon scene was meant to make the audience uneasy. Hecuba uses the right words but not in the right way. Later on, the bloodiness of her revenge, the spectacle of Polymestor as wounded animal, and the sheer mockery of the trial scene before Agamemnon as corrupted judge, will bring the audience's earlier unease to a point of strong discomfort; and Euripides, as so often, will leave them there.

It would not be difficult for a well-trained actor to get across the idea that Hecuba's plea is "sophisticated," that she is speaking more like the *poikilophrōn* Odysseus than like her earlier, simpler self. Euripides' audience knew all about words as weapons. But it remains for the reader and the literary critic to spell out two further implications of Hecuba's pleading that the audience can only have experienced in part and, as we said, with a vague unease. One is that *her character has changed*. She has been brought down to the level of her oppressors, a double-minded level—although she is single-minded in her desire for revenge.[11] But Hecuba's tricky, ambiguous language also affords us glimpses of a *confused*[12] *and disintegrated world*, a world stripped of gods, of morals, and of meanings, a world where chance rules supreme and where people struggle darkly for power to gratify momentary passions as best they can. The Greek, the civilized decencies are only skin deep. Beneath appearances, the universe has turned Thracian; it has returned to chaos and old night.

Has it really? Or are these shapes of chaos only the projection of Hecuba's inner turmoil? I think not; for suffering can give people drastic clarity of insight about certain things. Certainly, it would be rash to speak of Euripides' own world-picture as chaotic; we would not say, after all, that Shakespeare regularly perceived the world as "a tale / told by an idiot, full of sound and fury, / signifying nothing." Time and again, however, Euripides makes us feel a correspondence between the deterioration of human character and some larger disappearance of values and meanings out of the world. Sometimes there is a clear cause-and-effect relation between the two. In the *Medea*, to which I keep returning because it offers such a close parallel with the *Hecuba*, Medea collapses into savagery after Greece loses faith:

> Χο. ἄνω ποταμῶν ἱερῶν χωροῦσι παγαί,
> καὶ δίκα καὶ πάντα πάλιν στρέφεται.
> ἀνδράσι μὲν δόλιαι βουλαί, θεῶν δ᾽
> οὐκέτι πίστις ἄραρε·
>
> Holy rivers run uphill,
> Justice and all things
>   are twisted backward.
> Men have deceptive plans; the gods
>   inspire no certain trust. (410–414)

In a similar way, Hecuba collapses into savagery, and into spiritual slavery, not just because she is mistreated by men but because her mistreatment opens her eyes to the brutal, chancy, and godless world in which they all are living, oppressors and oppressed alike.

Although Euripides is best compared with Euripides, the sense of breakdown that I have been describing is fully documented by Thucydides (and also by another writer whom I have been keeping in reserve). Thucydides seems to regard history as the interplay of two incalculable forces.[13] One is chance, as seen in the play of wind and tide, rain and fire, and ignorant armies clashing by night. The other is human passion. At best, passions are restrained by the power of reason and kept in precarious equilibrium. At worst, under pressure of plague or war, all restraints break down: not just religious or moral sanctions, but even the control of the reasoning intelligence. Thus, at Corcyra (which has become, like Troy, a universal symbol of disaster), words lose their meaning and reason gives way to passion, notably the will to vengeance over one's enemies. Nothing holds in the darkness of revolution at Corcyra: not religion, not morality, not social and familial ties—not even enlightened self-interest. People's actions become totally irrational. One close parallel with the *Hecuba* is Thucydides' description of war as a "harsh teacher"; compare Odysseus' cold rebuff, "Hecuba, be instructed." Another is Thucydides' observation (3.83) that "the quality of simplicity, to which nobility most largely contributes, was laughed to scorn and altogether disappeared." This statement sums up our play. It was the quality of "simplicity," *to euēthes*, that went to the grave with Polyxena. She was the heart of nobility (*to gennaion*): of Hecuba's nobility too. Nobody laughs at her, to be sure; but the loss, the vanishing of an older and lovelier style of life, seems, at such a moment, altogether complete.

Let me confess now that I came to my reading of the *Hecuba* in my own perverse way, not from Thucydides but from Aristophanes' *Clouds*. I am continually amazed at how much the two plays stand back to back. It is not just that Aristophanes parodies the *Hecuba*, as when Strepsiades bellows to his son, "O child of mine / hie thee from the house / harken to thy father!"[14] In its comic and vulgarizing mode, the *Clouds* sets before us, step by step, the same radical vision of an increasingly demoralized world: from (a) the expulsion of Zeus and the old gods from heaven, through (b) the disappearance of justice and morality, which are replaced by sophistic persuasion; to (c) the arbitrary play of instinct and brute force: beating up your father. In all this, Aristophanes is responding to contemporary ideas, not least the ideas of Euripidean tragedy. He knows all about that chaotic universe. And he responds marvelously, with laughter and with hope. I must admit, though, that I worked backwards: that it was the *Clouds* that first made me realize the terror of Euripides' *Hecuba*.

This terror comes when we feel the full power of blind chance over the lives and minds of human beings. Before that power the qualities we cherish, such as nobility, are like straw. The special case of Hecuba is the typical case; we are all at the mercy of wind and tide,[15] and ultimately of chance, *tuchē*. No wonder the play is so full of words such as *tuchein, eutuchein, dustuchein*, with their related nouns and adjectives. Most everything that happens in *Hecuba* is a matter of chance, blind chance. It would be more reassuring, almost, if we could see some specific dark power at work in this play, like

Aphrodite in the *Hippolytus* or Dionysus in the *Bacchae*. Then evil would have a face. There are times, to be sure, when the timing of events seems diabolical. The maid, going for water to bathe Polyxena's corpse, finds the mutilated corpse of Polydorus rolled upon the shore. The winds are stilled—perhaps, as was alleged, by Achilles' unquiet ghost; certainly they do not stir until Hecuba's vengeance is complete. As I say, it would be almost reassuring to discover a specific demonic power behind these events; for what is most terrifying of all is the cold indifference of the universe to human suffering. Simone Weil, from whom I took my epigraph, speaks of human suffering again and again in words that apply extraordinarily well to the vision of Euripides:

> Si le mécanisme n'était pas aveugle, il n'y aurait pas du tout le malheur. Le malheur est avant tout anonyme, il prive ceux qu'il prend de leur personnalité et en fait des choses. Il est indifférent, et c'est le froid de cette indifférence, un froid métallique, qui glace jusque' au fond même de l'âme ceux qu'il touche. . . .
>   Les crimes humains qui sont la cause de la plupart des malheurs font partie de la nécessité aveugle, car les criminels ne savent pas ce qu'ils font.[16]

I do not think that we, as readers and critics, can respond adequately to the *Hecuba* if we do not feel and recognize the chill of which Simone Weil is speaking, for without it, our still vital categories of pity and terror must remain mere catchwords. Euripides draws out from our inmost being a *pity* for human lives, a generous pity that weeps for Spartan wives and mothers, yet loves our own Athens the more dearly because it is perishable. Kindness, decency, nobility, civilization: all these are the more precious to us when we realize how easily they can be corrupted or destroyed. Yet pity, as Euripides knew, and Thucydides, is no sure guide to action. Nor do advances, or apparent advances, in knowledge bring us any nearer to the good. The best education is shadowed by the worst propaganda. Inevitably, Euripides' tragedies of modern life and thought bring us not just to pity, but to *terror*: for we ourselves seem at times to be living in that same world—call it Thracian or Corcyrean, but it is also Athenian, and American—where all the lights of trusted value, and of trusted meaning, go out at once, and we are left in the dark. We have, then, pity and terror. They are not a guide to life. How could they be? They are only a brief response to tragedy, and to what tragedy sees and shows us of life. Still, they are human; and though they cannot keep us human, they have their place.

Logos and *Pathos*:
The Politics of the *Suppliant Women*
PETER BURIAN

Euripides' *Suppliant Women*, written in wartime about war and its aftermaths, dramatizes an incident regularly cited by the orators as among Athens' finest hours; its protagonist, Theseus, is a national hero explicitly portrayed as the founder and chief ideologist of the Athenian democracy. This play, more than any other in the canon, cries out for a political interpretation, and it has received many.[1] Traditionally, however, such interpretations have amounted to little more than mining the text for nuggets of political wisdom with which to prove Euripides' adherence to this or that faction, or the endorsement of some contemporary figure or program which is then said to constitute his message. But attempts to isolate politics *in* the play mistake the object of their enquiry. It is the politics *of* the play that demand attention, the politics encoded in the structure of its discourse. This paper attempts a close sequential reading of the *Suppliant Women* from the point of view of its political codes without assuming a priori that its politics constitute a commentary on contemporary affairs, but open to the likelihood that what Euripides saw in the world around him profoundly influenced his expressive choices. Moreover, we will grant at least as a working hypothesis that his choices are made for intrinsic reasons; that is to say, we will not lightly invoke events, persons, or concerns outside the drama to explain whatever in it may at first seem irrelevant or ill-conceived. In the last analysis, we take Euripides seriously as a political thinker only if we take him seriously as a dramatist.

Although the first scenes of the *Suppliant Women* contain relatively little that could be called overtly political, they offer two con-

trasting *kosmoi*, two orderings of reality fundamental to an appre-
hension of the play's political concerns. The first might be called
concisely the *kosmos* of emotion, and is embodied chiefly in the
suppliant women themselves; the second *kosmos*, that of intellect,
is represented above all by Theseus, whose aid the women seek. As
the play begins, a situation fraught with immediate and powerful
emotions is thrust upon the spectator. Theseus' mother, Aithra,
standing at an altar of Demeter and Persephone at Eleusis, is interrupted by the mothers of the Seven who fell at Thebes in the midst
of celebrating the solemn Proerosia, a sacrifice for good crops performed each year at the time of tillage.[2] The mothers are performing
a clashing rite of their own: they supplicate for help in reclaiming
the bodies of their sons from the Thebans, who have refused to give
them burial. The suppliant women surround Aithra and hold her fast
with a "chain that is no chain" (31) of wreathed suppliant branches.
Their presence at the altar threatens pollution.[3] Their shorn heads
and tattered robes of mourning are visual reminders that, as they
themselves say, they come "not in a holy manner, but out of need"
(63). Their tears and laments for the dead are ill-omened in the context of Aithra's attempt to ensure new life from the earth. All these
discords underline the fact that the natural order of the suppliant
women's lives has been overturned. They are, paradoxically, "child-
less mothers" (35); they seek to "bury those who should have buried
them" (174–75), but who instead now "lie prey to mountain beasts"
(47). In such circumstances, the suppliant women abandon themselves to powerful but futile gestures of despair, the ritual beating of
breasts and tearing of cheeks (48–51, 73–78), and to the antiphonal
cries of their dirge (71–72, 79–82), "for the rites of the dead are
kosmos to the living" (78): the ecstatic death-dance is their orna-
ment, and the ordering principle of their shattered lives.

This remarkable parodos looks beyond the mothers' appeal for
the recovery of the children's corpses to the intricate rituals of mourning around which the second half of the play is built, where the
kosmos of emotion will be once again, and decisively, thrust to the
fore. For the moment, however, the entrance of Theseus, the young
king whose aid the mothers hope to enlist with *his* mother's help,
unexpectedly changes the focus and direction of the drama. Until
now, the suppliants' suffering and need have monopolized our attention, and although Aithra has deferred to her son's judgment, the

sympathetic concern expressed in her prologue implied tentative acceptance of their suit.[4] But Theseus brusquely reopens the issue and
overturns the conclusion. The encounter of mothers gives way to a
confrontation of rulers, the claims of pity yield to deliberation, and
the *kosmos* of emotion is replaced by that of intellect.

Theseus is evidently distressed by the unexpected sights and
sounds of lamentation that greet him within the sacred precinct
(87ff.), but rather than engage the mothers, he turns to their ostensible leader Adrastos, the Argive king who led the Seven against
Thebes to defeat, who has huddled in misery at the back of the stage
throughout prologue and parodos (cf. 20ff.).[5] There is an abrupt change
of mood and tone: no longer is mother pleading with mother, now
the "glorious king of the Athenians" (113) interrogates a fallen king.
Theseus begins his peremptory cross-examination: "Speak. Uncover
your head and stop wailing. Without speech (*mē dia glōssēs ion*) no
goal is reached" (111–12). Not only the tone, but also the emphasis
on speech, has significance. Theseus does not look kindly on the old
man's inarticulate self-pity. He believes in the efficacy of speech to
produce understanding, in *glōssa* as the messenger of *sunesis*, as he
later puts it (203–4). His questions are directed to understanding the
causes of Adrastos' plight, and they are notably hard-headed in comparison with the show of emotion in the opening scenes. Theseus
will not be swayed by the sight of suffering until he has established
the responsibility for it, and will not sacrifice the moral and political
bases of his statecraft to assuage a sense of pity. His interrogation
moves swiftly from the immediate cause of the supplication to the
more remote causes of the expedition against Thebes, mercilessly
exposing Adrastos' own folly as the source of his woe. Adrastos interpreted the riddling words of an oracle too hastily and married his
daughters to two exiled strangers; ignoring the signs of sacrifice and
prophecy, he made war against Thebes on behalf of one of them,
Polynices. Theseus concludes the demonstration of Adrastos' error
with a judgment that has larger significance for the play's political
themes:[6] "you chose stout-heartedness over good sense" (*eupsuchian
espeusas ant' euboulias*, 161)—in terms of the antinomy we have
been developing here, emotion over intellect.

Adrastos cannot dispute the truth of this judgment, and so must
fall back on pathetic pleas and political arguments unlikely to sway
Theseus. He emphasizes his own misery (164–67), and associates it

with that of the mothers (168–75), but can offer no justification for the conduct that Theseus has shown to have caused it. What may be called Adrastos' first political point is simply another argument *ad misericordiam*: rich and poor must be examples to each other, the blessed should help the wretched since they themselves may one day need aid (176–79).[7] More obviously political is Adrastos' flattery of Athens' reputation as the only city willing to undertake burdens such as the one he prays for; but Adrastos omits to show why Athens should stake that reputation on him (184–92).

Theseus's reply, the so-called theodicy of lines 195–218, has long troubled commentators because of its supposedly irrelevant philosophizing.[8] In fact, on close inspection, it emerges as a tightly reasoned rebuttal of Adrastos' position formulated on the basis of what we have been calling the *kosmos* of intellect. There is nothing in it that does not relate to the immediate context or to the concerns of the play as a whole. Theseus begins with the general (but highly germane) observation that man's misfortunes are neither inevitable nor necessarily worthy of pity, because men "live in the light" (200) of understanding and are therefore responsible for their own actions. The gods have brought man out of bestial confusion through the gifts of *sunesis* and its interpreter, *glōssa* (203–4). Theseus then catalogs the gods' other gifts: the bounteous earth, rainfall, the seasons, and commerce to make up for whatever may still be lacking (205–10). The gods even guide men, when intelligence is insufficient, by prophecy and sacrificial divination (211–13).

The conclusion of this list of blessings with the mantic arts is certainly not accidental, although some have found it strange that Euripides, the scourge of Delphi, should so heartily endorse them. But surely we must insist on the logical priority of the question, why does Theseus speak these lines here, over the question, why did Euripides write them. And the obvious answer is simply that Adrastos' initial error was his disastrous failure to heed omens and prophecies. Theseus first makes a general observation, then applies it to his suppliant. Those who find the gifts by which the gods brought order to human life insufficient reveal only their own foolishness in pretending to more than divine wisdom (*daimonōn sophōteroi*, 218). This was precisely Adrastos' failing. He showed himself unwise (*ou sophos*, 219) by assuming that he understood Apollo's oracle, and by using it to justify what no wise man (*ton sophon*, 224) would ever attempt, the mating of justice and injustice. Furthermore, although he invoked the gods in making a foolish match for his daughters, he flouted their will when he led an expedition against Thebes, and "destroyed his city by dishonoring and slighting the gods, led astray by youths who take joy in glory and spread war unjustly" (229–33).[9]

Mention of the reckless and self-seeking young men who won Adrastos to their cause leads directly to the much-discussed "digression" on the three classes of citizens (238–45), a passage that can only be understood as an integral part of Theseus' answer to Adrastos. Adrastos argued that the fortunate have both a moral and practical obligation to help those in need (176–79). Theseus rejects Adrastos' plea by overturning its premise, the division of society into rich and poor, dependent upon each other for survival. These two groups are rather the self-seeking, mutually destructive extremes. Only the middle order can preserve the state:

> Of the three classes, the middle one saves communities, guarding whatever order (*kosmon*) a city establishes. (244–45)

Adrastos delivered his city to the cause of self-seeking extremists, disastrously mingling foul with fair, unjust with justice (*lampron de tholerōi . . . summeixas*, 222; *adika dikaiois . . . summignunai*, 224). In asking for Athens' aid, Adrastos asks for another such mingling: Theseus rejects it as bad and dangerous policy.

Theseus' "theodicy" and his political analysis, then, are clearly designed to demonstrate Adrastos' responsibility for his own misfortune and to provide a reasoned answer to his emotional plea. At this point, however, we cannot help observing that the action of the drama has taken a peculiar turn. It is entirely consonant with the story pattern of a suppliant drama such as this that the ruler have great doubts about accepting the suit of his suppliants (as Pelasgos does in Aeschylus' *Supplices*), but it is out of the question that he finally reject it. And, of course, Theseus does agree to help the mothers at last, but only after his own mother intervenes forcefully on their behalf. In effect, Euripides produces a second plea scene to reverse the "impossible" consequence of the first. This remarkable reduplication has, as we shall see, a number of significances, including a direct bearing on the politics of the play.

The transition to Aithra's plea is made in a scene that recalls the *pathos* and religious awe of the opening. Adrastos prepares to depart, ordering the women to leave their branches at the altar and to call Demeter and all the gods as witnesses that their prayers have been rejected (258–62). Thus, the threat of pollution inherent in the mothers' rite is evoked once more as they turn to make a last, emotional appeal. Even a beast (*thēr*, 267) has a cave for refuge, they say, and we are reminded of Adrastos' unfortunate alliance with Polynices and Tydeus, supposed to be the *thēres* to whom the oracle bade him marry his daughters (145); of the *thēriōdes biotos* from which Theseus asserted that the gods lifted mankind (202); and indeed of the fallen children of the suppliants, who lie prey to the *thēres* of the mountains (47). Altogether the mothers' appeal contains nothing new, and does not even touch the grounds for Theseus' refusal of aid. Yet the same sorrowful strains we have heard from them before, the same compelling gestures accompany their pleas for pity, and call the refusal into question. Theseus, in his exchange with Adrastos, set out his belief in a comprehensible, morally simple order in human affairs. He rejected Adrastos' appeals by showing that his actions had violated the tenets of that order. But in treating misfortune as a problem for ethical and political judgment, he overlooked the awesome, disordered *pathos* of the mothers, the human reality of their misery.

Contact with this reality is made at last, but in a deliberately limited, even circuitous way, as the mothers press their claim upon the young king's pity. Throwing themselves at his feet, embracing his knees in supplication (271–79), they repeat their anguished pleas. Just as they had earlier appealed to Aithra's maternal fellow-feeling, now they turn to Theseus as *teknon* for the burial of children his own age (282–83). But unlike Aithra, whose concern was immediately clear, Theseus resists the impulse to sympathy. His obvious distress is caused by his own mother's tears, which he interprets as a sign of pity for the suppliants. Although he feels pity too, he attempts to dissuade his mother from conduct that ill befits the shrine of Demeter and the misfortune of mere strangers (286–92).[10]

Aithra reopens the mothers' case with her tears and groans, but her argument is not a restatement of their pathetic pleas, or a plea for pity at all. (It is no part of the design of this play that Theseus yield to such a plea, whereas the influence of parents upon their children, and the duties of children toward their parents, are crucial.)[11] If the mothers' plight has reduced Aithra to tears, the distress that those tears cause her son gives her the opportunity to offer reasons much more likely to sway him than any display of emotion. Aithra's appeal is based on a complex chain of religious, political, and personal considerations. By the time Theseus makes his reply, cries of woe have been supplemented by persuasive discourse, and the suppliant's need is subsumed into the *kosmos* of intellect.

The first step toward interpreting Aithra's appeal is to recognize that it is not a compendium of separate contentions, but a complex arrangement of related ideas.[12] Aithra begins by offering to tell Theseus "something fine (*kalon*, 293) for you and for the city," and Theseus replies that women often speak wisely (*sopha*, 294). We are reminded of Aithra's remark in the prologue that "women who are wise" (*haitines sophai*, 74) get things done by men, and of Theseus' condemnation of Adrastos' lack of wisdom (*ou sophos gegōs*, 219) in flouting divine will. Part of Aithra's wisdom here is to convict Theseus of the same failing. Just as Adrastos erred than (*'sphalēn*, 156), so has Theseus now (*sphallēi*, 303); just as Adrastos dishonored the gods (*atimasas . . . theous*, 230–31) by ignoring the seers, so Theseus dishonors them (*ta tōn theōn . . . atimasas*, 301–2) by rejecting the suppliants. The consideration of religious duty then leads seamlessly to the political necessity of enforcing human law. Aithra says that she would not have ventured to speak had the suppliants not been wronged, but the phrase "I'd have kept silent" (*kart' an eichon hēsuchōs*, 305) introduces a term that will shortly gain a precise political significance (*hēsuchoi . . . poleis*, 324; cf. 509, 952). The injustice done the suppliant mothers leads Aithra to a legal point: violent men have deprived their enemies of burial and this violates a law respected by all the Greeks (*nomima te pasēs . . . Hellados*, 311). But she introduces this theme with a straight appeal to Theseus' sense of honor (*hosēn timēn pherei*, 306), and indeed her forceful statement of the need for Theseus to intervene (cf. 310) is grammatically and logically subordinated to this personal appeal.

The question of Theseus' reputation cannot be reduced to a matter of personal pride because it is wholly inseparable from the ethical and political considerations inherent in the terms of Aithra's argument. Thus, she makes a strong general case for enforcement of the law as the condition of social order (*to gar toi sunechon anthrōpōn poleis*, 312), and follows it with the warning that Theseus will be accused of cowardice if he shuns this duty. Even this personal argument, however, has strong political overtones. Theseus should not shirk a chance "to win a crown of glory from the city" (315); cowardice is countered by a term that has in this play a strong political flavor: *ponos*. Theseus was not dismayed by the trifling task (*phaulon . . . ponon*, 317) of slaying a wild boar; will he prove a coward when called upon to struggle (*ekponēsai*, 319) in battle? This appeal to heroic pride leads directly to the demands of political responsibility: the city grows by undertaking tasks (*en gar tois ponoisin auxetai*, 323); quiet, inactive cities (*hēsuchoi . . . poleis*, 324) remain obscure out of excessive caution. It is the argument for heroic action recast in overtly political terms, as an avowal of the policy known to the Athens of Euripides' day, and to her enemies, as *poluprogmosune*.[13] Concern with the contemporary flavor of this passage has, however, obscured its place in Aithra's argument, and its dramatic relevance. It is worth noting that Aithra's words echo Adrastos' claim that Athens is the only city capable of undertaking the *ponos* of burying his dead (184–92, a passage also notably "contemporary" in tone). The real difference between these two appeals is contextual. Adrastos' remarks come after he has been discredited and thus the argument that Athens alone *can* help is isolated from any compelling reason why she *should*. Aithra's political considerations, on the other hand, are linked to powerful religious, ethical, and personal arguments in a chain of reasoning that leads to her call for action.

Theseus' reply must be understood in the context of Aithra's plea. The young king responds directly to the evocation of his heroic reputation, but he subsumes the essential elements of her ethical and political arguments as well into his decision to aid the suppliants. He sets out to defend a reputation not merely for action, but for noble action (*polla gar drasas kala*, 339) and the punishment of the wicked (342). He identifies this reputation specifically with the policy of activism that Aithra endorsed (*oukoun apaudan dunaton esti moi ponous*, 342), making her endorsement itself grounds not to refuse (343–45). In accepting the suppliants' suit, he speaks for himself, but also for the state whose constitution he established and whose support he feels sure to win (349–57), for he now sees that the task corresponds to his own nature and that of Athens. He had earlier insisted that Adrastos shoulder responsibility for his own folly; now he accepts responsibility for a noble deed. There he shunned the mating of foul and fair; here he seeks a victory of fair over foul. He will try persuasion, but be prepared to fight, sure that if he must wage war, the gods will take no offense (346–48).

The dialectic of the multiple plea scenes yields a conception of personal and political heroism which the play as a whole will put to the test. Out of complex arguments and conflicting emotions Theseus distills at last a simple, unified image of self and state toiling for the right. Aithra has led him to it not by overturning his *kosmos*, but by correcting and extending his understanding of it. Theseus had treated Adrastos' plea for pity (*sōson nekrous moi*, 168) as a threat to the social fabric, but Aithra shows him that in so doing he neglected divine and human law, just as Adrastos had, and so himself failed to uphold the very basis of community:

τὸ γάρ τοι συνέχον ἀνϑρώπων πόλεις
τοῦτ᾽ ἔσϑ᾽, ὅταν τις τοὺς νόμους σώζῃ καλῶς.

This is what holds cities together: someone who nobly
preserves the laws. (311–12)

Theseus can now accept his destined role as the suppliants' savior, for he now sees in the task of preserving the laws an extension of his own principles, a reflection of his own nature, and a mark of his city's greatness.

Theseus does not, however, change his mind about Adrastos. Aithra argues the mothers' cause without attempting to justify the old king's foolish war, and he begins his reply to her by reaffirming his earlier condemnation (334–46). He will continue to resist association with Adrastos, forbidding him to answer the Theban herald (513–16) and ordering him to take no part in the battle (591–93).[14] Indeed, this emphatic separation of just and unjust causes is often invoked to explain the initial rejections of Adrastos' plea.[15] This is correct as far as it goes, but it does not go far enough. Theseus' very insistence upon the dangers of mingling his cause with that of the Argives raises questions to which the remainder of the drama will provide unsettling answers. In rejecting Adrastos' suit, and then in accepting the mothers', Theseus never wavers in his certainty that the right can be ascertained and, once known, can be put into action. But is it possible to keep the innocent separate from the guilty, right forms of action from wrong? Can the onward rush of events still be governed by the discriminations that offered a rationale for action at the start? After Theseus wins victory in battle, successive waves of lament, eulogy, and desire for revenge will submerge the distinctions won so laboriously here. Theseus' ordered world of intellect will yield to the mothers' world of emotions, bringing into question the assumptions upon which it was founded.

For now, however, the successful conclusion of the mothers' suit has released the tensions that the conflict of passion and reason had engendered, and at last the suppliants remove their branches from about the altar. In prompting this gesture, however, Theseus turns our attention not so much to the mourning mothers as to his own mother and her release from the bondage of their "awesome wreaths" (*semn' aphaireite stephē mētros*, 359–60). Theseus' arrival was motivated by his concern for Aithra (89–91); now he makes the obligation to see her safely home the focus of his departure, ending his speech and the episode with a *sententia* on filial piety:

> That child is wretched who does not serve his parents in return,
> the noblest tribute; for, having given, he receives in turn from
> his own children what he has given to his parents. (361–64)

Those who have remarked on the unexpected emphasis given this theme have tended to see in it "priggish sententiousness" designed to reflect on the character of Theseus.[16] But the point is not primarily ethopoetic. Filial devotion has been established as an important component of Theseus' decision to act (cf. 320, 343–45) and he reasserts it here in a form that not only caps the scene, but looks beyond it to the duty that the children of the Seven will feel to avenge their fathers' deaths by waging a new war against Thebes (1144–52). Here as so often in this play, personal emotion spills over into political signification.

The merging of personal sentiment with politics is evident also in the brief choral ode that now follows. The mothers appropriate the ethical and political atmosphere of Theseus' exchange with Aithra in a confident appeal to Athens, as a bulwark of justice, to preserve the laws (*nomous brotōn mē miainein*, 378). What the dead sons are to their mothers, a "blood-stained delight" (*agalma phonion*, 371), the rescue of the corpses will be to Athens: "A pious task is a noble delight for cities" (*kalon d'agalma polesin eusebēs ponos*, 373).[17] This assertion in turn is linked to a wish for bonds of friendship between Argos and Athens (372–76), foreshadowing the treaty with which Athena herself will bring the play to a close.

The second episode, which contains the famous (or perhaps one should say notorious) debate between Theseus and a Theban herald concerning the relative merits of democracy and tyranny (399–466), is naturally the focus of most discussion of political themes in the *Suppliant Women.* Before we turn to the debate itself, however, we should attempt to place the whole episode in the context of Euripides' larger dramatic choices. The war declared at the end of the episode was not forced on Euripides by his legendary subject. There is clear evidence that he has preferred the version in which Athens and Thebes do battle to one that he and his audience must have known in which the recovery of the bodies is accomplished peacefully.[18] In so doing, Euripides adheres to the expected pattern of events in suppliant dramas: the suppliants' protector is forced to wage war on their behalf.[19] Paradoxically, however, Euripides has eliminated the violent confrontation of enemy herald and suppliants which is otherwise such a prominent feature of these plays.[20] One result of this is to make the enemy herald a very different figure from his counterparts. By the simple expedient of letting him enter while the king is present, Euripides removes the occasion for that wanton violation of suppliant rights which so discredits the other heralds, and provides instead the opportunity for an extended and elaborate "contest of words" (*hamillan . . . logōn,* 428) between the representatives of two political systems. This is no casual choice, for the replacement of violence by political discourse offers a test of the power of that discourse to prevent violence. *Logos* here becomes, as we shall see, not only the medium of the agon but one of its central subjects as well.

This point can be seen right from the start. The herald's first words, "who is the ruler of this land?" (399) correspond to similar questions asked by other heralds only after they have attempted violence.[21] This herald has so such designs. Theseus, however, treats the words as a verbal challenge, opening a debate that locks the adversaries in irresolvable conflict before the issue at hand is even mentioned. In the other suppliant dramas, the enemy's violence prefigures and even causes armed conflict. In the *Suppliant Women,* war results from the inability of men who desire peace to achieve it by rational deliberation. The debate on government is part of a larger failure to reach understanding or even fruitful discussion. The failure is the point as well as the result of the entire agon, a fact only emphasized by beginning it with this unproductive and seemingly irrelevant exchange.[22] Here, as throughout the agon, the antagonists speak not so much to as past each other's points. The debate on government seems not designed to settle an issue but to establish the bounds of an opposition that will brook no compromise. The herald caps it with the only possible conclusion: "on these disputed matters, hold your view, but I still hold the contrary" (465–66). The debate is generally held to have little or nothing to do with the drama and, therefore, to be designed solely to reveal Euripides' own political views. What we have observed so far, however, suggests a different possibility: Euripides has deliberately staged a debate that will not reveal any view as correct beyond doubt or qualification. If this is so, the debate may be relevant to the drama in a manner not usually suspected.

We deduce from a famous passage in Herodotus that the comparison of constitutions was a subject of discussion in the second half of the fifth century.[23] There is no reason to doubt that the topic intrigued Euripides as much as the next man but every reason to be skeptical of the claim that his interest in it caused him to lose control of his play. Can we make sense of the undeniably "contemporary" tone of the debate without some such assumption? The observations of those scholars who treat the *Suppliant Women* as political allegory, if stripped of the a priori assumption that Euripides must be writing about contemporary affairs rather than alluding to them for dramatic ends, can help us here. It has been convincingly demonstrated, for example, that the "constitution of Theseus" portrayed in the play embodies an ideal most nearly approached under Pericles.[24] Theseus is depicted, with an anachronism that need not trouble us,[25] as the founder of a regime in which the people are sovereign, but follow the will of a high-minded leader.[26] The herald opposes this ideal by contrasting to it the grating reality of Athenian democratic practice during the ascendancy of demogogues such as Cleon. The inconclusive quality of the debate stems largely from the fact that Theseus upholds his ideal without confronting this reality. Thus, a clash of political ideologies, couched in the language of current factional dispute,[27] largely shapes the agon. It at once explains the failure of Athens and Thebes to settle their disputes peacefully and offers a significant comment on that failure.

Logos as the fundamental tool of political life is at the heart of the debate on government. Theseus, who called speech the messenger of understanding (203–4), defends democracy by defending the value of rational discourse to civic life:

> This is freedom (*touleutheron*): "Who has a useful counsel to bring before the city?"[28] And he who wishes to, shines forth; he who does not, keeps silent. What greater equality (*ti isaiteron*) could there be in a city? (438–41)

Here democratic slogans of freedom (*eleutheria*, cf. 405) and equality (*isotēs*, cf. 408, 432, 434) find proper expression in discourse for the good of the community as a whole. The picture counters but does not really answer the herald's portrayal of the abuse of language under democratic rule, where a demagogic seeker after private gain can "puff up" the mob with words (*ekchaunōn logois*, 412), hide his earlier errors with new slanders (415), and thus win control of the populace with his tongue (*glōssēi kataschōn dēmon*, 425). The effect is to emphasize the idealism of Theseus' position with a view of contemporary reality not only possible but disturbingly plausible when one thinks of a figure such as Cleon. Furthermore, the failure of discourse to serve the common good will be demonstrated by the very futility of the agon itself. For the second "round" of the agon will relentlessly transform the ideological impasse into a declaration of armed hostility.

The herald's arguments against intervention on behalf of the suppliants run squarely into positions established in the plea scenes. The contention that this is an Argive matter in which Theseus has no part (472) is not unlike Theseus' own initial response to his mother's tears and groans (291–92). Now, however, Theseus repeats Aithra's argument that he is acting to preserve a Panhellenic law (526, 538–41; cf. 310–13). To the claim that it would be impious to bury those Zeus has singled out for destruction (494–505), Theseus responds explicitly by calling burial "an ancient law of the gods" (*nomos palaios daimonōn*, 563; cf. *nomima theōn*, 19; *ta tōn theōn*, 301), and implicitly in his depiction of restoring the bodies to earth as part of a cosmic return of each element to its source (531–36). The herald's arguments are refuted by restating conclusions reached earlier and valid for the play as a whole. But the herald has much more to say, and more persuasively, about the joys of peace and the horrors of war (479–93). It would be a mistake to regard this passage as a condemnation of the war that Theseus is about to undertake, for "the Theban is illustrating the failings he describes" when he opposes Athens' lawful and pious decision to bury the fallen.[29] Nevertheless, the herald's depiction of foolhardy, thoughtless men who abandon the blessings they know peace bestows for the false lure of war has a significance beyond the context of the agon. The second half of the play, as we shall see, provides distressing confirmation. For the moment, the herald's pacifism, by raising the question of the efficacy of any war to achieve desired ends, suggests a possible limitation of Theseus' heroic ideal.

The theme of language, whose prominence in the debate on government we have already noticed, reappears in a different form in Theseus' attack on the Theban fear of burying fallen enemies, "a stupid waste of words" (skaion . . . analōma tēs glōssēs, 547). Yet the ironic question, "do you think they'll engender children in some recess of earth to visit vengeance upon you?" (545–46), does not describe so irrational a terror after all when one recalls the young Epigonoi, who have been on stage since the beginning of the play (cf. 106–7), in whom the sight of their fathers' ashes will stir up passion for a new war (1143ff.), and whose mission of vengeance Athena herself will confirm at the close (1213ff.). Nor, for all Theseus' displeasure at the herald's loquaciousness, can what he says be dismissed simply as "idle words" (logous mataious, 583; for Theseus' criticism of the herald, see 426, 459–62, 567). The themes of this "contest of words" are too complex for that. Theseus' actions are vindicated in principle, but doubts have nonetheless been sown about their consequences and final significance.

The acrimonious stichomythy with which the agon ends displays a number of the specifically political themes of this play. The herald, who earlier praised the "quiet" leader as wise (hēsuchos kairōi sophos, 509), taunts Athens and her king for their polupragmosune (prassein su poll' eiōthas hē tē sē polis, 576). Theseus in reply accepts the war that has been thrust upon him as his ponos (cf. 573) and the charge of polupragmosune as the emblem of his city's greatness: ponousa polla poll' eudaimonei (577). All this closely reflects the core of Aithra's political argument for accepting the suppliants' suit. The issue has been joined, but its full implications are only beginning to be understood.

The expected exchange of insults, boasts, and threats brings this encounter to a close on another arresting note. To Theseus' sneer at the prowess of the Thebans, a race sprung from serpent's teeth, the herald replies: "You shall learn it by suffering, for you are still a young man" (*neanias*, 580). Youth has political overtones in the *Suppliant Women*. Although Theseus' youth is elsewhere seen as a virtue (cf. 190, 232) and he himself contrasts democracy, which rejoices in the young (*hēdetai neaniais*, 443), with tyranny, which destroys them (*apolōtizēi neous*, 449), the rashness of the young (*neōn . . . andrōn thorubos*, 160; cf. 232, 250, 509, 738) leads to the disastrous expedition against Thebes. In the second half of the play Theseus will ask an older and wiser Adrastos to instruct the young (*eipe g' hōs sophōteros neoisin astōn tōnd'*, 842–43) by the example of those whose youthful folly he earlier condemned; Athena will sanction vengeance for their deaths by a new crop of *neoi* (cf. 1217), the children they left behind. The theme of youth, then, helps to articulate a disturbing suggestion of the action as a whole, that the cycle of generations is perpetually caught in a cycle of conflict.[30]

The battle sequence that ensues, although in many ways splendid of its kind, does not add much to our picture of the politics of the *Suppliant Women*. Still, it is worth noting how Euripides, by emphasizing Theseus' moderation as much as his valor, makes the battle not only a military triumph but also a triumph of ideal heroism. Before he departs to muster his troops, Theseus insists again on the sanctity and purity of his mission by ordering Adrastos to stay away from the battle "and not to mingle your fortunes with mine" (*kamoi mē anamignusthai tuchas tas sas*, 591–92). He still emphatically rejects any "mingling" (cf. 222–24) of just and unjust causes that might jeopardize the favor of the gods. Before the fighting starts, Theseus' herald makes a last plea for peaceful restoration of the corpses, which the Athenians have come to bury "upholding Panhellenic law, and not wishing to prolong the bloodshed" (671–72). He is answered by silence; the contest of words is at an end and there is no choice but to fight. When the battle is over, we are given further proof of Theseus' moderation:

It was possible to enter their walls, but Theseus held back, for he said he had not come to sack the city, but to reclaim the dead. (723–25)

The messenger concludes his speech with an encomium of Theseus, which has often been taken as electioneering for one or another Athenian candidate for a generalship but which fits the dramatic situation and the political concerns of the play far better than any of the "real world" hypotheses:[31]

This is the kind of general that must be chosen, one who is brave amidst dangers and hates the arrogant folk (*hubristēn laon*) who, seeking to scale the topmost rung of the ladder, destroy the happiness they had before. (726–30)

Theseus' heroism has been shown to be exactly what is here recommended: a combination of bravery and limited ambitions. But the particular form of the encomium adds to its effect. The speaker is an Argive, taken prisoner by the Thebans when they defeated the attack of the Seven (cf. 635–39); when he speaks of the arrogant people who destroy their own happiness he can be referring only to the mistaken ambitions of Argos which he has lived to regret.[32] If the situation itself were not enough to make this clear, an obvious allusion would. Scaling the top of a ladder as a metaphor for overreaching ambitions inevitably evokes Kapaneus, one of the Seven leaders of the original expedition against Thebes, whose blasphemous boasts provoked Zeus to topple him from his ladder with a lightning bolt and made him the very emblem of hubris at least from the time of Aeschylus, and more than once in this very play (cf. 496–99, 639–40, 934, 1011).

To the suppliant mothers, the outcome of the battle is a vindication of divine justice (731–33), and Adrastos, too, draws the obvious lesson: Zeus indeed rules (734–36) and hubris has been punished, first that of Argos, now that of Thebes (739–44).[33] Yet the matter does not rest here. Both of Adrastos' reflections are loaded in a manner that transforms his apparently neat moral into a disturbing commentary on past and future. Euripides has saved until this moment a startling fact, evidently of his own invention, about Adrastos' expedition: Eteocles had offered to settle the dispute on fair terms, but Adrastos and the Seven refused (739–40).[34] This no doubt emphasizes the folly of Argos, which the gods have duly chastised, but it also casts its shadow over Adrastos' general reflections on human foolishness and frailty, and over the coming "rehabilitation" of the fallen heroes, as well. The tone of Adrastos' speech is curiously despairing. Why do men claim to have the power of thought (*phronein*, 735), he asks at the outset, and goes on to formulate the characteristic civic failure that results from men's stupidity, the penchant for settling disputes by war instead of by words (*phonoi kathareisth' ou logōi ta pragmata*, 749). This has an immediate application to the Thebans, who answered Theseus' final call for a peaceful solution with defiant silence (673–74), and, as we have just learned, it applies to the original Argive expedition as well. But beyond that, Adrastos' pessimism negates the one great truth that the action up to this point seemed to have established, that men can order their lives in accordance with reason. Adrastos' response to the triumph of Theseus' heroic idealism is to put in doubt again the very foundation of Theseus' *kosmos*. Like the Theban herald's condemnation of war, Adrastos' reflections raise nagging questions about the final meaning of the action we have just seen so brilliantly succeed.

In this way, Adrastos' speech forms a bridge between the two main parts of the play. The recovery of the fallen warriors has been accomplished; what follows is not simply a grateful celebration of Athenian benevolence, or a pathetic restoration to bereft mothers of their children's ashes, though both elements are present. Rather, a series of startling and disturbing scenes, linked by the presence of the longed-for dead, constitutes a second action which, like the first, will move from the personal to the political, and from sentiments to deeds.[35] Lamentation and the rites of burial are its matrix, much as the pattern of suppliant drama underlies what went before.[36] In the second action, the expected resolution evaporates in new tensions, and questions seemingly closed are opened once more by a lengthy, intricate process of displacement. The comfortable conclusions of the successful rescue operation are never denied, they simply disappear from view, yield to lament, to consolation, and finally to a renewal of vengeance.

The restoration of the corpses, for which the war has been fought, brings no joy and even little relief. Adrastos wishes only that he had died with the others (769), a sentiment that will be voiced repeatedly in these scenes and turned into action by Evadne. The mothers, in the stasimon that formally closes the battle episode, sound a note of unrelieved gloom. The Athenian triumph they mention only to contrast it with their own sorrow (779–81); victory has brought them the sight of their lifeless sons, "an agony to see, lovely sight though it be" (783) and "the greatest pain of all" (785). The only lesson they seem able to draw is that it would have been better not to marry and give birth than to lose one's children (786–93). This theme, too, resounds throughout the remainder of the play; for the moment, it ushers in a kommos that rises to an almost ecstatic pitch of grief. Adrastos leads in the funeral cortege, and as they see it the mothers pray for death (796–97). They renew the mourning of their childlessness (809–10) and the outcry against marriage (822–23). They begin once more their gestures of self-defacement (826–27). The winning of what they so passionately sought has reduced them to the misery with which they began the play (cf. 71–86).

There is more to the kommos, however, than lament. One crucial key to its thematic function is the "reversal of point of view about the dead"[37] implicit in it, and developed explicitly in the funeral oration which follows. As at the beginning of the play, Adrastos first laments his own defeat (808; cf. 22–23) and he goes on to speak of the "blood-stained bodies of those ill-fated men slain unworthily by the unworthy" (811–13), apparently unmindful of the earlier demonstration of his and his companions' responsibility for all that they suffered. Adrastos renews his wish to join the Seven in death by praying for a fate like that of Amphiaraos or Kapaneus, earlier portrayed as victims of divine wrath:

Let earth snatch me down, whirlwind tear me asunder, let Zeus's fiery bolt fall upon my head! (829–31)

The chorus ends the kommos by laying the blame for their loss on the Furies who destroyed the house of Oedipus (833–37). By such means, amid the passion of mourning, the reasoned separation of just and unjust causes, elaborated and enforced in the suppliant action, begins to fade.

This process continues in Adrastos' funeral speech, but far more disturbingly, for here the change in viewpoint is conveyed by comfortable rhetoric rather than powerful lyric. Indeed, the juxtaposition of Adrastos' frigid eulogies with the passions of the preceding kommos is so jarring that it cannot be accidental, and their content is so eccentric (seen against what we may call the mythological background, as well as in context of the rest of the play) that it cannot be meant to pass without attracting attention. Critics have long since divided on whether to take the funeral speech at face value or to treat it as some form of satire.[38] These need not, however, be the sole alternatives. A reading of this speech as a failed attempt at genuine praise, although it offers the most direct way to account for (not dismiss) its peculiarities, seems never to have been attempted. This approach avoids the assumption, necessary to a "straight" reading, of Adrastos' self-recognition and moral rehabilitation, for which the play provides only the most equivocal of evidence.[39] The funeral speech itself, as we shall see, suggests that he has understood very little and can offer precepts of at best dubious value to the young who are his intended audience. Adrastos, caught up in the overmastering grief of the kommos, reconstitutes his friends in memory as model citizens, but the terms of his praise, the unmediated contrast between what is said here and elsewhere about the Seven, even the sharp contrast in tone between this scene and its surroundings, conspire to prevent an uncritical acceptance of his political wisdom.

The change in tone between the kommos and the funeral speech is abrupt and not without significant irony.[40] Theseus asks Adrastos to speak out of his superior wisdom (*hōs sophōteros*, 842) about the origins of the stout-hearted men (*diaprepeis eupsuchiai*, 841) whose bodies now lie on stage, for the benefit of the young.[41] Adrastos' fault, as Theseus told him in their first encounter, was to prefer *eupsuchia* to *euboulia* (161). Theseus' words here, even as they politely suggest his reconciliation with Adrastos and the Seven, keep the original condemnation before us as the formal praise begins. More than half of Theseus' invitation to Adrastos to speak consists of a warning against attempting to describe feats of arms in detail (846–56), a passage often taken to be literary criticism, but clearly relevant in establishing the tone of the scene. Theseus (like the audience) expects an account of the deeds that made the Seven a byword for *eupsuchia*; the details Adrastos provides of their domestic and civic lives will be all the more startling.

Adrastos' oration has a general analogy of subject and setting to the *epitaphios logos* pronounced at the Kerameikos in Athens in honor of those who fell in battle, but the differences in detail are also striking.[42] The differences permit an aesthetic distance from hallowed custom at the very moment that the general analogy thrusts a comparison upon the audience. Those who stress the analogy seem to assume that the association must have engendered a mood of reverence. Given the contents of these eulogies, it is far likelier to have inculcated a spirit of critical detachment. Adrastos promises to speak "truly and justly," beginning with Kapaneus, "whom the violent bolt transfixed" (859–60). Kapaneus had wealth, but never flaunted it or gave himself airs. He avoided gourmandizers, believing as he did in the value of moderation. He was loyal to his many friends, had a courteous tongue, and kept his word (861–71). Can this be the Kapaneus universally known as the boaster who challenged Zeus and was destroyed? The traditional picture is not simply ignored, it is stood on end, not subjected to mere *variatio*, but deliberately put into glaring contrast with other references in the play.[43] Eteoclos was an honest man, though poor, and loved his city (871–80). Hippomedon, as his name suggests, preferred horses and the rugged outdoor life to the softer pleasures of the Muses (881–87). Parthenopaios was a foreigner who served his adopted city well (888–98). Tydeus was not a sophist with words, but with his spear (901–3).[44] This last encomium touches on one of the central themes of the play, the failure of *logos* to resolve conflict. Adrastos earlier lamented this failure on the part of entire cities: "you accomplish your business by bloodshed, not by discourse" (*phonōi kathaireisth', ou logōi ta pragmata*, 749); now seeking to praise a comrade fallen in battle, Adrastos reverses the terms: "he did not shine in discourse but was a formidable debater with the shield" (*ouk en logois ēn lampros all' en aspidi deinos sophistēs*, 902–3).

To this remarkable catalog, the old king adds a lesson of deeply ironic significance:

> Courage can be taught, since even an infant learns to speak and hear the things he does not know. And whatever he learns, he treasures up into old age. So train children well. (913–17)

The irony does not lie merely in the examples that precede the maxim of men "who were not afraid to die before the walls" (910), given the folly of their war and the disaster that came from it. We are soon to see the pattern of these men's lives emerging in their sons. What the Epigonoi "learn" from their fathers' lives (and deaths) shows with disheartening clarity the failure of reasoned discourse, the foundation of Theseus' optimistic *kosmos*, to change the pattern. The children assume the role of their fathers' avengers not as a concession to legendary tradition, but as an outgrowth of the process illustrated by the funeral speech. The custom of honoring the dead, time-honored and comforting, entails a disastrous suspension of judgment. In the second part of the *Suppliant Women*, all the distinctions hammered out in the suppliant action are swept away and its positive outcome, the result of Theseus' heroic moderation, is mingled with the chaotic products of ancient and unmastered passions.

The mothers respond to Adrastos' evocation of the training that prepared their sons for an honorable death by the lamenting that they raised them for such a fate (*iō teknon, dustuchē s' etrephon*, 918–19). Their labors (*ponous*, 920, of birth pangs; cf. 1135) have been in vain. After these moving lyrics, Theseus briefly continues the eulogies by commemorating the two warriors whose bodies cannot be present for burial, Amphiaraos, swallowed up by a sudden rift in the earth, and Polynices, buried at Thebes by Antigone. If it was plausible for Adrastos to speak the funeral oration proper in all sincerity, the same cannot so easily be said of Theseus here, and in any case the praise is curiously stinting and diffident.[45] Of Amphiaraos, Theseus says that the gods have spoken his eulogy clearly when they took him under the earth still alive (925–27),[46] and he adds nothing more. Polynices he does not praise at all, merely offering the otherwise unknown detail that Polynices was bound to him by an old tie of guest-friendship (928–31). The effect is extraordinarily flat, and like Theseus' invitation to Adrastos, suggests critical detachment rather than emotional commitment.[47]

The commemoration at an end, there is once again a sharp change in tone. When Adrastos bids the mothers approach their children's bodies, Theseus rebukes him: "They would die to see how their sons have changed" (944). With this abrupt shift from the rhetoric of eulogy to the ugly facts of blood, wounds, and bodily decay, the pathos of loss resurges unabated, and remains unassuaged by the physical contact for which the mothers have longed (cf. 69–70, 815–18). The episode closes, as the corpses are carried off to the pyre, with a somber outburst from Adrastos that reintroduces two of the play's crucial political terms:

> O wretched mortals! Why do you take spears and bring slaugh-
> ter upon one another? Rather stop, leave off your toils (*lēxantes
> ponōn*) and keep your cities safe in mutual tranquility (*hēsuchoi
> meth' hēsuchōn*). (949–52)

Here is the last bitter irony. The orator forgets the optimistic sentiments of his own oration, contradicts the implications of its lesson
in courage, and returns to deploring the folly that leads men to war.
And in so doing he reverses the crucial terms of Aithra's appeal
(cf. 323–25), the terms under which Theseus had shouldered a noble
and heroic task and brought it to an apparently triumphant conclusion. Adrastos here confounds one of the play's crucial distinctions,
not in order to convey Euripides' private opinion,[48] but to show us
how far the drama has moved away from Theseus' *kosmos* of intellect. *Ponos* cannot achieve an end of unmixed good for the same reason that men cannot learn to live in *hēsuchia*. "Why do men claim
to have the power of thought?" Adrastos asked at lines 734–35. The
funeral oration itself is one token of the disheartening failure of
reason.

Ponos and *hēsuchia* unleashed from the control of a common
discourse are in a sense the subject of the next episode, in which the
extreme of heroic action is embodied by Evadne's leap to death on
Kapaneus' pyre, the extreme of passivity by Iphis' despairing decision
to die by starvation. This spectacular scene has often been criticized
as intrusive,[49] despite its strong thematic links to the rest of the play.
Those who defend it do so by pointing to its extension of the *pathos* of
the mothers to other sufferers whose lives are wrecked by the downfall of the Seven,[50] but many and perhaps more important connections still require attention. Iphis and Evadne are father and daughter, and their encounter is in many ways the reversal of the fruitful
dialogue of mother and son (Aithra and Theseus) in the first episode.
Like the mothers of the Seven, Iphis' old age is shattered by the loss
of his children; but young Evadne is more like one of the Seven
themselves in her rush to destroy herself to win glory. Indeed, Evadne
does not see herself as a figure of *pathos*, however much we are
inclined to see her that way.[51] True, she seeks to end the life that

Kapaneus' death has made wearisome toil (*ponous*, 1005), but she sees transcendence of her misery precisely in her decision to rejoin him in death. Indeed, in the passion of her attachment to Kapaneus there is more than a little of his self-destructive fury. She comes running like a Bacchante to share his pyre and tomb (1000–1003; cf. 1015). Denied marriage on earth (cf. 1025–30), she chooses indissoluble mingling of her body with her husband's in the flame (*sōma . . . posei summeixasa*, 1019–20).[52] Above all, Evadne is consumed by the ideal of heroic fame. She rushes to her death "for glory's sake" (*eukleias charin*, 1015), arrayed not in mourning but in a dress that "means glory" (*thelei ti kleinon*, 1055). Her leap will make her victor (*kallinikos*, 1059) over all women in a contest of valor (*aretēi*, 1063).[53] Her death is no doubt a product of war, but it is emphatically self-chosen, ecstatically sought and embraced as a triumph.

Iphis' horror when he understands what Evadne plans, and his numb grief when she has put her plan into action, show by contrast a *pathos* that issues in extreme passivity. Iphis comes to recover the body of his son Eteoclos (1036–37), but in the end he sees nothing to be gained by touching those bones (1107); he comes to find his daughter, only to discover when he does that he cannot prevent her, either, from a violent death. Unlike Aithra, who successfully persuades her son to undertake noble action, Iphis futilely tries to forbid (1068) an action his daughter regards as noble, but for him is the final, shattering blow.[54] Bereft of his children, his life means nothing. Evadne at least could find meaning in her choice of mingling her body with her husband's in death; Iphis can only hope to "waste away my old body by fasting and destroy it" (1105–6). It is the perfect pendant to Evadne's kind of heroism, the equally genuine expression of his very different temperament, and equally destructive. The contrast of his passivity and her activity also reflects on the theme of youth and age, introduced explicitly when Iphis responds to Evadne's suicide with the wish that men could have a second youth to correct the mistakes of the first, and then grow old again (1080–86). But Iphis' own mistake was simply to want children, and his life seems only to have taught him that he would have been happier without them than enduring their loss (1087–93; this is an echo of the mothers' laments at 792–93, 804–10, 922–23). Iphis leaves the scene with the bitter comment that those who are no longer of any use should die and get out of the way of the young (1112–13). This complete renunciation cannot but cast a bleak light on the hopes the play has held forth of learning through experience and example.[55]

Evadne and Iphis, then, extend the *pathos* of the suppliants, but in a complex and equivocal way, by embodying a heroism, born of grief, that can only destroy, and a passivity, born of despair, that can accomplish nothing at all. The tragedy here takes an intensely private form, but the public and political implications of extreme responses to loss are displayed in the startling second kommos. The children of the Seven bear their fathers' ashes to the mourning mothers. For the mothers, this is the greatest *pathos* of all (1120–22), but they no longer react with wild lament or gestures of frenzied grief. Like Iphis, they are numb from grief, and have not even the strength to stand as their children's ashes are borne in (1114–17). The *ponos* and *charis* (1135–36) of childbearing have brought them only loss. But the heroic impulse cannot be stilled, and it suddenly bursts forth from the children as a cry for vengeance (1143–52). Their vision of a new war comes as a shock; for the attentive spectator it is the shock of recognition. It is an impulse that arises from the very fabric of the play, and its every detail has been prepared. "Courage can be taught" (913–14) was the lesson of Adrastos' oration and now his instruction of the young begins to bear fruit in a reenactment by the sons of their fathers' lives. They will follow in their fathers' footsteps to Thebes and destroy their fathers' enemies.

But the passage evokes not only the spirit of the headstrong young warriors who fell at Thebes. Their children's passionate identification with the object of their grief reminds us also of Evadne, whose fiery death repeated her husband's fate, and who sought a total mingling with him. Just as her heroic resolve was forged from overwhelming grief, so the children's vision of vengeance arises from their laments. Iphis left the scene to make way for the young (1113), and the youths enter as if to confirm his bleak view of the human condition. The mothers, for their part, join in the wish for vengeance (1145, 1152) while at the same time they dread what the resurgence of bloodshed may bring (1147–49).

The children's vision of their fathers recedes, the fathers' words are borne away on the air, the children themselves are once more crushed by the numbing weight of grief (1159).[56] But the point has been fixed in the spectators' minds and will soon be confirmed by the authoritative voice of Athena. New violence, new loss, new grief will issue from the grief and loss the old violence had wrought. The passions of this kommos, which permit no distance from the object of mourning and so displace all the careful distinctions of Theseus' *kosmos* of intellect with unbridled emotion, guarantee the outcome. We see the process clearly in the sons' identification with their dead fathers, whose ashes are everything for them (*en d'oligōi tama panta*, 1126) and yet a pathetic exchange for lost glory (*plēthos oligon anti sōmatōn*, 1130–31). The need they feel for vengeance is thus imaged as an impulse to restore balance in an unequal exchange, and presents in an extreme form Theseus' notion that the children are obliged to serve their parents (361–64).

By the time Theseus returns to take leave of the suppliants whose prayers he has granted, the play has left his noble ideal of a *kosmos* based on *logos* far behind. His words here epitomize the same gallant moderation with which he triumphed; the epiphany of Athena, which brings the drama to a close, serves as a corrective and shows the essential limitation of Theseus' political wisdom. Theseus freely bestows the ashes "of these noble fathers I took up for burial" (1167) upon their sons, asking in return only that the favor (*charin*) be remembered and successive generations taught to honor Athens for it (1169–73). Adrastos promises "unaging thanks" (*charin*) and the return of noble deeds for noble deeds (1178–79). But Athena, who appears unannounced as Theseus and Adrastos exchange good wishes, will not allow the ashes to be "so easily let go" (1186). In return for Theseus' and Athens' labors, Adrastos must swear a formal oath committing Argos to a defensive alliance, and Athena specifies its terms and the rites attendant upon it in precise detail (1187–1212).[57] She then goes on to foretell the successful expedition of the Epigonoi.

Athena's epiphany is at once an epilogue to the action and a commentary upon it. Those who speak of it as the natural conclusion of Theseus' mission neglect the fact that it emphatically corrects the simple exchange of *charis* for *charis* with which Theseus tries to obtain a satisfactory outcome for his city. If the purpose of the exodos is to end the play on "a note of promise and trust,"[58] why does Athena insist that promise and trust are not enough? Those who argue that Athena's intervention undercuts the nobility of Theseus' mission by turning it to profit for Athens[59] miss the crucial point that the need for oaths and sanctions is established by the action itself, in its demonstration of man's inability to preserve *logos* unaltered, to learn from past mistakes, to let reason govern emotion. Theseus' trust in *charis* rests on his old devotion to *logos*, with which he wants the record of his deeds preserved so that future generations can guide their conduct by "these very same words" (*tousde tous autous logous*, 1171). Athena tells him what the play has shown us, that another kind of *logos* is needed (*tousd' Athēnaias logous*, 1183), an oath to be broken at incalculable peril. For the memory (*mnēmēn*, 1173) on which Theseus relies, Athena substitutes the concrete token (*mnēmeia*, 1204) of a bronze tripod Heracles had given to Theseus, now to be inscribed with the oath and set up in Delphi as an unchanging witness of what happened there.

Something similar must be said about the expedition of the Epigonoi. The actions of the play, with its emphasis on the groundlessness of the first expedition against Thebes and above all on its disastrous human consequences, cannot help but color our reaction to Athena's urging of a new war of revenge. On the other hand, the charge that Athena foments an unnecessary war[60] ignores the vision of vengeance that welled up spontaneously within the children before she appeared. Athena is not here to reform human nature. The expedition of the Epigonoi belongs to history; the play has analyzed its causes. Athena gives it the divine sanction of prophecy.[61] In instructing the children and in correcting Theseus, Athena does what a god should do: she tells the truth.

History, the world outside the play of endless slaughter and suffering, of a political order precariously maintained by the strongest available constraints, confirms the tragic consequences of the play's inner workings. Theseus' *kosmos* of intellect is never rejected, just as the expedition he undertakes at its behest is never shown to be mistaken or a failure in its own terms. His reasoned discriminations and high-minded moderation define a legitimate ideal, but one whose limitations are obvious in its failure to master the *kosmos* of emotion that dominates the second half of the play. The dramatization of a proud moment in Athenian history does not deny legitimate grounds for pride, but it makes the old story more than a vessel for patriotic sentiment. The *Suppliant Women* is a work of the kind Stanley Fish describes, in a very different context, as "dialectical":

A dialectical presentation . . . is disturbing, for it requires of its readers a searching and rigorous scrutiny of everything they believe and live by. It is didactic in a special sense; it does not preach the truth, but asks that its readers discover the truth for themselves.[62]

Those who have tried to understand the play as patriotic drama, and equally those who have seen in it a thoroughgoing satirical or ironic intent, seem to expect it to preach its truth. It withholds that comfort, insisting that even admirable aspirations and achievements are beset by uncertainty and subject to distortion by passion and the passage of time. Its complex structure corresponds to a complex vision. The *Suppliant Women* is not a tract masquerading as tragedy, and its politics cannot be found in isolated allusions or interpreted as advocacy of a particular Athenian policy. It is nevertheless political to the very core, a tragedy of men and women doomed not to heroic isolation, but to an imperfect society, for better or worse.[63]

The *Bacchae* as Metatragedy
CHARLES SEGAL

Dionysus is the god of wine, madness, and religious ecstasy; he is also the god of the drama and the mask. His worship breaks down the barriers not only between god and beast and between man and wild nature, but also between reality and illusion. In the tragic theater, as in the Bacchic ecstasy, the participant "stands outside" of himself: he temporarily relinquishes the safe limits of personal identity in order to extend himself sympathetically to other dimensions of experience.

The audience's identification with the mythic persona on the stage is, of course, very different from the Bacchantes' fusion with their god in the dancing and leaping on the mountainside in torchlight processions. Yet the little evidence we have suggests that the ancient spectator knew very well the joy of full surrender to the illusion of the dramatic mask. The anecdote that the appearance of Aeschylus' Furies made children faint and pregnant women miscarry, though doubtless exaggerated, nevertheless indicates a high degree of responsiveness to the theatrical spectacle (*Vit. Aesch.* 7).

In the *Bacchae*, I suggest, Euripides uses the figure of Dionysus as god of the tragic mask to reflect on the paradoxical nature of tragedy itself. Paradoxical, because by creating illusion tragedy seeks to convey truth; by causing us to lose ourselves it gives us a deeper sense of ourselves; and by representing events filled with the most intense pain it gives us pleasure. The paradoxes of Dionysus, therefore, his "liminal" status, his place *between*—between truth and delusion, sanity and madness, divinity and bestiality, civilization and the wild, order and chaos—are in part also the paradoxes of tragedy.

Arguably the play embodies a fin-de-siècle self-consciousness, a reflectiveness on a literary form that was now nearing the end of its creative life. Similar preoccupations seem to occur in Aristophanes' *Frogs*, in which Dionysus is also a major figure, and in Sophocles' *Oedipus at Colonus*.[1] On the other hand, concern with the question of illusion and reality in art is nothing new in Euripides: it is a major issue in the *Helen*, written less than a decade earlier.[2] That such problems concerned Euripides and his contemporaries is also attested by the *Helen* of Gorgias.[3]

Viewed in this perspective, the "problem" of Dionysus in the *Bacchae* is, in part, the problem of the relation between imagination and reality in both art and life. By bringing Dionysus himself on the stage and symbolically enacting the power of Dionysiac illusion, Euripides raises and explores the question of how the "falsehood" of (dramatic) fiction can bring us truth; how, by surrendering ourselves and losing ourselves to the power of imagination, we can in some measure find "ourselves," discover or recover some hidden, unfamiliar part of our identity.

The entire play is both a symbolic and a literal epiphany of Dionysus. Dionysus functions as both a religious and a literary symbol: he is the god of religious ectasy and the god of the lesser ecstasy of the dramatic performance. Euripides, characteristically, exploits the tension between the religious meaning of the epiphany and its more intellectualized significance as a literary symbol of tragedy. How Dionysus "appears," in what form he reveals himself, both within the framework of the play and within the theater of Dionysus, depends on each spectator's predisposition to the god.

In another sense too, the play is a symbolic enactment and distillation of the two contradictory aspects of Dionysus which the paradox of the *Bacchae* contains. The relationship of reflexivity between the Dionysus who is a character in the play and the Dionysus who is outside the play as the god of the dramatic festival and of the theatrical illusion parallels the tension between the "terrible" Dionysus (*deinotatos*, 861) who brings wild joy or wild madness and the tamed Dionysus who is the patron of the tragic performance.

The play gives the participants in the dramatic spectacle, the audience in the theater of Dionysus, the opportunity to encounter the power of the Dionysiac experience without having to suffer what Pentheus, Agave, and Cadmus suffer. As the scapegoat-king within

the play is a surrogate victim for the entire community in its contact
with the wild ecstasy of the god, so the play as a whole is a surrogate
for the real violence and chaos that the Dionysiac frenzy brings to
the ordered structures of civilization. In witnessing the represented
rite, the city is spared the potential destructiveness of the actual
rite. By sacrificing the mythical representative of order, the poet
makes it easier for the city and the citizens to surrender something
of their own need for order and to confront their own Dionysiac impulses without the violent and bloody rendings of a literal or an
emotional *sparagmos*.

Two scenes are more or less explicitly concerned with the boundaries between imagination and reality and hence with the illusion-
creating power of the dramatic spectacle. These are the so-called palace miracle and the robing of Pentheus.

The palace miracle takes place shortly after Pentheus orders the
imprisonment of the Lydian stranger, the god in disguise. The youth
is led off in chains, the chorus sings the second stasimon, and immediately Dionysus' voice is heard off stage (576ff.). "Goddess Earth-
quake, shake the earth," he cries, and the chorus replies that the
Theban palace will collapse. "Do you see the stone beams here
gaping (with cracks) upon their columns?" they ask. Bring fire and
burn the palace, the god's voice says. "Don't you see, don't you behold, the holy fire around Semele's tomb?" the chorus answers.

How realistically was this scene presented? At one extreme in a
1930 performance at Cambridge, England, "the miracle," according
to Dodds, "was indicated by the partial collapse of an architrave of
the castle and a burst of flame from the smouldering fire."[4] At the
other extreme Verrall and the early Norwood, with a rationalism
Euripides himself anticipates and parodies in the sophistries of the
prophet Teiresias, suggested that the whole miracle was a hoax per-
petrated on the Thebans by the stranger who is not Dionysus at all,
but a charlatan possessed of hypnotic powers.[5] As Dale, Dodds, and
others have suggested, probably little or nothing happened on the
stage. Certainly the facade of the palace was still standing, as it
forms the scene at the back.[6]

The Verrall-Norwood hypothesis, however, has one small grain
of validity. By creating a tension (though not necessarily a total contradiction) between the chorus' words and what is shown on the
stage, Euripides brings home to us the power of the dramatic illusion,

the power of his art, which is also in part the power of Dionysus, to create a fictive and yet gripping and convincing world. Even if there was some visual representation of the destruction of the palace, the discrepancy between what could probably be shown on the stage and the stranger/god's remark at 633, "He [Dionysus] has broken the palace down to the ground; it has collapsed entirely," forces us to recognize the symbolic nature of what is shown onstage. The very contradiction self-consciously calls attention to the symbolic dimension of the dramatic action.[7] This discrepancy not only makes manifest the invisible inner workings of Dionysus, but enacts the realm of symbol itself as the only means of representing that hidden, but nonetheless very evident power of the god.

Dionysus' show of force, then, is a religious epiphany; but it is also the force of the tragic spectacle, the power of the dramatic illusion, the power of a fiction to embody truth through symbolic meaning. This power is also "Dionysus," and it is akin to the other powers associated with the god: the religious ecstasy of the Maenads, the sudden epiphany, the power of wine as a *pharmakon* or drug that can bring joy and forgetfulness of sorrows.[8] The repeated verbs for "seeing" in the so-called miracle (591–97) call attention to dramatic illusion per se and the possible discrepancy between what actually *is* there and what *appears* to be. That this scenic aspect of Dionysiac illusion coexists with the illusionistic power of the god in general is made probable by the Dionysiac stranger's trochaic speech immediately after the miracle: Pentheus "thought he bound him"; he "thought the palace was burning"; he "seemed" to be stabbing his enemy, and was puzzled that the prisoner "appears" before him outside. Expressions such as *dokein*, "seems," *phainesthai*, "appears," *phasma*, the "seeming image," *hōs eoike*, "as seems likely," all keep in the foreground this concern with the power of Dionysiac illusion (605, 616, 624, 629–30, 638, 646).

The robing scene, some two hundred lines later, clarifies this parallelism between the religious and specifically "theatrical" aspects of Dionysus' power. As a religious-ritual symbol acted on the stage, the robing transforms Pentheus from king to scapegoat, male to female, human to beast-victim. As a metatragic symbol it also represents the power of the tragic mask to reveal a truth hidden beneath surface appearance and to disclose an identity of opposites beneath apparent differentiation.[9] By putting on a foreign garb, as the actor puts on a foreign mask, Pentheus lays bare a truth about himself hidden beneath the regal robes he wears.

As a religious symbol Dionysus' mask is, in Walter Otto's phrase, the god's "strongest symbol of presence,"[10] the means of the most immediate confrontation with the terrifying otherness of deity in tangible and physical form. But the mask is also a man-made artifact which embodies the human power to create and use symbols. The stage action, in which the doubly masked (because disguised) god is now masking (but also unmasking) his spellbound human victim, dramatizes how fine is the division between the symbolic world as it is controlled or controlling. The realm of the symbol is one of power. Like all such power for the Greeks, it is bound up with divinity and therefore dangerous as well as useful, just as Dionysus is himself "a god most terrible and most gentle to mankind" (861).

The robing scene is thus a symbolic microcosm of the illusion-creating effects of the drama itself. It invites us to view the working of the dramatic fiction as if in a series of mirrors. Pentheus is a "spectator" (*theatēs*, 829) who would "look upon" the Dionysiac rites (811–15) "seated in silence" in a secure vantage-point where he is not seen (816). But this spectator, against his will, becomes a participant. His participation, furthermore, will prove necessary to the full performance of the rite he would witness. Symbolically effacing the distance between spectator and actor, the robing scene is a sinister mirror image of the play's effect upon its audience, its *theatai*. In order for the "sacrifice" at the center of the rite-spectacle to work for them, they too must relinquish some of their distance; they must become, at least to some extent, participants, if the *penthos*, the pain or grief of this spectacle, is to be fruitful as cathartic sympathy.

There is much in the language of this scene that suggests the art of the theater—not only the word *theatēs*, "spectator," and the recurrent *sophia*, "skill or wisdom," which may refer too to the poet's "craft,"[11] but also the rare verb *ekmousoō* which specifies the nature of that "craft" in 825. "Yes, I am wise (*sophos*)," we may translate, "for Dionysus gave me this music instruction (*exemousōsen*)."[12] With this "music" power Dionysus will make Pentheus "see with pleasure things which are painful" or "bitter" (*pikra*, 815), a line that could refer to the paradox of tragedy as well as to the paradoxes of identity within Pentheus which Dionysus' robing serves to unmask. Theatrical illusion, wine, and the religious ecstasy of the *thiasos* all belong to Dionysus' power to release the impulses or "desire" (*erōs* is Dionysus' word in 813) governed by what we usually conceive to be our real selves.

In the Dionysiac performance of which Pentheus would be a "spectator" (829) the reversal will be double. Not only will the spectator move from his secure periphery to the exposed and violent center, but Dionysus' initial proposal of the theatrical situation also implies an analogous reversal for the "audience": "Do you want to see them sitting together (*sunkathēmenas*) on the mountains?" the stranger asks Pentheus at the crucial point (811). The "participants" are here described with a verb more appropriate for an "audience" in the theater. The fact that the same verb is applied to Pentheus as spectator five lines later (*kathēmenos*, 816) confirms this interchanging of the two roles. The spectacle, of course, will take place not in the enclosed civic space of a theater, but on the exposed wild mountainside; and the pretense of the "actor" who plays the part of a character he knows to be fictitious gives way to the madness of the newly masked king whose "disguise" confuses appearance and reality. Thus beneath the conscious and intentional fiction of the dramatic performance, a fiction wherein we willingly and indeed eagerly submit to a domination of "reality" by "appearance," runs a less controllable and more dangerous power of delusion, the hypnotic power of the god which completely takes over this "actor's" mind. In the fused spectacle and rite for which Pentheus is robed, the civilized accouterments disappear and the power of illusion oscillates between the two poles of divine epiphany and confused bestial shapes.[13]

Pentheus will take off the god's *mitra* and resume his civic, nontheatrical identity for a moment of recognition or *anagnōrisis* as he cries out, "Mother, I am yours, your son Pentheus," (1118–19). But this return to "reality" only finds him at the center of the spectaclerite where his identity is totally dissolved, figuratively in the fusion of human king and bestial victim and literally in the rending and scattering of his body. Yet this play, which lays such heavy stress on the power of illusion, also allows us a return to reality, albeit painfully, in the anagnorisis of Agave at the end. Early in the scene she asks, "Of these things what is not well? What then is painful?" (1263). This line echoes and then acts out Dionysus' paradox about "seeing with pleasure that which gives you pain" in the first robing scene (814). For the spectators who remain spectators—that is, for us, the audience—the anagnorisis functions as part of this paradoxical "pleasure" that tragedy confers. For Agave the anagnorisis may signal a deeper knowledge of the god, but it is a "hard and painful truth" she acquires (paraphrasing *dustēn' alētheia* in 1287). For Pentheus, who remains trapped in the fusion of spectator's and actor's roles, the moment of anagnorisis coincides with the moment of his death.

The "truth" that tragedy bestows through its fiction contains and transcends the truth of the ecstatic Dionysus. The Dionysiac ritual brings a total subjection to the power of the god; but the tragedy simultaneously imitates that experience and through its symbolic structure holds it at a distance and reflects upon its meaning. The "drugs" or *pharmaka* of Dionysus the enchanter (*goēs*, 234) can take away pain, but they can also bring the degrading madness of Pentheus and the murderous delusion of Agave. The Asian Maenads both see serene beatific visions and invoke the god in his terrifying beast-shapes. Both extremes are, of course, comprised in that confusion of the familiar limits of reality which belongs to Dionysus.

As actor and spectator exchange roles within the plot and as the god of the informing principle of the drama, the power of illusion itself, becomes a visible and tangible presence on the stage, the epistemological status of the symbolic discourse also changes. Dionysus exists as a character among characters, that is, as an integral part of the dramatic fiction, and as a privileged symbol (marked by his shift from human to divine status within the work) of the very process that makes possible the dramatic fiction. In other words he is both an object of the process of symbol making and the process itself, both a signifying term in the symbolic representation of reality and a principle of the convertibility of objects into symbols. In the language of Saussure he is both signifier and signified, just as the action of the play, centered as it is upon the question of disguise and revelation, masking and unveiling, at the same time refers to itself (what I call its metatragic aspect) and denotes something beyond itself (the problem of the meaning of Dionysus in all the various areas involved in the play, religion, society, the nature of man, personal identity).

One of the indications of this epistemological fluidity is the relative sparseness of metaphor and simile in the play. Pentheus may be "like a giant" (534), but he also *is* a "savage monster" (542).[14] To

Pentheus the hubris of the Maenads "blazes up *like* fire" (778), but that simile only marks his own distance from Dionysus' fusion of appearance and reality in the miraculous fire that burns at the palace or around the Maenads' hair (597ff., 757f.; cf. 1083). The dressing of Pentheus as a Maenad involves the language of likeness and resemblance (*prepeis,* "you resemble," 917; *eikasthēsomai,* "be made like," 942). But Dionysus who "seems" to lead him as a bull (*dokein,* 920) is actually "present as one made a bull" in the verb *tetaurōsai* (922; cf. 1017, 1159). Pentheus compares the Maenads to birds with a simile in 957, echoing the messenger's simile of 748; but when they are fully caught up in their Dionysiac ecstasy they are simply "hunting dogs," with no "as" or "like" (731, 977). When Pentheus is totally drawn into his "likeness" to a human Maenad, he actually becomes the beast of the Maenadic *sparagmos,* the beast that he does not merely resemble but "is," just as in the likeness of his disguise he is already "dedicated" as an offering to the god (*anakeimestha,* 934).

This question of dramatic illusion and truth, of uncovering hidden depths by disguising and covering the surface, is but one of several areas in which the *Bacchae* reconstitutes symbolically the basic elements of tragedy only to stress their most ambiguous and problematical aspects. The first of these has already been discussed, the mask. The robing scene, as we have suggested, reflects in various ways on the paradoxical relation between imagination and reality. It is a symbolical condensation of the mimetic art of drama, in which the actor steps out of his own personality and with the mask literally puts on another. The mask is also a symbol both of the "pure presence" of Dionysus and of the elusiveness of that presence, as of any divine presence in the time-bound mortal world. In this respect the mask is also a symbol of the mystery attaching to the process by which the divine can be made manifest in human life. In primitive ritual the act of putting on the mask, experienced as a sacred object, transforms a man into a god. In the *Bacchae,* however, the sacral disguising of the king transforms him into a beast and fuses celebrant and victim.

The play also designates in two senses the privileged and ambiguous quality of the space circumscribed by tragedy. First, its action and setting isolate and intensify one of the essential symbolic properties of tragic space as the field where order and chaos, city and wild, protected and exposed areas intersect and overlap. What in fact initially motivates the protagonist is the attempt to keep out of the city foreigners, barbarians from Asia who come with exotic rites. Enclosure or imprisonment, the protection of walls and gates, the destruction, real or imagined, of the palace, and the movement between city and mountain delineate the basic stages of the action.[15]

The second aspect of the problematical quality of theatrical space brought into focus by this play consists in the relation between seen and unseen, which, as we have already noted, is another facet of the relation between reality and imagination, truth and fiction. The plot structure heightens the tension between the tangible theatrical space and the imagined but more vivid space behind the *skēnē* where in fact the most exciting action occurs, namely, the events on Cithaeron narrated in the two long messenger speeches. By making us especially aware of the two spatial fields, the seen and the unseen, this device underlines the symbolic and mimetic dimension of tragic representation and thus functions in a manner analogous to the robing scene.

The *Bacchae* also calls into question the familiar role of the chorus as a voice of the community and a representative of ethical and political norms. This is one of the very few Greek plays in which the chorus does not represent such values. Instead of being citizens or confidantes of the chief protagonists, this chorus of Asian Bacchantes has its proper place in the wild, is hostile to Thebes and its king, and embodies the very antithesis of everything for which the Greek polis stands. True, the Persian chorus of Aeschylus' *Persae* and the chorus of Phoenician women on their way to serve Delphic Apollo in the *Phoenissae* offer some parallel; but even those choruses are in sympathy with the protagonist and, more important, have the moral values and sentiments with which civilized men, that is, Greeks, can identify. Not so in the *Bacchae*, whose choruses violently challenge these values, are emotional, ecstatic, devoted to no human city and no human house, and are free of male control. When the members of this chorus praise wisdom, moderation, the right attitude toward the gods, justice, a calm and peaceful life devoted to beauty and serenity, we are left puzzled. The discrepancy between the traditional gnomic wisdom of these utterances and the personae who utter them widens as the play goes on.

This tension, in turn, reflects a deeper disharmony and disequilibrium between form and content in these odes generally. The choral lyrics veer between hauntingly beautiful poetry full of the beauty of nature and violent cries for vengeance and bloodshed.[16] The second stasimon, for example (509–75) moves from the evocations of Pentheus' chthonic savagery to Orphic song in a landscape of remote mountains and verdant river valleys. Later, within the hundred lines between the third and fourth stasima (862–911 and 977–1016) the chorus' song changes from gnomic reflectiveness in a lovely sylvan setting to a fierce hunting cry, spitting rage and hatred. On the one hand this split within the choral lyrics is the most extreme development of the freer relation of chorus to action with which Euripides experimented in his later plays (by "freer" I do not mean to imply that there is no relation or that these odes are merely decorative). On the other hand this split is especially characteristic of the *Bacchae* itself and has a counterpart, for example, in the movement from Golden Age bliss to the bloody rending of living creatures in the first messenger's speech. It obviously corresponds to that polarity between horror and beauty, revulsion and fascination, which Euripides perceived in the Dionysiac cult. On the "metatragic" reading, however, this gap marks Euripides' awareness of tragedy's complex relation to the established moral values of the city. Given the chorus' ambiguous relation to traditional wisdom, *sophia*, the play lacks a firm, clear voice of civic reason, restraint, authority. Instead we are at every moment pulled in different directions, pulled beyond the civic *sophia* to the beauty or the horror of the wild.

It is perhaps for this reason that the play is called "Bacchae" and not "Dionysus" or "Pentheus." In the absence of any single center of values or meaning, the vacuum is filled by the Maenad-chorus in their ambiguous, problematical way. Behind that tension in the function of the chorus lies Euripides' awareness, in this latest stage of his work, that his art contains a deep ambivalence between reason and humane sensibilities on the one hand and the untrammeled, potentially beautiful but also potentially destructive life of the instincts on the other. Having a band of Maenads serve as the chorus enables him to pose this dichotomy with special clarity and with a clearer relation to the form of tragedy per se, for the chorus usually functions as the major link between civic values and tragic heroism.

The erosion of clear civic values, the fluctuation in the nature of the chorus, and the radical change in the relation between Pentheus and Dionysus in the play also serve to question the role of the hero.

The play contains no single center of heroic action, no dominant personality (or at least human personality) whose strength of spirit is somehow tested, discovered, or affirmed through suffering. The play, we remember, is called "Bacchae" not "Pentheus." The tragic suffering, though centered upon Pentheus, is distributed among the three main figures, a device that recalls plays such as the *Trojan Women* and *Hecuba*.

From the illusionistic role of hero whose intransigent will brings him into conflict with the gods and the realities of life they embody, Pentheus slips into the metatragic role of the actor playing different parts, trying on different roles, masks, and costumes, until his final role is to become only the mask, the empty *prosōpon*, carried by the original of one of those figures he was impersonating, the Maenad Agave. It is, then, the logical consequence of Pentheus' taking on the role and garb of the Maenads in the robing scene that he is present onstage in the last portion of the play only as the severed head with which Agave enters at 1168. Her grisly trophy could well have been the mask that Pentheus wore, now daubed with red. When Cadmus asks Agave, "Whose *prosōpon* do you hold in your arms" (1277), the word may connote "mask" as well as "face," although the former meaning is not clearly attested until Demosthenes and Aristotle.[17] Agave's reply, "A lion's, as these hunting women say" (1278), calls attention once more to the illusionistic convention of the stage. The play-within-the-play effect of "masking" Pentheus is now answered by this scene of unmasking, in which Agave's delusion that the *prosōpon* she carries is that of a lion mirrors the theatrical illusion itself, that the masked actor is Pentheus. On the level of symbolization of the theatrical illusion, this movement from the costume of king to that of Bacchante to mask alone parallels Pentheus' movement in the plot from king to sacrificial victim. Psychologically, the multiplicity of roles/costumes/masks also parallels the multiplicity of unintegrated character traits in his fragmented and conflicted personality. Torn apart emotionally as well as literally, he is also torn apart metatragically, dismembered into a sequence of costumes that ends up as the empty mask, the disembodied *prosōpon* (1277).

The revelation of truth by the severed head/mask, however, also serves to "unmask" the Maenads and their god, for it shows the homicidal potential in their ecstasy and delusion. Like his double and opposite, Dionysus too plays roles. But when he changes the mask of the stranger for that of the powerful deus ex machina at the end, it is to demonstrate the helplessness of the human "actors" and to introduce another myth of men changing shape and losing identity (1330–39).

The bloody "visage"/mask revealed as Pentheus' head in 1277 contrasts with the "laughing visage" with which Dionysus, once the hunted beast, will now ensnare the hunter, Pentheus:

> Come, beast Bacchus, over the beast-hunter of the Bacchanals
> cast with smiling countenance (*gelōnti prosōpōi*) the noose of
> death when he has fallen among the herd of Maenads. (1020–23).[18]

The *prosōpon* in this choral prayer is possibly a reference to the "mask" as well as the "visage" of the smiling stranger in the early scenes of the play. The reversals of hunter and hunted, king and beast, agent and victim, therefore, are bound up with the reversals in the Maenads and their god and visually enacted in the change from the smiling *prosōpon* of the stranger in the first half of the play to the grisly, blood-flecked *prosōpon* of Pentheus carried onstage at the end.[19]

Unlike Hippolytus, Pentheus does not survive his *sparagmos* long enough to make any sense of his suffering. His *anagnōrisis*, reported secondhand by the messenger and not acted out on the stage, is but a momentary return to lucidity, at once snuffed out by the murderous madness of Agave and her Maenads (1114ff.). Confronting Agave, "the priestess of his slaughter" (*hierea phonou*, 1114f.), he is virtually a helpless infant, paralyzed by fear before the nightmarish image of the Evil Mother who looms over him with distorted, maddened features, foaming mouth, and rolling eyes (1122–24). Not only does the hero-king become a passive victim, but the adult warrior becomes, as it were, a small child, his most fearful anxieties realized in this encounter with the dark, destructive mother.[20] Like the tragic suffering in the *Trojan Women, Phoenissae,* and even the *Hecuba,* the anagnorisis is fragmented among several characters. The momentary and futile recognition for Pentheus is drawn out in the slow and painful exchange between Agave and Cadmus at the end, but here too both characters experience their suffering as victims rather than heroes.

Not only does the figure who should occupy heroic status regress from king to victim and from adult ruler to terrified infant, but his very name calls attention to the inversions of agent and sufferer. This persecutor of the god will come to "suffer" (*paschein, pathos*, and related words) the "grief" (*penthos*) contained in his name. "Tell me what must be suffered; what terrible thing will you do to me?" Dionysus, disguised as the stranger, asks in his first interview with Pentheus:

εἴφ᾽ ὅτι παθεῖν δεῖ· τί με τὸ δεινὸν ἐργάσῃ; (492)

But in the next scene it is Pentheus who complains, *pepontha deina*, "I have had terrible things done to me." Ironically it is the king's hyperactivity that betrays his helplessness before the apparent passivity of the god's "calm" (cf. *hēsuchos* in 623 and 636; also 647). In the long messenger's speech the women "do terrible deeds" (*deina drōsi*, 667, 717), whereas Pentheus exclaims soon after, "This exceeds all limit if what we suffer (*paschomen*) we suffer from women" (*peisomestha*, 785f.).

This inversion of active and passive in the ambiguity of the hero's role appears also on the syntactic level in a whole series of juxtapositions of the active and passive forms of the same verb. Not only is the "doer" (*drōn*) the "sufferer" (*paschōn*), but the leader is the "one led" (*agomemos*, cf. 439, 518, 618, with 855); the one who hopes to "see" is "seen" (cf. 1050 and 1075); the one who takes or captures (*lambanein*) is the one "taken" (cf. 239 and 355 with 960); and so forth. These syntactical inversions are the microcosmic expression of that fluctuation between leadership and helplessness, discipline and inner chaos, which characterizes the royal protagonist in his failure to achieve a heroic identity.

Read at another level, these inversions are also analogous to the splitting of the heroic role (and the heroic personality) between two characters who are doublets, but doublets who stand in a complex and ambiguous relation to one another, as the opposite and the same, antagonists and doubles. The god of ecstatic rites is, of course, the authoritarian king's repressed alter ego, as the bull is the bestial double of Dionysus' Olympian divinity. Both literally and symbolically the hero-king becomes the surrogate for the god, changes places with the beast-victim who actually *is* the god. This crossing of the boundaries of social status, of ritual function, and of individual personality is basic to Dionysus as god of the Bacchantic rite and of the dramatic illusion. Symbolic meaning becomes terrifying as we see it acted out on the stage, where illusion and imagination become visible and visual "reality." Placing Dionysus himself and Dionysiac "masking" at the center of the action, the play reveals not the grandeur of a human king who could emerge as the bearer of the god's pathos, but the confusing identification of the king with a helpless victim who has lost touch with both reality and divinity and is either child or beast. Simultaneously this masking/unmasking reveals the emptiness of the mask as fiction and its full power as symbol.

The *Bacchae* is much concerned with change of shape or form, *morphē*, a word which, along with terms for "change" or transformation, occurs frequently in this play.[21] Pentheus accuses the stranger of being an enchanter; his word (*goēs*, 234f.) implies a sorcerer who changes form (cf. Hdt. 4.105).[22] The god actually appears (at least to his worshipers) in the form of snake, bull, and lion—and so, eventually, does Pentheus (539, 1174, 1185), who also undergoes a spectacularly theatrical change of sex (cf. *gunaikomorphos*, 855 and cf. 917). By bringing the disguised Dionysus onstage[23] as god of the Maenadic ecstasy and of the tragic mask, Euripides calls attention to the fluidity of identity and the reversibility of circumstances that tragedy explores.[24]

In this play the normal tragic peripeteia effects a fusion of opposites as Dionysus appears increasingly as the hidden alter ego of Pentheus. Thus the play not only reveals the possible coexistence of opposites in our subconscious mental life, but also isolates the mysterious principle of conversion and reversibility which lies at the heart of our symbol-making and myth-making capacities. By these capacities the drama can explore the fluidity of "reality" we experience once we leave the secure moorings of our everyday logic of non-contradictions, the safe, fortified, heavily defended walls of Thebes. With its 180-degree reversals in syntax, physical appearance, personal identity, and action, the play provides a model of the tragic inversions and focuses on Dionysus as the active force behind these inversions; he is the god of the mask, of the crossing of boundaries between city and wild or man and beast, and of the disintegration of the clear limits and boundaries of the personality.

In Teiresias' sophistic lecture on Dionysus, the "change of name" (*onoma metastēsantes*, 296) serves as a rationalistic instrument for purging the Dionysiac religion of some of its illogical, irrational elements, in this case the "myth" that Dionysus was born from the thigh of Zeus. But the change of name that the play *enacts* shows a very different level of Dionysiac transformation and takes place not in "words" but in bloody deeds as Pentheus becomes a female bacchant and lives out the hidden meaning of his name, *penthos* (cf. 367).

Early in the robing scene Dionysus tempts Pentheus with the question, "Would you see with pleasure things bitter to you?" (815). Near the end, as Cadmus is about to bring Agave out from the spell of the Dionysiac illusion, he says:

> Alas, when you become sensible (*phronēsasai*) of what you have done you will suffer a fearful suffering. But if you continue to remain in this state in which you now find yourself, though not happy you will not think that you are miserable. (1259–62)

Sanity, in this situation, does not bring happiness, but then neither does delusion. What this scene illustrates, however, is the paradoxical process by which the illusion created by tragedy can bring self-recognition and clarification. Tragedy immerses us in illusion only to break through that illusion by a "recognition" or anagnorisis of the underlying horror and cruelty of existence.[25] The madness of the Dionysiac illusion is not allowed to triumph or persist to the end, even though, as Cadmus says, Agave might be "happier" thus.

If the Dionysiac ritual brings the intoxicating ecstasy that unites man with nature, the tragic performance brings the recognition-through-illusion wherein man discerns the painful reality of his life and can confront his own suffering and the suffering he has inflicted. As in other Euripidean tragedies—one thinks especially of *Hippolytus* and *Heracles*—a purely human encounter and human dialogue between *philoi* contrast with the mythical machinery of remote and cruel divinities.[26]

On a metatragic reading, Agave's awakening from the Dionysiac delusion symbolizes the process by which drama frees itself from the bondage of ritual. The play thus condenses into a single action the long and complex process by which the Dionysiac ritual no longer merely breaks down the barriers separating man and nature, human and bestial, but in the form of tragic art restores man to himself as the bearer of his human self-awareness even as it threatens him with the loss of his humanity or his firm personal identity.

Yet the last scene is obviously far from being a humanistic comment on Dionysiac ecstasy. It is rather a symbolic representation of the painful way in which tragedy itself comes into being. As the agent of this process, Cadmus reverses his own earlier, superficial adherence to Dionysiac ecstasy (just as Dionysus' etymologizing of "Pentheus" replaces the glib sophistries of Teiresias' etymologizing of Dionysiac myth). Thus, paradoxically, Cadmus lives up to his original role as a culture-hero, though in a way very different from the past. The facile joyfulness of his initial enthusiasm for the god (178–89) is now answered by his knowledge of the price this Dionysiac ecstasy may entail. His earlier willingness to accede to useful lies (30f., 333–36) gives way to a courageous lucidity before the terrible truth he is called upon to unmask, despite the "happiness" offered by remaining under the spell of the illusion (1259–62).[27] Ironically, of course, Cadmus performs these civilizing and humanizing functions only as he is about to lose his human shape, revert to the form of the dragon he once conquered, and like Agave leave his native Thebes for exile in the wild.

Beyond the illusion-creating power of Dionysus, therefore, the *Bacchae* places the tragedy itself, which dramatizes the process of surrender to the power of the god's mask and madness yet also can contain that power within its own frame, reflect upon it as an element in the dramatic fiction, and represent a rejection of delusion for "reality" in the anagnorisis with which it ends. Taken together, the robing of Pentheus and Agave's return to sanity represent the two halves of a totality. The robing scene acts out the process by which the spectator-participant submerges himself in illusion; Agave's anagnorisis enacts the process of emerging from illusion to reality, as all spectators must do as they leave the theater and return from the characters with whom they sympathize or identify to their own selves. Pentheus has his anagnorisis too (1115–21), but it is abortive and is not represented on the stage.

Agave's gradual return to sanity (1264ff.) can be viewed not only as a "psychotherapy scene," as Devereux suggests, but also as a representation of the inner anagnorisis that takes place within each spectator as we attempt to integrate the fiction now ending into the reality of our own experience and self-understanding. Agave's successful return from delusion to reality completes and makes good the failed anagnorisis of Pentheus. Pentheus, as we have noted, becomes only the illusionistic role, only the mask or *prosōpon*. Agave comes to see the illusion behind the *prosōpon*, and recognizes that the *prosōpon* she carries is not a lion's but her son's (1277–84). At that point she breaks through the illusionistic spell of the Dionysiac symbol to a "recognition" of the terrible reality, "the greatest pain," which it contains (1282).

Here again Pentheus and Agave's acts of submission to the illusion of the Dionysiac spell complement one another as reflections upon the paradoxes of tragedy. Pentheus, "luxuriating" (968f.) in the robes of illusion/delusion, will "unmask" himself ("He flung from his hair the god's *mitra*," 1115f.) to the horror of his death as the god's victim, not his worshiper; Agave, who entered with cries of joy in the insanity of her infanticidal "hunting," will cry out to "truth, unhappy" which she unmasks, thanks to Cadmus' guidance, in giving up the illusion behind the *prosōpon* she carries. Under the spell of Dionysus, Pentheus "would see with pleasure what is painful" (815). But Agave's rejection of Dionysus' delusion within the frame of Dionysiac illusion is the other half of the tragic paradox reflected in the play: we willingly, even eagerly, submit to an illusion which will leave us with searing pain, the *algos deinon* or *megiston algos* of which Cadmus speaks repeatedly in this scene (1260, 1282).

Like the Dionysiac ritual, the Dionysiac art form enacts the power of the god, but it also reflects on the limits of that power. The play both is and gives us the *pharmakon*, the drug which, like wine, makes us forget our pain in the *terpsis*, "delight," of its fiction.[28] Yet this power of illusion, be it through wine, religious ecstasy, or illusionistic art, brings pain along with its pleasure; *algos*, *ponos*, or *penthos* along with *terpsis* or *hēdonē*. Unlike the other manifestations of Dionysiac power, however, the "drug" of the theatrical illusion is its own antidote, for it contains the process of awakening from illusion to reality. Unlike the god whose rites it so vividly represents, the play proffers both madness and sanity. Dionysus' rites have their "wisdom" too, of course, and perhaps the play is saying that tragedy is the appropriate form, probably the only form, that can hold these contradictions in solution, the wisdom and the folly, the "pleasurable" and the "painful" spectacle which are one and the same (815; cf. 861).

All art, insofar as it purports to present "reality" through illusion, contains these paradoxes, but in the *Bacchae* and its god they lie particularly close to the surface and are, I believe, particularly self-conscious. Euripides here is playing, seriously, with paradoxes which perhaps are echoed, in a different mood, in a perhaps not entirely frivolous *paignion* of his contemporary, Gorgias, who remarked apropos of tragic illusion ("deception"), "By its myths and passions tragedy creates that deception in respect to which he who deceives is more just than he who does not deceive, and he who is deceived is wiser than he who is not deceived."[29]

Abbreviations and Short Titles

A&A	*Antike und Abendland*
AC	*L'Antiquité Classique*
AJP	*American Journal of Philology*
Annales ESC	*Annales (Économies, Sociétés, Civilisations)*
Arktouros	G. W. Bowersock, Walter Burkert, M. C. J. Putnam, eds. *Arktouros: Hellenic Studies Presented to Bernard M. W. Knox on the Occasion of his 65th Birthday.* Berlin 1979.
AUMLA	*Journal of the Australasian Universities Languages and Literature Association*
BCH	*Bulletin de Correspondance Hellénique*
BICS	*Bulletin of the Institute of Classical Studies of the University of London*
BIFG	*Bollettino dell'Istituto de Filologia greca dell'Università di Padova*
CAH	*Cambridge Ancient History.* Cambridge 1923–39.
CAF	Theodor Kock, ed. *Comicorum Atticorum Fragmenta*
CCC	*Civiltà Classica e Cristiana*
CJ	*Classical Journal*
CP	*Classical Philology*
CQ	*Classical Quarterly*
CR	*Classical Review*
CSCA	*California Studies in Classical Antiquity*
CW	*Classical World*
DK	Hermann Diels, ed. *Die Fragmente der Vorsokratiker*⁶. Rev. Walther Kranz. Berlin 1951–52.
Entretiens Hardt	*Euripide, Entretiens sur l'antiquité classique.* Vol. 6. Fondation Hardt. Geneva 1960.
E. Segal, ed. *Euripides*	Erich Segal. *Euripides: A Collection of Critical Essays.* Englewood Cliffs, N.J. 1968.
FGrH	Felix Jacoby, ed. *Die Fragmente der griechischen Historiker.* Berlin 1923–Leiden 1958.

G&R	*Greece and Rome*
GRBS	*Greek, Roman and Byzantine Studies*
HSCP	*Harvard Studies in Classical Philology*
HThR	*Harvard Theological Review*
JbDAI	*Jahrbuch des deutschen archäologischen Instituts*
JHS	*Journal of Hellenic Studies*
Kern, *Test.*	Otto Kern, ed. *Orphicorum Fragmenta.* Berlin 1922.
LEC	*Les Études Classiques*
LSJ	*Liddell and Scott's Greek-English Lexicon*⁹. Rev. H. Stuart Jones. Oxford 1925–40.
Mélanges d'arch.	*Mélanges d'archéologie de l'école française de Rome*
Mnem.	*Mnemosyne*
MPL	*Museum Philologum Londiniense*
N^2	August Nauck, ed. *Tragicorum Graecorum Fragmenta*². Leipzig 1889.
NJbb	*Neue Jahrbücher für Wissenschaft und Jugendbildung*
PMG	D. L. Page, ed. *Poeti Melici Graeci.* Oxford 1962.
PP	*Parola del Passato*
QUCC	*Quaderni Urbinati di Cultura Classica*
RE	*Paulys Realencyclopädie der classischen Altertumswissenschaft.* Stuttgart 1894–1963.
REG	*Revue des Études Grecques*
Rev. Phil.	*Revue de Philologie*
RFIC	*Rivista di Filologia e Istruzione Classica*
RGVV	*Religionsgeschichtliche Versuche und Vorarbeiten*
RhM	*Rheinisches Museum*
Riv. Fil.	*Rivista di Filologia*
RSC	*Rivista di Studi Classici*
Schwinge, ed. *Euripides*	E.-R. Schwinge, ed. *Euripides.* Wege der Forschung 89. Darmstadt 1968.
SCO	*Studi Classici e Orientali*
TAPA	*Transactions and Proceedings of the American Philological Association*
TrGF	Bruno Snell, ed. *Tragicorum Graecorum Fragmenta.* Göttingen 1971–.
Word and Action	B. M. W. Knox, *Word and Action: Essays on the Ancient Theater.* Baltimore, 1979.
WS	*Wiener Studien*
YCS	*Yale Classical Studies*

Notes

Rhesus: *Are Smiles Allowed?*

1 Two major exceptions are the articles of Hans Strohm, "Beobachtungen zum *Rhesos*," *Hermes* 87 (1959) 257–74, and Guido Paduano, "Funzioni drammatiche nella struttura del *Reso*," *Maia* 25 (1973) 3–29 and "Ettore e la frustrazione del piano eroico," *SCO* 23 (1974) 5–30.

2 D. W. Lucas, in a review of a Utrecht dissertation (*CR* n.s.1 [1951] 20), concluded, ". . . in spite of all, many will remain disinclined to believe that Euripides could ever have written such a work so intellectually null, so completely devoid of the play of ideas, of the clash of argument, and of verbal nicety, and precision." Nevertheless, A. C. Pearson, in "The *Rhesus*," *CQ* 20 (1926) 80, ended a note by remarking, "the curious thing is . . . that the play is not nearly so bad as it ought to be," and this Eduard Fraenkel (*Gnomon* 37 [1965] 239) quotes as hitting the nail on the head. He adds, "Es ist auch nicht zu leugnen dass der Verfasser ein sehr begabter Theatermann war."

3 There are many faults in the Goossens-Grégoire thesis ("Il ne s'agit pas ici d'une suggestion indirecte ou furtive d'événements contemporains, mais d'une transposition systématique, dans le mythe Troyen, de toute l'histoire de Sitalkès," Henri Grégoire in "L'Authenticité du *Rhésus*," *AC* 2 [1933] 91, cf. Roger Goossens, "La Date du *Rhèsos*," *AC* 1 [1932] 93ff.) and some of them are pointed out by Th. Sinko, "De causae Rhesi novissima defensione," *AC* 3 (1934) 91–133; 411–29 (though this author ends by proposing a fourth-century propaganda play!). Grégoire responds to Sinko with "Sitalkes et Athènes dans le *Rhésus* d'Euripide," *AC* 3 (1934) 431ff. without being able to answer all of Sinko's objections. The largest single failure of the Goossens-Grégoire hypothesis, however, is simply that it cannot produce either a unified play or an even moderately intelligent piece of propaganda. At one point the piece is supposed to be an attack on Sitalkes for slowness, at another a criticism of Athens for a Hector-like overconfidence after Sphacteria, but never is there a paraphrase of the final political resolves that the play is supposed to encourage; and the fact that a Rhesus-

Sitalkes equation supposes a parallel Trojan-Athenian equation is never directly faced.

4   See Friedrich Klinger, "Über die Dolonie," *Hermes* 75 (1940) 337ff. for an analysis of the structure and composition of Book 10, and note his summation: "Was hier erzahlt ist, hat durchaus das Verstohlene, Sonderbare, Abenteurerliche nächtiger Vorgänge" (p. 361).

5   In the meantime Athena has intervened in minor ways, lending special force to Diomedes at 366 and 482, imposing a nightmare upon Rhesus at 497, and deciding that the exploit should end, at 509. Note however Bernard Fenik, "*Iliad X*" *and "The Rhesus": The Myth*, Collection Latomus 73 (Brussels 1964), who finds Athena's activities external to the tale; for him she is a legacy from a Cyclic source prior to Book 10 (pp. 52ff.).

6   The Scholiast T at the head of Book 10 reports that the song was included in the *Iliad* at the command of Pisistratus, and if this is true, it is an interesting indication of his literary taste. Whoever chose it, the lateness of the addition seems to have influenced both the *Rhesus* poet and his critics, making the one more willing to take semicomic liberties, and causing the others to extend their suspicions of bastardy from the source to the play itself.

7   Notice also the gift of a black sheep from each chieftain for the Greek heroes (10.215), and on all these animal motifs, see Klinger (above, n. 4) 351 and 357ff.

8   Characteristic of this moralizing impulse is the extreme difference in the depiction of the two sides: the Trojans are all wind and boastfulness, the Greeks all care and counsel (until the killing begins); cf. Klinger (above, n. 4) 347.

9   The word *orphnē* is used seven times in *Rhesus*, six times in the eighteen Euripidean plays, and not at all in the extant plays of Sophocles and Aeschylus; its frequency here is doubtless caused by the thrice-repeated *nukta di' orphnaiēn* at *Il.* 10.83, 276, and 386. Paduano 1973 (above, n. 1) 15 points out that whereas night, in Book 10, is a simply physical factor to be overcome, it has been transformed, in *Rhesus*, into a symbol of mortal incapacity and uncertainty. Strohm (above, n. 1) 260 likewise refers to the darkness of *Rhesus* as representing the "schicksalsblindheit der Handelden."

10 But note the ambiguity in Book 10, where once Rhesus, once Dolon, is counted as the thirteenth.

11 Or one might compare the entrance of Orestes and Pylades on "quest" at Eur. *IT* 67.

12 Strohm (above, n. 1) 261 notes this little *aristeia* as a moment in which Odysseus accomplishes something without the help of Athena, but he does not try to adjust this observation to his overall view that no one here is anything but the puppet of Athena.

13 Victor Steffen, "Der Hilferuf in den *Netzfischern* des Aisch.," *Eos* 55 (1965) 1ff. Compare also the comic parallels cited by Oliver Taplin, *The Stagecraft of Aeschylus* (Oxford 1977) 251.

14 Strohm (above, n. 1) 261 notes the link between this confused parodos and the epiparodos to come at 675ff.

15 There may of course have been an iambic prologue speech preceding the opening lines of the play as we have it. Two such were known in antiquity, but one

was considered even then to be spurious and the other (which may also have been a later addition) was lost by the time the hypothesis was written. The frankly spurious speech was spoken by Hera to Athena (as the other may also have been) and it probably predicted Rhesus' arrival. Critical opinion is divided as to whether or not the original *Rhesus* had a trimeter prologue; Strohm (above, n. 1) 275, argues that the lack of such a speech is typical of the nonformal structure of the whole, and he is followed by Fraenkel (above, n. 2) 235.

16   Cf. Strohm (above, n. 1) 265 and 258, who would classify Aeneas as Mistaken Warner, comparing Polydamos and Hector at *Il.* 12. 61, and Creon and Eteocles at *Phoen.* 706ff. Taplin (above, n. 13) 147 n. 3 remarks on the latent absurdity of greeting a man who comes seeking information with the tragic commonplace "he comes, bringing news for his friends" (*Rhes.* 86).

17   Pearson concludes that Hector is "changeable and fatuous" ("The *Rhesus*," *CR* 35 [1921] 58). Usually his boldness is questioned, and he is judged to be a mere glory-seeker, but J. Geffcken, "Der *Rhesos*," *Hermes* 71 (1936) 401 finds him to be a decisive leader, and Guido Pagani ("Il *Reso* di Euripide," *Dioniso* 44 [1970] 31) admires a "prudent" Hector.

18   Compare the coming of Lamachus, Ar. *Ach.* 1095ff. A question of whether or not to arm comes up in the crypto-comic scene between Iolaus and the messenger at *Heracl.* 698ff. Taplin (above, n. 13) 160 cites also Achaeus, *TrGF* 20F 37; he notes that if Hector does begin to arm he will be left with the process half completed, and so he in the end decides to regard *Rhes.* 70, 90, and 99 as "only figurative."

19   Taplin (above, n. 13) 57–58 n. 1 suggests that the loose usage of exit/entrance patterns in relation to episode divisions may be characteristic of satyr-drama.

20   In the early fourth century Eubolus wrote a comic *Dolon* (*CAF* 2.175).

21   A dim echo of Eteocles at Aesch. *Sept.* 414 makes him the more pretentious; cf. *Rhes.* 446, where Rhesus uses the same figure in scorn for Trojan ineffectiveness in battle.

22   In the Doloneia it is Hector who first speaks of a reward for Dolon (*Il.* 10.304); note also that Diomedes, there, instead of asking for a wage, asks for a companion (10.222).

23   The choice of a (modest) reward is a fairy-tale motif (e.g., Beauty and the Beast, The Gifts of the Magician, *The Merchant of Venice*) related to the refusal of gifts motif found in popular lives of the philosophers (e.g., Socrates and Alcibiades, Diog. Laert. 2.24.5; Diogenes and Alexander, Diog. Laert. 6.38).

24   However, for Paduano 1973 (above, n. 1) 23, the exchange proves that Dolon is rational and practical, a man without values, and therefore a good match for Odysseus.

25   It is possible that Hector withdraws into his tent, but if he does so, he will have to come out again during the choral ode. At any rate, he exits in spirit; see the discussions of Strohm (above, n. 1) 259 and William Ritchie, *The Authenticity of the "Rhesus" of Euripides* (Cambridge 1964) 115–18.

26   Note line 510, where Rhesus inadvertently gives Dolon a negative label: "no brave man would kill his enemy by stealth."

27   The suit is not the invention of the Rhesus poet, for Dolon wears something of

the sort on a kylix in Munich (ca. 480 B.C.) signed by Euphronius and attributed to the Panaitios painter. On the vase, however, the spy walks upright, carries a sword, and wears a helmet that shows his human face, whereas the Dolon of *Rhesus* means to pull the animal's head over his own like a mask (209). Note that Hermes turns away from Dolon in the painted scene, as Apollo and Hermes do in the play. See J. A. K. Thomson, "Dolon the Wolf," *CR* 25 (1911) 238–39.

28   Gilbert Murray, *The Rhesus of Euripides* (London 1913) xvi; cf. Carl Ruck, "Duality and the Madness of Heracles," *Arethusa* 9 (1979) 72.

29   The word *mimos* occurs at Aesch. fr. 57 N² where the meaning cannot be determined exactly; otherwise it is used in the fourth century, not for the act of mimicry, but to designate an actor or a piece; see Ritchie (above, n. 25) 261. Dolon's movements, while wearing his wolf-suit, are likewise evoked and marked by a second invented phrase, *klōpikois bēmasin* at 205; *klōpikos* occurs only here and at *Rhes.* 512, where it refers to Odysseus.

30   Paduano 1973 (above, n. 1) finds tragic irony in these reminders, but this could be their tenor only if Dolon's coming death were solemn or at least dignified; because it is not, the ironies of the Dolon scene are merely cruel and paratragic, if not comic.

31   Whether or not the Lycian Apollo was really a wolf-god, his name was often explained in that way in antiquity (Serv. *ad Aen.* 4.377), and it cannot be an accident that it is the Apollo of the Lycian Shrine who is to watch over the wolf-spy; cf. W. E. Higgins, "Wolf-god Apollo in the *Oresteia*," *PP* 168 (1976) 201ff.; R. P. Eckels, *Greek Wolf Lore* (diss. Univ. Penn., 1937) passim. The epithet, *thumbraios*, gives Apollo a rustic Asiatic flavor (Strab. 13.598), and his Delian name connects him with the Hyperboreans.

32   Note that the word *lēma* is also used to denote the choral tendency to boast in the satyr-drama *Cyclops* (596).

33   No single Trojan decision or action comes to anything: Hector's decision to arm and attack is discountenanced by Aeneas; Aeneas' advice to obtain information is frustrated by Dolon's failure, as is Hector's promise of a reward; Dolon's resolve to kill the Greek chiefs is blocked by Odysseus and Diomedes; Hector's decision to reject Rhesus is set aside by the shepherd's advice; Hector's decision to accept Rhesus as an ally is undone by Odysseus and Diomedes, as are Rhesus' plans to kill all the Greeks and invade Greece; the charioteer's accusations against Hector are dissolved by the Muse's words; Paris' intention to warn Hector is baffled by Athena; the choral attempt to stop the getaway of Odysseus and Diomedes is defeated by their own foolishness and indirectly by Dolon who gave the password away; and finally, Hector's ultimate action in leading out his forces will be blocked by the Greek army and the eventual Greek victory.

34   Wilamowitz announced categorically that such things could not have been said in the fifth century (*Glaube der Hellenen* 2 [Berlin 1932] 259), and Albin Lesky, *Greek Tragic Poetry* (trans. Matthew Dillon, New Haven 1983) 397 (third German ed. [1972] 527), treats "the greeting of Rhesos as Zeus Phanaios . . . unthinkable in the fifth century" as one of the main reasons for doubting the authenticity of the *Rhesus*.

35 For evidence of a Thracian Ares cult in Roman times, see *RE* s.v. "Thrake," 6.A.1. (1936) 522.

36 Cf. Hellanicus, *FGrH* 1.125 n. 73; Strab. 16.2.39; Plut. *Apophth. Lac.* 224E = Kern, *Test.* no. 203. See also Mircea Eliade, *Zamolxis* (Chicago 1972) 21–75.

37 M. P. Nilsson, "Early Orphism," *HThR* 28 (1935) 209–10.

38 The epithet *kalligephuros* at 350 has been supposed to point to a post-Hagnon date; see P. Perdrizet, "Le pont d'Amphipolis et la date du Rhesos," *In Memoria Lui Vasile Parvan* (Bucharest 1934). Nevertheless, Herodotus (7.114) records bridges across the Strymon at the time of Xerxes' passing.

39 Cf. *RE* s.v. "Bedy," supp. 3 (1918) 202, and D. Detschev, "*Bedu* als makedonischer Gott," *Glotta* 16 (1928) 280–85.

40 Parth. *Amat. Narr.* 36 (ed. Martini, *Myth. Gr.* 2.1 [1896] 48ff.).

41 See P. Perdrizet, *Cultes et mythes du Pangée,* Annales de l'Est 24, 1 (Nancy 1910) 13–28, esp. 39–40, citing an Attic white-ground lekythos (*JHS* [1888] pl. 16) and a red-figure vase from Berlin (Furtwaengler, *Berlin Winkelmannsprog.* 50) for representations of Thracians in fox-skin caps.

42 Porph. *Vita Pyth.* 14; cf. Perdrizet (above, n. 41). The name Zamolxis was supposed to derive from the Thracian *zalmos,* hide or pelt.

43 They appear in Hipponax fr. 41D, and in the Pindaric version as well as in *Il.* 10.

44 See G. Seure, "Le roi Rhésos et le heros chasseur," *Rev. Phil.* 2 (1928) 106–34.

45 J. Gagé, *Dieux Cavaliers,* Mélanges d'arch. 43 (1926) 103–23; R. Mouterde, *Dieux Cavaliers, Mel. Univ. de Beyrouth* 11 (1926) 309–22.

46 For the sun-god in Thracian religion, see G. I. Kazarou in *CAH* 8.548; for Orphic sun worship, Nilsson (above, n. 37). As a sunlike god who would kill Achilles, Rhesus must necessarily become a rival of Apollo's.

47 See *Arch. epigr. Mitt.* 15.95.15 for an altar inscribed *Nemes[ei Adra]steiai;* cf. Bernhard Schweitzer, *JbDAI* 45 (1931) 206.

48 Cf. Ar. *Ran.* 962, and see also *Rhes.* 499, where a boasting Odysseus is scornfully called a *krotēma.* This seems to have been a tragic commonplace for Odysseus; cf. Soph. fr. 913 P and the discussion of Ritchie (above, n. 25) 201, which stands, despite the criticism of Fraenkel (above, n. 2) 233.

49 Taplin (above, n. 13) 77 calls this a "chariot-borne" entrance and as such typically fourth century, but I can find no hint of a conveyance in the texts. There is no point in the present scene at which Rhesus could step down, and yet he and Hector go off together. In addition, if we saw the car, we would see the horses as well, and no actual pair could be presented as the most beautiful in the world (after Achilles').

50 Fraenkel (above, n. 2) 233, objects strongly to the expression, but its awkwardness calls attention to the awkwardness of the apology.

51 See G. Seure (above, n. 44) 106–34, where it is argued that this represents the earlier strand in the Rhesus legends (in contrast to that found in Philostratus).

52 Compare Menelaus, Eur. *Andr.* 733ff., also Polymestor, at Eur. *Hec.* 963ff. In more general ways the scene, with its reproaches, is similar to the first meeting of Medea and Jason (note the rhetorical likeness of *Rhes.* 438 and *Med.* 555).

53   There was a tradition of warlike achievement available for Rhesus to call upon, but the poet has refused to let him use it; cf. Schol. at *Il.* 10.435A.

54   It is the contention of Paduano 1973 (above, n. 1) 3–29 that the figures of Dolon and Rhesus are purposely coordinated in such a way as to enhance Dolon, but even he is forced to admit (p. 19) that the interaction *might* work in the opposite way, in which case Rhesus, and indeed everyone else in the play, is being reduced, by means of Dolon, to a ridiculously nontragic stature.

55   Herodotus (5.11) remarks that Thracian funeral games featured single combats.

56   For Pagani (above, n. 17) 35 these ambitions are evidences of "l'idealità eroica del giovane guerriero."

57   Other Persian touches are added in his account of his march to Troy, which becomes a Xerxes expedition in reverse, with its emphasis upon the crossing of the Hellespont and the sacrifice there (428ff.), and its insistence upon storms and bad weather (440; cf. Hdt. 7.42). If it is true that Rhesus is supposed to suggest a sun-god, this will make a further similarity to Xerxes; see Hdt. 7.54. There is an echo of the Aeschylean Xerxes at *Rhes.* 430–31; cf. *Pers.* 816–17; also *Rhes.* 54 and *Pers.* 481; *Rhes.* 741 and *Pers.* 44; *Rhes.* 441 and *Pers.* 501; and especially *Rhes.* 309ff. and *Pers.* 429f. The "hymn" to Rhesus might also be compared to the song for Darius at *Pers.* 647ff., esp. 665–66. Joshua Barnes, in the Glasgow edition of Euripides (vol. 5 [1821] 325) noted Persian touches in the choral praise of Dolon.

58   Otto Gruppe, *Griechische Mythologie und Religionsgeschichte* (Munich 1906) 214, proposed that his name meant "prophet"; others (Seure [above, n. 44] and E. Boisacq, "L'Étymologie de gr. RESOS" *REG* 39 [1926] 332–34) derive it from *rāj-* and make it mean "king" or *kurios* or hero without name.

59   Scholiasts at *Il.* 10.435.

60   Fenik (above, n. 5) argues that *Rhesus* reflects not so much Book 10 as a pre-Homeric Cyclic version of the Rhesus tale which, he believes, was also the basis of the Pindaric poem. He reconstructs this "old" version by simply lumping together what he takes to have been the Pindaric, the "oracle," and the *Rhesus* fictions, without seeing that some of the elements of such a combination would be mutually incompatible. Only *without* the oracle (as mentioned in the second part of Schol. *Il.* 10.435A) can Rhesus have the day of glory which is the cause of his death in the "Pindaric" treatment (Townley Schol., Schol. B, and the first part of A). The two versions to be discriminated are thus not "Pindar" + "oracle" + *Rhesus* (Fenik's Cyclic version), on the one hand, and Book 10 (Fenik's "new" version), on the other. Rather, we must recognize one in which a mortal Rhesus fought for one day (Pindar + Hipponax + traditions of death in battle), and another in which a more-than-mortal Rhesus could not be allowed to eat or pasture his horses or fight. Book 10 is a rationalized telling of the second of these, and *Rhesus* follows it, while yet showing an acquaintance with the alternative tale. Obviously the latter, magical version must be older than Book 10; probably the former, with its *aristeia* for Rhesus, is as old or older than the latter, but neither can be dated. It must be noted in particular that there is no hint of an oracle in *Rhesus*; this particular motif is known only from late oracles (Serv. *ad Aen.* II.3 and the A Schol.) and it could even have been a post-*Rhesus*

invention. Fenik cites the Cyclic love of great prophecies about the fall of Troy as an indication of its great age, but this is not telling evidence.

61 Cf. Eur. *Cyc.* 437.

62 Ritchie (above, n. 25) 357: the play "dwells upon the pathos of untimely death in a spirit of pity." See also Pagani (above, n. 17) 36.

63 He can be compared only to the singing, barbarian, eunuch messenger of Euripides' *Orestes* (1369ff.).

64 His words are made particularly grotesque by a parody, at 791, of Clytemnestra's famous phrase (Aesch. *Ag.* 1390) about receiving a shower of blood.

65 The word *klōps* is used four times in these 996 lines, only thrice in all received Euripides, and never in the surviving lines of Aeschylus or Sophocles; *klōpikos* is used twice here (205, 512) and nowhere else; see Fraenkel (above, n. 2) 230.

66 The dream is the technical fulfillment of Dolon's fantasy, for in it horses are mastered by wolves.

67 Note his extraordinary introduction (730): "Shh! Somebody's about to fall into our net!" Having let the assassins go, the chorus "catches" this messenger. Strohm (above, n. 1) 272 remarks: "Einen Exangelos der nicht Klärung sondern Verwirrung bringt kennt das attische Theater sonst nicht." Even Pagani (above, n. 17) 38 is forced to admit, "questa vorebbe essere un encomio del morto eroe e invece ha gli accenti di un lamento smarrito e avvilito."

68 Offensive freedom, on the part of someone of low station toward a master, belongs to comedy and to satyr-drama; cf. e.g., the attack made by Silenus on Dionysus in Aeschylus' *Isthmiastae*. Satyr-drama also provides a parallel to this messenger who attempts to enter into the action, for Odysseus, in Eur. *Cyc.*, is a protagonist who also acts as messenger (382ff.).

69 The praise that Nestor used, in the Doloneia, to put a positive seal upon the action has been translated into this sordid piece of calumny. It might be remarked in passing, however, that if Hector *had* betrayed his ally, Rhesus' death would have been potentially tragic, as his death at the hands of enemy assassins is not.

70 Extended justification for choral movements is thought to be typical of satyr-play; see Steffen (above, n. 13) 41, and compare the Old Comedy examples cited by Taplin (above, n. 13) 251.

71 Strohm (above, n. 1) 263 speaks of it as an independent "Gegenspiel" and compares it to Eur. *IT* 1153–1233.

72 On this song, see G. H. Macurdy, "The Dawn Songs in *Rhesus* (527–56) and in the Parodos of *Phaethon*," *AJP* 64 (1943) 408ff.

73 Note Fenik (above, n. 5) 20 n. 1, who observes that "this entrance scene, with its hurried, furtive whispering ending with the decision to get away while they can . . . borders on the comic." The two Greeks cast further doubt on the seriousness of the earlier prince-and-counselor scene, for Diomedes is to Odysseus as Hector was to Aeneas.

74 The question of what is and is not fated (and what is and is not known about that fate) is not central to the play's explicit concerns, but it must nevertheless be considered if we are to appreciate the poet's use of tradition. In the Doloneia there was no hint of a special fate or indeed of a special force for Rhesus, but

here the case is different. Two creatures in *Rhesus* claim some knowledge of fate: in the past the Muse knew that if Rhesus went to Troy he would die there (934–35)—she knew, in other words, of a contingent, negative, place-fate; Athena now knows that if Rhesus survives this night, no Greek will be able to stand against him—she knows a contingent, positive, time-fate for the Thracian prince. When these two pieces of information are conflated, Rhesus' destiny looks like this: since he has come to Troy, he must sooner or later die here; he may die at once or he may live through the night and having done so defeat the Greeks, afterwards dying at some future time at Troy. The "great harm to the Greeks" of the Pindaric version has on the one hand hardened into complete battlefield success for Rhesus, but on the other hand it has been softened from actuality into mere hypothesis. It must be emphasized that there is nothing in the words of either goddess about victory in a single day; nothing about death's necessarily following that day immediately; nothing about oracles or about eating and drinking or pasturing horses at Troy (as at Schol. *Il.* 10.435A and Serv. *ad Aen.* II.3). The dramatist has selected his motifs so as to leave the fate of Rhesus as open as possible, while he yet reminds his audience of the alternative possibilities offered by the lyric and the epic traditions. The flexibility of Rhesus' fate is emphasized by another detail as well, when Athena tells Odysseus and Diomedes that they may not kill Hector or Paris, because their deaths are fixed (cf. *Il.* 674–75, where Odysseus must not kill Sarpedon for the same reason). When she goes on to tell them that they should kill Rhesus, the natural conclusion is that his death is not so precisely fixed, and we therefore feel that we are watching divinity as it constructs "what is" by conflating divine will with "what had to be."

75   She works a river into her description, 618; cf. *Il.* 10.437, where the comparison is with snow and wind.

76   Mechanically speaking, she is more like the priestess at Eur. *Ion* 1320, in that she stops a specific motion on the part of the actors.

77   Paris announces his own comic foolishness by saying that he has not heard the rumors quite straight (*ou torōs*, 656); cf. Soph. *Ichn.* 108.

78   Murray (above, n. 28) 63: "Of course the voice will change too." W. N. Bates, "Notes on the *Rhesus*," *TAPA* 47 (1916) 10: "It is likely too that Athena steps out at 641 for a moment to disguise herself as Aphrodite, that is, by dropping her spear and helmet and throwing her cloak about her."

79   Compare Eur. *Bacch.* 487, where *sathros* is associated with *dolios*.

80   Strohm (above, n. 1) 265 notes the frequent use of forms of *peithein* in the play, especially "wenn das Ziel ein verkehrtes oder unheilvolles ist," citing 330–31, 594, 663, 666, 838, 937, 943.

81   The comparison is frequently made; see especially A. D. Nock, "The End of the *Rhesus*," *CR* 40 (1926) 173, and Strohm (above, n. 1) 261. I would agree with Fenik (above, n. 5) 24 n. 1, that the two scenes may derive from some common, perhaps Cyclic, source, but are not directly related to one another.

82   Pagani (above, n. 17) 37 likens her to the Athena of *Troades*: the *Rhesus* goddess allegedly "stimmatizzata . . . per la sua desinvolta delittuosa crudeltà," the *Troades* goddess allegedly "bollata per la sua calcolata perversità."

83 In a lost comedy by Amphis (fr. 47; *CAF* 2.236) Zeus seems to have appeared
dressed as Artemis on his way to Callisto's bed, and it may be that the same
occurred in the earlier *Callisto*, by Alcaeus comicus (cf. *Hyg. Poet. Astr.* 2.1;
Schol. lat. Arati 38 Buhl).

84 Pearson (above, n. 2) 60: "Athena's interference is that of a mischievous stage
puppet."

85 Strohm (above, n. 1) 263 notes that the audience will have been expecting a report or message to complete the "Ersatz-Aktion" of Dolon's departure, and that
they get such a "report" when they see the wolf-skin on Odysseus' back.

86 Odysseus' costume is reemphasized by the contrived reference to another disguise of his (503)—contrived, because it violates the accepted chronology of the
war; see Schol. at 503 and *Od.* 4.252–58.

87 It has been supposed, for example, by Lesky (above, n. 34) 398, that it is Odysseus who speaks the end of line 689, giving false directions to the chorus, but
this would necessitate a group of silent soldiers who rush off at this point, leaving the chorus and Odysseus just as they were, which makes no scenic sense
and gives the Greeks no way to escape.

88 So J. A. Hartung, *Euripides restitutus* I (Hamburg 1843) 37; cf. Bates (above,
n. 78) 7–8.

89 *Inachus*, *PTeb.* 692, 16ff.; see Richard Carden, *The Papyrus Fragments of
Sophocles* (Berlin/New York 1974). In *Ichneutae*, line 94, the cry is *theos theos
theos theos*. Compare also Xen. *An.* 5.7.21: *paie paie balle balle* and Alcman fr.
26.2 Page, *bale dē bale*.

90 But notice the statement of G. C. Richards, ("The Problem of the *Rhesus*," *CQ*
10 [1916] 197): "Though there is thrill and sensation, there is nothing comic."

91 This I take to be the intent of 686, "Perhaps you've killed Rhesus then?" spoken
by Odysseus in a tone of outraged triumph, with the implication, "You could
only presume to mistreat me, a 'Thracian,' and get away with it, if you had already (which is of course ridiculous) killed my protector, Rhesus." The response
is harder to make out. Does the Trojan answer, "No, but I'm going to kill you,
for you are obviously a killer"? Richmond Lattimore (*Euripides*, vol. 4 of *Complete Greek Tragedies* [Chicago 1960]) writes: "Odysseus: Was it you killed
Rhesus? Leader: No. You tried to kill him. We'll kill you!" This seems impossible, as the actual killing of Rhesus is still unknown at this point.

92 Louis Gernet, *Anthropologie de la Grèce antique* (Paris 1968) devotes a chapter
to Dolon ("Dolon le loup," 189–208) but he seems not to notice this reappear-
ance of the wolf-suited figure, though it bears out his suggestion that behind the
Dolon episode there is a rite of pursuit. G., in fact, suggests two sorts of rites:
the first, one of initiation (in which the costumed figure is a pursuer or killer
and may gain a kind of invisibility from his mask or hat); the second, one of
expulsion (in which the costumed figure is a *pharmakos* who is pursued and
maltreated). It would seem that the *Rhesus* poet has played with both of these
patterns, assigning one to Odysseus and the other to Dolon. Dolon thinks that
he is an initiate-wolf (i.e., he will cut off a head, will come back to a new status
in the army, will have Hermes and Apollo as his guides and companions), but in
fact he is a *pharmakos*, caught and killed by Odysseus and Diomedes and

beaten, in proxy, by the Trojan host. Meanwhile Odysseus plays the true initiate: he kills (or at least Diomedes kills for him), he enjoys a kind of invisibility because of his costume and the password (the charioteer sees wolves, not men, and Odysseus and Diomedes slip away from their capturers into the night). Thus, from the Trojan standpoint, a rite of driving out a *pharmakos* figure has been mis-performed, and the bad-luck demon has returned upon the community. Meanwhile, from the Greek standpoint, two warriors have undergone an initiation and returned strengthened to a strengthened community.

93 Odysseus is *dolios* at 894.

94 This of course is true only on a symbolic level; on the fictional level the chorus repeats and concludes the misdeed of Dolon; he gave the password to the Greeks; the chorus receives it back from them, thus giving it its effect.

95 So Geffcken (above, n. 17) 399f.

96 In addition, it is the Lycians, the people of Apollo, whose absence draws the chorus offstage and allows Odysseus and Diomedes access to the Trojan camp.

97 C. W. Keyes, in a paper summarized in *TAPA* 59 (1928) xxix, argued that Apollo's role in *Rhesus* showed Euripides' "well-known hostility" to that god. It might be more accurate to say that the play represents a process somewhat similar to that of Euripides' *Iphigenia among the Taurians*, in which a divinity mythically sheds barbarian cults and attributes, to become more purely Hellenic.

98 In the prologue they vacillate between panic-stricken haste (23ff.) and sober caution (76); at 327 they approve Hector's rejection of Rhesus, at 337 they urge his reception; at 251 they anathematize as an effeminate fop anyone who does not honor their alliance, at 342ff. they worship such a one as a god, and so on.

99 Compare Murray (above, n. 28) ix: "I feel in *Rhesus* a good deal of that curious atmosphere, not exactly comic but wild and extravagant, which the Greeks felt to be suited to the satyr horde. . . ."

100 There seem to have been similar situations in Sophocles' *Inachus* and *Ichneutae* and in Euripides' *Autolycus* and *Sisyphus Drapetes*.

101 Rhesus' cult of Adrasteia may be compared with the Cyclops' Doctrine of Necessity (*Cyc.* 316ff.)

102 The full lists of tragic echoes are given by Ritchie (above, n. 25) in the chapter on style (pp. 193–258), though he of course does not suppose a parodic purpose.

103 Compare the drunkenness of Heracles in *Alcestis*, where, however, it is given a real function in the plot, as it is also in *Cyclops*.

104 Many critics have complained of her coolness, e.g. L. K. Valckenaer *ad* 870: "Sithonia nive frigidior est versus." Strohm (above, n. 1) 274, notes that the Muse gives the situation only a "Pseudo-Tiefe," and Henri Patin (*Études sur les Tragiques Grecs* [Paris 1873] 166) was reminded of the Aeschylean *Psychostasia*.

105 At 909 her *aristotokoio* parodies the *dusaristotokeia* of Thetis (*Il.* 18.54).

106 On Thamyris, see Paus. 6.33.3; 10.30; 9.30.2; he appeared in an Orphic context in the Nekyia of Polygnotus and there was a statue to him on Helicon (A. Keramopoullos, "Epigraphikon Sēmeiōma ek Boiōtias," *BCH* 30 [1906] 467).

107 This line is sometimes read as a claim that Orpheus introduced the Eleusinian mysteries, but the argument of Ivan Linforth on this point is circular: the refer-

ence "must be to rites which were essentially Athenian, otherwise there would be no point in the allusion" (*The Arts of Orpheus* [Berkeley, Calif. 1941] 63). Nothing in the Muse's speech makes undeniable reference to Eleusis, and in the context it is more natural to hear a reference to private mysteries which can be disrupted by an absence of foreign personnel. There is great difference of opinion over the actual introduction of Orphic ideas and practices at Eleusis, but the myth of Zagreus, at any rate, can only be localized there toward the end of the fourth century (see Solomon Reinach, "Une allusion à Zagreus dans un problème d'Aristote," *Mythes, cultes et religion*, vol. 5 [Paris 1923] 66ff.). Pausanias, 8.37.5, speaks of Onomacritus as one who introduced Orphic-style Dionysos worship, but Erwin Rohde (*Psyche* I³ [Tübingen 1903] 350) sees this as the introduction of private mysteries, and Lobeck (*Aglaophamus* 1.239) took the *Rhesus* passage in the same way, as referring to random *teletai*, not the mysteries of Eleusis.

108 This is the first evidence of a move to claim that Musaeus was Athenian; Plato can still call him the son of Selene (*Resp.* 2.364e), but during the fourth century he was insinuated into the history of Eleusis by being made the father of Eumolpus, and Diodorus (4.25.1–4) reports that Musaeus himself was a hierophant there (see Kern, *Test.* nos. 161, 166–72). The Muse's words at 945–46 seem to reflect a fairly early stage in this process, as there is no mention of Eumolpus or of Eleusis, while the reference to Apollo brings non-Eleusinian associations, and is reminiscent of the vase-painting representations of the second half of the fifth century; see Nilsson (above, n. 37) 192; *RE* s.v. "Musaios," 16.1 (1933) 757ff.; and P. Boyancé, *Le Culte des Muses* (Paris 1937) 25.

109 Line 949 has been variously translated. Vater thought the Muse was saying that she would bring in "no other learned person to certify that I have given these gifts"; Leaf wrote, "I will call in no other skilled pleader to speak in my behalf"; Murray had the Muse say that she would call in no professional mourner but would do her mourning herself; Lattimore made the speech end, "I need no advocate, Athene"; and Richards mysteriously gives the words as, "I am not going to bring down on my head another musician." None of these statements makes very good sense, and none carries out the threatening tenor of the Muse's remarks, and so Paley proposed, "I will take care not to bring to Athens any more teachers of religion and art." The problem with this interpretation is the middle voice of *epaxomai* which would seem to place the Muse where the *sophistēs* had been or might be brought; it may be, however, that the verb has been influenced by the interest of the Muse (these are teachers of her sort of subject; cf. 890, where she says she is honored by the *sophoi*), or by the past situation, when she presumably visited Athens.

110 On the bad reputation of Onomacritus, see W. C. K. Guthrie, *Orpheus and Greek Religion*² (London 1952) 13f. and Nilsson (above, n. 37) 195.

111 His general fate is thus parallel to the fates of Memnon and Achilles (Proclus *Chrest.*, Allen 106, 6–7 and 14–15) but his particular future as a prophet in a cave has a northern flavor.

112 See Rohde (above, n. 107) 161 and Seure (above, n. 44) 131ff., on Philostr. *Heroicus* 680.

113   There are two ways of reading these lines: one, with *hōste* at 972, produces a god
       Bacchus, an unnamed prophet, and Rhesus in an indeterminate capacity; the
       other, with *hoste* or *hos ge*, is more economical, since it identifies Rhesus as
       the prophet. In the first case, discussion must arise over the person of the
       prophet: F. Vater (*Eur. Rhesus* [Berlin 1837] 280) believed it was Lycurgus; Wil-
       liam Ridgeway ("Euripides in Macedon" *CQ* 20 [1926] 17ff.) thought it was Di-
       onysus; E. Maass (*Orpheus* [Munich 1895] 61ff., 134ff.), and Otto Kern (*Orpheus*
       [Berlin 1920] 26, 28), said that the prophet was Orpheus; Nock (above, n. 81) 184
       argued that the prophet was Zamolxis. In the second case this problem is avoided
       (as is also the problem of the prophet who is himself a god); cf. Perdrizet (above,
       n. 41) 27 n. 10: "Rhesos serait le prophète du dieu des mystères, lequel a pour
       trone les cimes rocheuses du Pangée," and Wilamowitz, "Lesefrüchte," *Hermes*
       61 (1926) 285.

114   Paus. 8.37.5 = Kern, *Test.* no. 194. See Nilsson (above, n. 37) 202 and 221ff.;
       Perdrizet (above, n. 41) 21ff.

115   So the initiates of the Thracian mysteries were represented in Aeschylus' *Bas-
       saridae*; see Nilsson (above, n. 37) 203–4. It might be noted that Aeschylus also
       wrote a satyr-play *Lycurgus*.

116   If, like *Alcestis*, this play was performed in fourth position, the Trojans' coming
       day will be an actual night!

117   The difficulty with this argument is that Hagnon's transfer of the bones may
       possibly be a late invention, as it is recorded only at Polyaenor 6.53; see F. Pfis-
       ter, "Der Reliquienkult im Altertum," *RGVV* 5 (1909) 197–98 and n. 730. Most
       scholars accept the historicity of the translation, however (see, e.g., Grégoire,
       [above, n. 3] 116), and Walter Leaf even claimed that the *Rhesus* was "a political
       piece, intended to encourage the expedition" of Hagnon, and to support and jus-
       tify the "body-snatching at Troy," though how insisting that there were no relics
       was to do this he did not explain; see "Rhesos of Thrace," *JHS* 35 (1915) 1ff.

118   Fraenkel (above, n. 2) 228ff. noted paratragic usages as points against authen-
       ticity. He also believed there were too many phrases that seemed to come from
       late Euripidean plays, but this objection (like Strohm's argument that certain
       structural phenomena correspond to late Euripidean structures) assumes that a
       poet's stylistic development is one steady forward progress, and it also pretends
       that there is a more complete sample of Euripidean and other tragedy than is
       actually available. What Fraenkel himself said about the danger of arguing from
       the *hapax* that may disappear with tomorrow's papyrus find applies as well to
       these developmental proofs. In detail, he objected to the many split lines of
       Rhesus, but these can be paralleled in the satyr-plays (cf. e.g. *Cyc.* 557–58). He
       also made much of the untragic *tharsei. tharsō.* at *Rhes.* 16, but cf. *Cyc.* 568,
       pher' encheon nun. encheō.

119   Note the observations of Fenik (above, n. 5) 27–28 n. 1, who studies the patterns
       of certain repetitions and concludes that they are an attempt on the part of the
       poet to create a pseudoformulaic style in the iambic lines, so as to give them
       something of the sound of epic diction.

The Power of Aphrodite: Eros and the Boundaries
of the Self in the Hippolytus

I acknowledge the good counsels and patient generosity of Glenn Most and David Quint and, above all, I owe more gratitude than I can express here to Marylin Arthur, Ann Carson, Helene Foley, and Jack Winkler.

1   The following books and articles will be cited in abbreviated form:

Avery	Harry Avery, "My Tongue Swore, But My Mind Is Unsworn," *TAPA* 99 (1968) 19–35
Fauth	Wolfgang Fauth, *Hippolytos und Phaidra: Bemerkungen zu religiösen Hintergrund eines tragischen Konflikts*, parts 1 and 2, Ak. der Wiss. und der Lit. in Mainz: Abh. der Geistes = u. Sozialwiss. Kl. 9 (1958), 8 (1959)
Frischer	Bernard Frischer, "*Concordia Discors* and Characterization in Euripides' *Hippolytus*," *GRBS* 11 (1970) 85–100
Knox	B. M. W. Knox, "The *Hippolytus* of Euripides," *YCS* 13 (1952) 3–31
Loraux 1978	Nicole Loraux, "La gloire et la mort d'une femme," *Sorcière* 18 (1978) 51–57
Loraux 1981	Nicole Loraux, "Le lit, la guerre," *L'Homme* 21 (1981) 37–67
Padel	Ruth Padel, "Imagery of the Elsewhere: Two Choral Odes of Euripides," *CQ* 24 (1974) 227–42
Pigeaud	Jackie Pigeaud, "Euripide et la connaissance de soi: Quelques réflexions sur *Hippolyte* 73 à 82 et 373 à 430," *LEC* 44 (1976) 3–24
Reckford 1972	K. J. Reckford, "Phaethon, Hippolytus, and Aphrodite," *TAPA* 103 (1972) 405–32
Reckford 1974	K. J. Reckford, "Phaedra and Pasiphae: The Pull Backward," *TAPA* 104 (1974) 307–28
Segal 1965	Charles Segal, "The Tragedy of the *Hippolytus*: The Waters of Ocean and the Untouched Meadow," *HSCP* 70 (1965) 117–69
Segal 1969	Charles Segal, "Euripides, *Hippolytus* 108–112; Tragic Irony and Tragic Justice," *Hermes* 97 (1969) 297–305
Segal 1970	Charles Segal, "Shame and Purity in Euripides' *Hippolytus*," *Hermes* 98 (1970) 278–99
Segal 1978	Charles Segal, "Pentheus and Hippolytus on the Couch and on the Grid: Psychoanalytic and Structural Readings of Greek Tragedy," *CW* 72 (1978) 129–48
Segal 1979	Charles Segal, "Solar Imagery and Tragic Heroism in Euripides' *Hippolytus*," *Arktouros* (1979) 151–61
Turato 1974	Fabio Turato, "*L'Ippolito* di Euripide tra realtà e suggestioni di fuga," *BIFG* 1 (1974) 136–63
Turato 1976	Fabio Turato, "Seduzioni della parola e dramma dei segni nell' *Ippolito* di Euripide," *BIFG* 3 (1976) 159–83

All textual references to the *Hippolytus* will be cited from the edition of W. S. Barrett (Oxford 1964).

2   On the relations between the first *Hippolytus (Kaluptomenos)* and the second,
    called *Stephanephoros*, see especially Barrett (above, n. 1) 1–45; Louis Séchan,
    "La légende d'Hippolyte dans l'antiquité," *REG* 24 (1911) 105–51; Fauth 1958,
    1959; C. Zintzen, *Analytisches Hypomnema zu Senecas Phaedra* (Meisenheim/
    Glan 1960); H. J. Tschiedel, *Phaedra und Hippolytus: Variationen eines tra-
    gischen Konflikts* (Warnsdorf 1969); Bruno Snell, *Scenes from Greek Drama*
    (Berkeley/Los Angeles 1967) 47–69; Hans Herter, "Theseus und Hippolytos,"
    RhM 89 (1940) 273–92, "Phaidra in griechischer und römischer Gestalt," *RhM*
    114 (1971) 44–92, and "Hippolytos und Phaidra," in *Kl. Schr.* (Munich 1975)
    119–56 (with exhaustive bibliography).
3   E.g., *Thesm.* 153, 497, 547, 550; *Ran.* 1043–52.
4   On this aspect, see Loraux 1978. On the possible correlation between Phaedra's
    concern with her *eukleia* and the cult of Artemis Eukleia at Athens to whom
    prospective brides and bridegrooms sacrificed (Plut. *Arist.* 20.5), see the inter-
    esting note of D. C. Braund, "Artemis Eukleia and Euripides' *Hippolytus*," *JHS*
    100 (1980) 184–85.
5   William Sale, *Existentialism and Euripides: Sickness, Tragedy and Divinity in
    the Medea, the Hippolytus, and the Bacchae*, Ramus Monographs (Victoria,
    Australia 1977) 58.
6   See esp. Segal 1970 and Avery.
7   See Reckford 1974, esp. 314–18, who makes an important contribution to this
    study of the play by proposing to read the second Phaedra in the light of her first
    self and that of her mother Pasiphae, as represented in the *Cretans*. He argues
    that Phaedra is caught between her rejection of her first self and "her inward
    fascination with becoming the kind of woman she denounces," but in the end,
    succumbs to the "pull backward" to become the "bad" Phaedra, so that she trag-
    ically replays and reenacts the experience of her earlier models. Reckford takes
    Phaedra as an example of "personal failure" in modern psychological terms
    rather than, as I would prefer, to recognize the issue as intertextual, less con-
    cerned with moral judgments on the character than with dramatic strategies
    and what they might more broadly imply.
8   A. Masaracchia, "Una polemica di Euripide con il suo pubblico (*Ippolito* 373–
    402)," *Studi Classici in onore di Quintino Cataudella* (Catania 1972) 1:289–
    302.
9   That is, of eros giving counsel in time of emotional difficulty. See François Las-
    serre, *La figure d'Eros dans la poésie grecque* (Paris 1946) 97. The concept of
    Eros as teacher is somewhat earlier than Euripides but the exact terminology is
    not.
10 On questions of teaching and learning as central to the play, see Gisela Berns,
    "Nomos and Physis: An Interpretation of Euripides' *Hippolytus*," *Hermes* 101
    (1973) 165–87, although her interest focuses more particularly on philosophical
    explanations.
11 On the subject of these rites de passage, see Pierre Vidal-Naquet, "Le chasseur
    noir et l'origine de l'éphébie athénienne," *Annales ESC* 23 (1968) 947–64,
    which has appeared in several versions, the latest of which is in *Myth, Religion,
    and Society: Structuralist Essays by M. Detienne, L. Gernet, J.-P. Vernant, and*

P. Vidal-Naquet, ed. R. L. Gordon (Cambridge 1981) 147–62, as well as his "Le cru, l'enfant grec et le cuit," in *Faire de l'histoire: nouveaux objets* (Paris 1974) 137–68, in its latest version also in Gordon's collection, 163–85 (with valuable bibliography). On hunting and adolescence, see Marcel Detienne, *Dionysos Slain* (English trans., Baltimore 1979) 20–52 (French ed., Paris 1977). On horse taming, see Claude Calame, *Les choeurs de jeunes filles en Grèce archaïque* (Rome 1977) 385–420 and passim. His discussion of the lyric chorus as the "site of education" for the young and his emphasis on the dual role of the leader as *didaskalos,* director and teacher-initiator, are especially relevant to the problems of teaching and learning explored here and further support my contention that the woman as the teacher of the young male is anomalous in the institutional structures of the culture. On the relation of the play to the experience of the adolescent male, see Segal 1978.

12   The nurse in her sophistic argument (443–56) reminds us of these traditional powers of Aphrodite: her cosmic sway over the domains of land, sea, and air, her connections with sexuality and generation, her irresistibility to gods, mortals, and animals. There are two odes that could be read, in fact, as hymns to the goddess and to Eros: 525–64, 1268–81. Cf. Soph. 855 N^2 and Eur. 431 N^2 (the first *Hippolytus*). See also Segal 1965, 118.

13   For a splendid study of Greek notions of exchange, see Laurence Kahn, *Hermès passe ou les ambiguïtés de communication* (Paris 1978) 126–46, whose discussion includes Aphrodite as a figure closely allied with Hermes in the erotic sphere.
      It is worth noting that for Greeks, words of "exchange" privilege the notion of a transaction with an other (*allos*), e.g., *allassō,* and its compounds. These words appear frequently in our text (360, 629, 652, 726, 935, 1181, 1256, 1385).

14   I have borrowed the phrase from Segal 1969, 302. Knox 40 points out the unusual construction of this play which assigns almost the same number of lines to Phaedra (187), Theseus (187), the nurse (216), and Hippolytus (271): "When the action is so equably divided between four characters, the unity of the work cannot depend on any one, but must lie in the nature of the relationship between all four."

15   Several critics have noted some of the instances of binding and weaving in the play, but none in systematic fashion and none in connection with the larger issues of the drama. See, e.g., Segal 1965, 133–35; Reckford 1972, 415; and Padel 229.

16   See Fauth 1959, 428–30, and Segal 1965, 147 n. 48, 166 with citations; see now also Walter Burkert, *Structure and History in Greek Mythology and Ritual* (Berkeley, Calif. 1979) 112–13 with appropriate bibliography. Burkert argues (in my opinion, unconvincingly) for another meaning, not a person but a "time, place, or occasion of unharnessing horses." In any case, given the remarkable frequency of *luo* words in the text, it would be difficult not to imagine that Euripides is exploiting the *nomen-omen* possibilities in the name of Hippolytus. It is interesting that the text shows him referring to the activity of binding (or yoking) horses, as if he were a Zeuxippos before he became a Hippolytus (111,

1183). On the importance of yoking/unyoking in the play as connected with both marriage and horse taming, see E. W. Bushala, "*Suzugiai Charites, Hippolytus* 1147," *TAPA* 100 (1969) 23–29 and Reckford 1972, 415–27. This whole vocabulary (111, 545, 548, 1131, 1183, 1389, 1425) should be connected with the motif of binding/unbinding.

17 *Lusimelēs* of Eros, Hes. *Th.* 911, Archil. 118, Alcm. 3.61 PMG Page; of sleep, *Od.* 20.57, 23.343; of death, Eur. *Supp.* 47 (where its use is modeled on the typical Homeric formula of loosening the limbs (*Il.* 4.469, 22.335, 5.176, etc.).

18 See, for example, Plato, *Pol.* 310a–b, which in the extended simile of weaving and statecraft, speaks of fashioning human bonds (*desmoi*) that include marriage and adoption of children. See also Plato *Resp.* 520a, *Leg.* 921c.

19 On Dionysus' activities in this capacity, see C. Ramnoux, *Mythologie ou la famille olympienne* (Paris 1962) 200–202; Kahn (above, n. 13) 114–16 ("the unbinding of Dionysus is itself a bond," p. 116). See now also Charles Segal, *Dionysiac Poetics and Euripides' Bacchae* (Princeton 1982) 21–22, 88–89, 100–101, esp. 92–93 n. 16, and "Etymologies and Double Meanings in Euripides' *Bacchae*," *Glotta* 60 (1982) 81–93.

20 Cf. the tragic poet Dikaiogenes 1.1 N² for the latter.

21 E.g., *Od.* 11.245, Eur. *Alc.* 177. See the discussion in Detienne (above, n. 11) 32–33 and Pauline Schmitt, "Athéna Apatouria et la ceinture: les aspects féminins des Apatouries à Athènes," *Annales ESC* 32 (1977) 1059–73.

22 I oversimplify here about the more general aspects of Dionysus which his theater, of course, continually represents, in order to emphasize my point, and am therefore using only the *Bacchae* as the foil to the *Hippolytus*.

23 See esp. Reckford 1972.

24 *Harmozō* in its matrimonial context, see e.g., Hdt. 9.108; Pind. *Pyth.* 9.13, 117; Eur. *Phoen.* 411. *Harmostēs* as a betrothed husband, Poll. *Onom.* 3.35, cf. 3.39. The function of Aphrodite as Arenta in Sparta is explained as *xenous harmottei pros mian sunapheian gamikēn* (ad Lycoph. 832 [266f. Scheer]). I am indebted for these references to A. Carson, "Wedding at Noon in Pindar's *Ninth Pythian*," *GRBS* 23 (1982) 122. The cognate *harmonia* is discussed in more detail later.

25 For the sexual connotations of the bull from the sea and the horses of Hippolytus, see Knox 6 n. 8, Segal 1965, 125, 144–48.

26 The last ode, 1268–81, directed this time to Eros, is sung just after the messenger speech and just before the entrance of Artemis. Now the chorus turns to a more lyrical and more benign celebration of the exalting powers of eros. Hippolytus has fallen and eros is ascendant, but the language also suggests the reconciliation to come, for eros embraces (*amphibalōn*) and it enchants (*thelgei*), 1270, 1274, and is golden-gleaming (*chrusophaēs*) 1275, suggesting the sweeter, the *glukus* aspect of *glukupikros* (bittersweet) Aphrodite.

27 Theseus' lament over Phaedra (807ff.) uses conventional terms of mourning but is nevertheless instructive in this regard.

28 Everything the nurse says about her relations with Phaedra as well as her general observations on the subject can apply just as well to the erotic and mirrors Phaedra's secret feelings for Hippolytus in a pointed series of ironies.

29 C. A. E. Luschnig, "Men and Gods in Euripides' *Hippolytus*," *Ramus* 9 (1980)

98, makes the interesting suggestion that Hippolytus' claim that the goddess had destroyed all three (1401, 1403) included Artemis as the third and not Phaedra. Thus Artemis appropriately and subtly offers the corrective that makes clear the identity of the trio to which she refers (1404).

30 Knox and Segal 1965 emphasize the import of the reconciliation scene at the end but in a different perspective. (Neither, however, stresses the fact that it is the goddess who gives this command for this scene). Words of contact, excluding those of binding, are *psauō*, 14; *haptō* and *sunaptō*, 187, 515, 606, 1026, 1359; *harpazō*, 1220; *helkō* and *proselkō*, 1084, 1221, 1237, 1362, 1432; *thigganō*, 310, 885, 1044, 1086; *athiktos*, 652, 1002; and other more general words of handling, touching, and their negatives.

31 It is worth noting that spatial language about boundaries and lines of demarcation are prominent in this play, beginning in the prologue where Aphrodite claims hegemony over the territory between the Black Sea and the *termōn*, the boundaries of Atlas (3), that is, the known world, beyond which boundaries lie the Hesperides to the west (746) and beyond which Theseus would send Hippolytus, if he were able (1053). As it is, Theseus sends Hippolytus to the boundaries, the *horoi* of the land (974) and makes his last address to the "renowned boundaries, *horismata*, of Athens and Pallas" (1459). At the beginning, Phaedra longs for the *terma*, the boundary of death (139–40) and later speaks of the *pathos*, the trouble, that is moving across the boundary of life in an ill-starred crossing (*peran dusekperaton*, 678). The shore, *aktē*, is another significant boundary (737, 742, 761, 1173, 1197, 1199, 1205, 1208, 1210). Finally, the position of Troezen is precisely fixed over against Athens as the outermost (*eschaton*) point of land (373–74, cf. 30–31).

32 This entire scene mixes images of both sexuality and childbirth. The great wave that swells up and seethes thick foam as the sea was spouted forth (1210–11) suggests a mighty ejaculation, and the specific mention of foam, *aphros*, recalls both the birth of Aphrodite and the semen of Uranus that created her (Hes. *Th.* 189–98). (On the relation of Poseidon anad Aphrodite here, see Segal 1965, 144–45.) *Kuma*, wave or swell, also means pregnancy, so the language suggests that the wave, *kuma*, is giving birth to the bull and has put it out on the shore (*exethēke*, 1214, a word commonly used for exposing a child), and the great roaring that fills up the whole earth (1215) might then recall the first cries of the newborn. *Kuma* also means that which is produced by pregnancy, namely the fetus, and this meaning too seems to subtend the messenger's first line when he speaks of the *aktēs kumodegmonos*, the shore that receives the wave/fetus (1173).

Next, the phrase describing how, once the thongs were cut, Hippolytus falls to the earth loosened from his bonds (1244) is suggestive of the delivery of the infant, where loosening of all knots and bonds was thought to facilitate childbirth (e.g., Pliny, *NH* 28.42, 59; see Kahn [above, n. 13] 103–4, with relevant bibliography). What is more, Hippolytus' cries of anguish when he is brought on stage (1350–51) suggest the suffering for himself, as I will discuss more fully below.

Finally, Artemis instructs Theseus to take the child into his arms (1432), as though she were here indeed the goddess of childbirth, as a result of which

Theseus finally acknowledges the legitimacy of his son. Support for this interpretation, I suggest, is found in the last antistrophe of the first stasimon (the
first ode to Eros and Aphrodite) where Semele is described as both bride and new
mother, wed to the flame-girt thunder and bringing forth in childbirth (*tokada*)
the twice-born Bacchus (*digonos*, 555–62). The context refers to Phaedra, but
the content, both theme and language, applies far more clearly to Hippolytus
(pace Segal 1979 who sees them as symmetrical)—both in terms of the supernatural destruction which also afflicted Semele and the condition of the child
who is brought forth as the "twice-born." It is therefore even more significant
that the chorus, just before the entrance of the messenger, refers to the poor
mother who bore him to no avail (1142–46), replying to Hippolytus' recent lament for his mother and his *pikrai gonai*, his bitter begetting (1082).

33   A brief word about the complex of binding and unbinding which has a vast range
of uses, both positive and negative, and which has been well treated by R. B.
Onians, *The Origins of European Thought* (Cambridge 1951) s.v. "bond," 316;
Mircea Eliade, *Images and Symbols* (New York 1969) 92–114; Marie Delcourt,
Héphaistos ou la légende du magicien (Paris 1957) chap. 1, 15–28, and passim;
Marcel Detienne and J.-P. Vernant, *Cunning Intelligence in Greek Culture and
Society* (Eng. trans., Atlantic Highlands, N.J. 1978) 270–326 and s.v. "bonds,"
330 (French ed., Paris 1974); Kahn (above, n. 13) 75–117 and 119–64. Detienne
and Vernant, and Kahn specifically discuss Eros and Aphrodite in connection
with bonds and related terms. See also H. Schreckenberg, *Ananke* (Munich
1964) 175 whose study of the word "necessity" defines the concept as an al-
lophone of *desmos*.

In addition to the various associations I have made concerning Aphrodite's
power and the construction of a plot (*desis/lusis* and *plokē*), some further observations are in order. First, let us not forget the association of knots and bonds
with love magic (*katadesmos*). Furthermore, Detienne and Vernant, and Kahn
have connected the activity of this unbinding/binding with the attribute of
Metis (cunning intelligence) as one of her most distinctive features, a trait
which Aphrodite and Eros share. Hence the semantic field to which binding/
unbinding belongs includes deceit (*apatē*), trickery (*dolos*), contrivance (*mēchanē*), ways and means (*poros*) as well as their opposites (*amēchania, aporia*). All
are terms belonging to our play, whose plot Aphrodite and ultimately Phaedra
have devised (*mēsato*, 592, 1400).

A further correlation can be found in the fact that a significant property of the
binding/unbinding mechanism is its continuous reversibility, so that binding is
always liable to unbinding and vice versa. "To exercise all its powers, the intelligence of *metis* needs the circular reciprocity between what is bound and what is
binding" (Detienne and Vernant, 305); this kind of intervention attests, in turn,
to a labile and ambiguous reality (see Kahn 93–94). From a wider cultural standpoint, therefore, the language of knots is particularly appropriate to the actual
situation and theme of the play.

34   See the discussion of J. M. Bremer, "The Meadow of Love and Two Passages in
Euripides' *Hippolytus*," *Mnem.* 28 (1975) 268–80 for the ambiguities of the
meadow; see also Segal 1965, 122. On its traits as coextensive with Hippolytus

himself, see Pigeaud 3–7, whose remarks are very pertinent (except for his mis-
taking the activity of the gardener as tending only the little sterile Gardens of
Adonis). For associations of the meadow with images of the Golden Age, see the
excellent analysis of Turato 1974, 136–51.

35 On the ironies, see Segal 1978, 138–39.

36 On this point see also Segal 1965, 137–38.

37 On the question of the female body as the model for male suffering, see now the
excellent study of Loraux 1981, 37–67, esp. 53. She appropriately cites Plato
Resp. 3.395e, who forbids all mimetic activity to the guardians but particularly
disallows the imitating of a woman—sick, in love, or in childbirth.

38 Northrop Frye, *The Secular Scripture: A Study of the Structure of Romance*
(Cambridge, Mass. 1976) 153. The distinguishing feature of the *parthenos* is not
so much her physical integrity but the fact of her independence, that she belongs to no man. For further discussion and citations, see Fauth 1959, 482–90.

39 See Reckford 1972, 414–21.

40 For another emphasis on the symbolic function of Phaethon, see Padel 235.

41 For various discussions of this passage in addition to Reckford 1972, see Segal
1965, 133–35, and Hugh Parry, "The Second Stasimon of Euripides' *Hippolytus*
(732–775)," *TAPA* 97 (1966) 317–26, who makes the excellent suggestion that
the ode reflects Phaedra's own thoughts, which I would reinterpret here as another form of intersubjectivity—this time between the chorus and Phaedra. See
also Padel 228.

42 Frischer remarks: "*Concordia* is realized by means of three devices: a character
is regularly associated with the same images as his polar opposite; a character
consistently repeats the words and deeds of his opposite; and the values which
generate his actions, the laws which regulate them, and the qualities which
they reveal are remarkably similar to the qualities, laws, and values observable
in the behavior of the other characters in the play" (pp. 86–87). In addition to
Frischer's systematic study, which includes both mortal and immortal characters, see, e.g., L. E. Matthaei, *Studies in Greek Tragedy* (Cambridge 1918) 76–
118; G. M. A. Grube, *The Drama of Euripides* (London 1941) 193; Knox; Segal
1965, 1969, 1970, 1979; and Berns (above, n. 10).

43 See, e.g., Segal 1965, 160, and Sale (above, n. 5) 35–36 (exhaustive, but often
overdone in its claims and modernizing zeal).

44 See the fine discussion of this passage in Loraux 1981, esp. 51–53.

45 For the implications of their respective genealogies, see R. P. Winnington-
Ingram, "Hippolytus: A Study in Causation," *Entretiens Hardt* 175–76; Reckford 1974; A. V. Rankin, "Euripides' Hippolytus: A Psychopathological Hero,"
Arethusa 7 (1974) 71–94; J. J. Smoot, "Hippolytus as Narcissus: An Amplifica-
tion," *Arethusa* 9 (1976) 37–51; and Segal 1970, 295; 1978, 135–39. On the
similarities between Phaedra and Hippolytus, see n. 42 above.
    It is interesting that two divergent types of criticism—psychoanalytic and
mythic-ritual—agree in their respective splitting of the feminine figure between Aphrodite (Phaedra) and Artemis (Amazon). In the view of the psycho-
analysts, splitting is a common defense mechanism against incestuous wishes.
The other group associates the same phenomenon with the pre-Greek Mediter-

ranean figure of the Great Goddess who combined both aspects within herself—
at once both benign and destructive, loving and/or destroying her consort. See
further the discussion of Fauth 1959, who points out that for the Greeks, the
"original homogeneity was split into a polarized tension" (p. 406). Oddly enough,
this new Phaedra invented by Euripides would seem, in her tension between
Artemis and Aphrodite, to express in social and contemporary terms what already may exist at a much deeper substratum of the myth.

46   Paraphrase of J.-P. Vernant, "Tensions and Ambiguities in Greek Tragedy," in J.-P.
Vernant and P. Vidal-Naquet, *Tragedy and Myth in Ancient Greece* (Eng. trans.,
Atlantic Highlands, N.J. 1981) 18 (French ed., Paris 1973).

47   Vernant, "Ambiguity and Reversal: On the Enigmatic Structure of *Oedipus
Rex*," in Vernant and Vidal-Naquet, *Tragedy and Myth in Ancient Greece*
(above, n. 46) 94, in speaking of the "logical schema of reversal, corresponding
with the ambiguous type of thought that is characteristic of tragedy," remarks
that it "offers the spectators a particular kind of lesson: man is not a being that
can be described or defined; he is a problem, a riddle, the double meanings of
which are inexhaustible."

The closest analogue to Hippolytus is another child of an Amazon-type
mother (Atalanta) whose name, Parthenopaios, reveals these ambiguities. In the
Seven Against Thebes of Aeschylus, he in fact carries the Sphinx on his shield
and encodes all the riddles of the drama in his person and position in the series
of warriors. See discussion in F. I. Zeitlin, *Under the Sign of the Shield: Semiotics and Aeschylus' Seven Against Thebes* (Rome 1982) 98–115, and 199–201.
For the contradictions within Hippolytus himself, see Segal 1978, 134–39.

48   See Hesiod *Op.* 59–82, and the discussion of this account and that in *Th.*
535–616 in J.-P. Vernant, "The Promethean Myth in Hesiod," in *Myth and Society in Ancient Greece* (Eng. trans., Atlantic Highlands, N.J. 1980) 168–85
(French ed., Paris 1974) 177–94, and Pietro Pucci, *Hesiod and the Language of
Poetry* (Baltimore 1977) 82–126.

49   On the mythic patterns of the Golden Age that underlie the world of Hippolytus, see Turato 1974.

50   The remarks of Tony Tanner, *Adultery and the Novel: Contract and Transgression* (Baltimore 1979) 13, are instructive here.

From the point of view of . . . society, adultery introduces a bad multiplicity
within the requisite unities of social roles. From another point of view, we
could say that the unfaithful wife is, in social terms, a self-canceling figure,
one from whom society would prefer to withhold recognition so that it
would be possible to say that socially and categorically the adulterous woman
does not exist. Yet physically and creaturely she manifestly does, so she becomes a paradoxical presence of negativity within the social structures, her
virtual non-being offering a constant implicit threat to the being of society.

51   Pigeaud 8–9 connects knowledge of the self to the experience of woman with
her own body, citing an excellent text from the Hippocratic *Diseases of Women*,
62 (8., p. 126L). The analogy he establishes is suggestive, but our text also seems

to contrast one kind of knowledge (the body) with the other (the cognitive),
• whose aim is to overrule the body and its instinctual demands.

52 On these various connections, see Segal 1965, 122, 124–25.

53 See Segal 1965, 125, who does not distinguish, however, between river/stream
and sea (on Oceanus as a fresh-water stream, see Barrett [above, n. 1] 184).

54 Segal 1965, 130–31, speaks of the fire of eros without reference to the "warm
sun" of the parodos.

55 *Electron* (amber) draws its name from *elektōr*, the sun, and the entire expression that characterizes these tears as *elektrophaeis augas*, "amber-shining
rays," marvelously distills the process (Phaethon's encounter with the sun) into
a product (the amber tears) and translates the experience from fire to water. See
also Padel 231 on this passage.

56 See Segal 1965, 133; Padel 233; and Parry (above, n. 41) 322. Padel remarks: "The
divine unattainable world is composed of the same forces that make real life
so painful: the marriage of Zeus and Hera parallels the unhappy marriage of
Phaedra: wings that might lift the imagination away from reality symbolize a
return to it." Parry points to the ambiguities inherent in the Garden of the
Hesperides, which promises immortality to the gods but is in the "westernmost
area where earth, heaven, and death are in closest conjunction."

57 The text describes her fasting as keeping "her body pure (*hagnon*) of the grain of
Demeter by the non-eating of her mouth." The Homeric expression, *Damatros
aktas* (cf. *Il.* 13.322, 21.76), is particularly appropriate to the context, for where
adulterous desire is present, Demeter, the goddess of legitimate marriage, most
emphatically is not. On the other hand, fasting indeed belongs to the cult of
Demeter, whether at the Thesmophoria or at the Eleusinian mysteries. As these
mysteries are mentioned in connection with Hippolytus' visit to Athens where
Phaedra first saw him and fell in love (25–27), we might also understand her
abstention from Demeter's grain as an indication of another kind of mystery
that is to take place, namely, that of Aphrodite. (The theme of the mysteries will
be treated later.)

58 This vocabulary includes *anoignumi* (open) 56, 793; *chalaō* (loosen) 807; *aphiēmi* (let loose) 991 (cf. 418, 1324 and *methiēmi*, 499, 1202); *katechō* (keep
back) 882 (cf. *echō* [hold] 660, as well as *sugkleiō* [lock up] 498); and, of course,
luō (unbind) 1060.

59 The *deltos* is closed up with seals (*sphragismata*) and requires unfolding (*exelixas*) of its wrappings but *luein* is also used for opening a *deltos* (Eur. *IA* 38,
109ff., 307). On the homology of mouth and door, see Artem. *Oneir.* 1.31.

60 Artem. *Oneir.* 4.30.

61 Frischer 92.

62 See the remarks of Padel 230 n. 1 and Avery 35. The first version of the *Hippolytus* was called *Kaluptomenos* because he veiled his head in shame at Phaedra's
propositions. As it is generally agreed that he was not brought back on stage in
that first play, the gesture of Hippolytus now echoes Phaedra's earlier gesture of
aidōs in this play. Death, like the robe (or the veil), covers the self, as if it were a
palpable cloud that by its contact effected the change of state in the person. (See
Onians [above, n. 33] 420–25.)

Hippolytus' *pepla* are also significantly mentioned here, recalling the *pepla* from which the nurse had intended to take a scrap for her love charm (514) and which he later will not allow her to touch when she pleads for his silence (606).

63   For a somewhat different formulation, see Avery 34.

64   For *delta* as female genitals, see Schol. *ad Lys.* 151 and Hesychius with remarks by Jean Taillardat, *Les images d'Aristophane* (Paris 1965) 77 and Jeffrey Henderson, *The Maculate Muse* (New Haven, Conn. 1975) 146. Etymologically, *delta* is probably related to *deltos*, both owing their origin to the Semitic *deleth* or door. Cf. Chantraine, *Dict. Etym.* 260. (Euripides *IT* 727 speaks of the *deltou . . . poluthuroi diaptuchai*, the "many-doored folding leaves of the *deltos.*") Other associations link the woman to the *deltos*: door (*thura, pulai*) is an obscene term for vagina (Aristophanes, *Eccl.* 962–63, 990, cf. 709; *Wasps* 768–69, *Thesm.* 424–25, *Lys.* 309, 265, 423, 1163). See Taillardat 77 and Henderson 137. From another point of view, the *deltos* and the woman are related through the metaphor of plowing, where *alox* or furrow refers both to the woman (Soph. *OT* 1211, Eur. *Phoen.* 18) and to writing on a *deltos* (Aristophanes, *Thesm.* 782, parodying Euripides' *Palamedes*). See also the observations on the *deltos* in Soph. *Trachiniae* by Page Dubois, *Centaurs and Amazons* (Ann Arbor, Mich. 1982) 98–99, although she does not remark upon the fact that the *deltos* is used both literally and figuratively (Soph. *Trach.* 47, 156, 683).

At the same time, the *phrenes* or inmost thinking parts of the self are imagined as a *deltos* on which one writes, records, and remembers (e.g., Aesch. *Supp.* 179, *PV* 789, *Eum.* 275; Pind. *Ol.* 10.1–3; Soph. *Phil.* 1325, *Trach.* 683, 597 N^2; and possibly Aesch. 530.21 and Eur. 506 N^2. (See also David Sansone, *Aeschylean Metaphors for Intellectual Activities* [Wiesbaden 1975] 60–63.) This representation is also appropriate in the ramifications of the secret in the play as both sexual and cognitive.

65   Artem. *Oneir.* 2.45. See also the comic fragment of Antiphanes' *Sappho* (196K, Ath. 10.450e–51b) which poses the riddle of a "she" who keeps her children under her bosom, and these cry out, although they have no voice. The answer is an epistle (*epistolē*) whose children are the letters.

66   On this last point, see, e.g., the famous double entendre of Clytemnestra in Aesch. *Ag.* 609–10 and Eur. 1063 and 320N^2. The women in Aristophanes' *Thesmophoriazousae* complain that as a result of Euripides' slanders against them, their husbands come home and search for hidden lovers, putting their wives under seal and iron bars (*sphragidas . . . mochlous*, 415), and henceforth carry with them the secret little keys (*kleidia . . . krupta*, 410–21) to the storerooms the women used to control.

67   The word for footstalls, *arbulai*, is unique in its semantic use here because, as Barrett remarks, 380, the term normally means "shoes or boots." The *hapax* is perhaps significant in two ways: its use transfers to the chariot what should belong to the self and it confuses the container (i.e., the space for the shoe) with that which is to be contained (the shoe).

68   *Trepō, tropos*, and *strephō* are related terms.

69   Loraux 1981, 58–59, in her superb analysis of lines 1351–53, sees only symptoms of the *ponos* of childbirth, while Segal 1965, 151, sees only the erotic

in 1375–77. But it is important to emphasize that both experiences merge for Hippolytus in this scene. Archilochus 104D, for example, when speaking of desire (*pothos*), says that he "lies wretched and faint (*apsuchos*), because of the harsh pangs (*odunēisin*) of the gods, pierced through his bones." Similarly, in regard to Loraux's fine discussion of Heracles' sufferings in Sophocles' *Trachiniae* (on pp. 59–64), I see these as combining both the erotic and the parturient, especially given the specifically erotic theme of the play. For the *Trachiniae*, see Dorothea Wender, "The Will of the Beast: Sexual Imagery in the *Trachiniae*," *Ramus* 3 (1974) 1–17. For the conflation of erotic and parturient terms and the relation to warrior violence, see also N. Huston, *Dire et interdire: éléments de jurologie* (Paris 1980) 41–51.

70 See Reckford 1972, 417–18 n. 14 where he offers convincing arguments for the divided chorus.

71 For an analysis of these sexual meanings, see Segal 1965, 144–48.

72 Just as the second stasimon, the "escape ode," can be construed with Parry (above, n. 41) 323 as the expression by the chorus of Phaedra's most intimate feelings at the moment when she is putting an end to her life, so this "anti-epithalamium" seems to me to perform a similar function for Hippolytus when he has reached his critical moment. Hippolytus, it has been suggested, has affinities with the figure of Hymenaios, the male who disappears on his wedding night (see Reckford 1972, 415), who in his ambiguities functions as both bride and bridegroom, *parthenos* and *kouros*. The device of dividing the chorus into male and female parts would thus correspond perfectly to the psychological status of Hippolytus. This attuning of chorus and character, in which the group identifies with the personage just at the time of his/her greatest isolation from society, further enhances the more general theme of intersubjectivity in the play. At the same time, using the loose associative techniques that are granted to choral poetry, the ode seems to imitate with remarkable fidelity the inner processes of subjective thought.

73 The vocabulary of concealment is, of course, especially prominent in this play, consisting of *kruptō, kruptos, kaluptō, keuthō, keuthmōn, lanthanō, lathra*. These words refer to the secret, to gestures of the body, and to spatial configurations: 139, 154, 191, 243, 250–51, 279, 330, 394–95, 403, 414, 416, 594, 674, 712, 732, 915, 1105, 1209, 1290, 1277, 1458.

74 I paraphrase here Jean Starobinski, "Je haïs comme les portes d'Hadès," *Nouvelle Revue de Psychanalyse* 9 (1974) 10, commenting on Achilles' remark in the Embassy, *Il*. 9.312–13 with particular attention to the notion of the *phrenes* as both physical and mental organ (mind, intelligence, "bottom of the heart").

75 In the scene with his father, he is tempted once again to "loosen his mouth," this time to save himself (1060), a point that critics persist in overlooking.

76 Coppelia Kahn, "The Providential Tempest and the Shakespearean Family," in Murray M. Schwartz and Coppelia Kahn, eds., *Representing Shakespeare* (Baltimore 1980) 220.

77 The marginal status of both is intensified by the fact that she is of foreign (Cretan) origin and he is the child of the barbarian Amazon mother.

78 The dispute over the interpretation of Phaedra's statement continues. Without

entering into the debate, I would only reiterate that the "doubleness" belongs to *aidōs* and not to *hēdonai* (pleasures). For the most recent bibliography, see M. Orban, "*Hippolyte*: palinode ou revanche?" *LEC* 49 (1981) 12–13 n. 26.

79   See Sigmund Freud, "The Antithetical Sense of Primal Words," in *On Creativity and the Unconscious*, ed. Benjamin Nelson (New York 1958) 60, citing the philologist Karl Abel.

80   For a discussion of *sōphrosunē* in this passage, see Helen North, *Sophrosyne* (Ithaca, N.Y. 1966) 81. She would translate 1034–35 as "Phaedra behaved with self control (*esōphronēsen*) although she had not the power to be chaste (*sōphronein*), while, I, who have the power, have not used it well." If we consider that the effect of eros is to produce *aphrosunē*, since eros takes away the wits (the *phrenes*), what Hippolytus says is clearer still: Phaedra was in the grip of eros and therefore did not have the capacity for *sōphrosunē*, while I, untouched by eros, did (and do) have the capacity, but did not use it well (i.e., the angry speech which he must now realize she had overheard).

In the more general discussion of *sōphrosunē* (for a recent one, see A. Schmitt, "Zur Charakterdarstellung des Hippolytos im 'Hippolytus' von Euripides," *Würzburger Jahrb. f. die Altertumswiss.* 3 [1977] 17–42), the fragment of Antiphon (39D) seems to me to be especially appropriate: "Whoever has not desired (*epethumēse*) or touched (*hēpsato*) the shameful (*aischron*) or the base (*kakon*), is not *sōphrōn*. For there is nothing over which he has gained the mastery (*kratēsas*) and proved himself well-ordered (*kosmion*)." (Cf. Pl. *Symp.* 196c.4–5.) In other words, genuine *sōphrosunē* is an active not a passive principle, and is won by the self through the experience of resisting desire.

On the question of inside/outside, Starobinski (above, n. 74) makes some excellent remarks in connection with Achilles and *Il.* 9:

> Wisdom . . . dictates a control which is not exercised only over the precious substance of life (*psuchē*), but over a proud spirit (*megalētora thumon*). To keep it (*ischein*) in the breast (*stēthessi*) can seem like the image-archetype of "repression." To "keep in the breast," just as to "hide in the heart," is made possible by the reality of a visceral *inside*, which the individual can make the receptacle of the "breath" that he actively refuses to exteriorize: in preventing the "haughty" from finding an external issue, the act which bars the passage requires an organic interior (the breath and its viscera) to make a space for the repressed discourse: thus, in the voluntary economy which rules, evaluates, restrains the quantity of passion which can be displayed outside, a wisdom is born, and it installs an interior dimension, a subjectivity. . . . This mastery such as Peleus had recommended to Achilles, is neither simulating nor lying: it invites him simply to keep his passion quiet, to rein it in, not to hold an *other* discourse in its place: this is the virtue called "retenue," . . . and which consists in having dealings with others, always deferring the gesture or word which would harm them. . . . We find everywhere the same lesson: the mastery exercised at the gates, the surveillance exercised over the lips, the voluntary suppression which proves (which creates)

the virtue of prudence (i.e., *sōphrosunē*), and which protects the "soul" (pp. 14–15).

81 The mysteries are called a *telos, teletē* (cf. 25) and so was marriage. For the Eleusinian mysteries, which were based on the Demeter-Kore myth, marriage as a *telos* might well bear a double charge. The condition of the *mystēs* is that of one whose eyes and lips are closed, two conditions that will come into play for Hippolytus as will be discussed further below. His witnessing, his *opsis*, of the mysteries (25) anticipates but does not prepare him for those of Aphrodite.

82 An important link between Aphrodite's mention of Hippolytus' initiation into the mysteries at Athens and what happens in the play is suggested in the nurse's remarks at 191–96: "But if there is something dearer (*philteron*) than this life, the embrace of darkness (*skotos*) hides it in clouds. We seem to be unhappy lovers (*duserōtes . . . phainometha*) of that which glitters upon the earth, through inexperience (*apeirosunē*) of another life and the non-revealing (*ouk apodeixin*) of what lies beneath the earth." That "other life" and the revelation of things "beneath the earth" evoke the context of the mysteries while events for Hippolytus will make him seem to be the one who is *duserōs* of those things here on earth.

   The mystic way of life is represented for Hippolytus in three ways: first, through this reference to the *opsis*, the sacred viewing at Eleusis; second, through his personal cult of Artemis in whose meadow it is *ou themis* for the *kakoi* to pluck its flowers (81); and last, in Theseus' interpretation of his son as a votary of the Orphic mysteries (952–54).

83 Turato 1976, 183. This important study, extending beyond Knox's formalist abstraction of alternating speech and silence among the characters, offers a rich and admirable analysis of the various, even competing, systems of communication at work in the play.

84 Claude Lévi-Strauss, *The Elementary Structures of Kinship* (New York 1967) 496. For the connections between language and kinship with reference to Eteocles, the son of Oedipus, who, like Hippolytus, utters a long tirade against women, see Zeitlin (above, n. 47), 29–36.

85 J.-P. Vernant, "Hestia-Hermès: sur l'expression religieuse de l'espace et du mouvement chez les Grecs," in *Mythe et pensée chez les Grecs* (Paris 1965) 106.

86 See the discussion of Knox and Turato 1976 as cited in n. 83, above.

87 Oliver Taplin, *Greek Tragedy in Action* (Berkeley, Calif. 1978) 70–71, notes that "the sustained scene of eavesdropping with its almost grotesque associations with listening at the keyhole, is quite without parallel in surviving Greek tragedy."

88 The variety of words for speech, voice, and utterance in this passage is remarkable. Nouns: *audē* (571), *logos* (751), *phēma* (572), *kelados* (576), *phatis* (578), *ia* (585), *boa* (587). Verbs: *throeō* (571), *boaō* (571, 581), *audaō* (582), *gegōna* (586), *exaudaō* (590).

89 Segal 1965, 146–47, sees Hippolytus' wish that the house could have a voice (1074–75) and the terrible sound of the bull and the sea as relating to Hippo-

lytus' earlier desire to refuse speech to women (645–46) but he takes the issue no further than the general trope of tragic irony and does not connect all these phenomena to Hippolytus' privileging of the auditory sense.

90   The chorus justifies its presence on stage as having just come as a mourner (penthēteria, 805). Greek ritual customs suggest that mourning is an antiphonal affair, involving both kin and nonkin (or those related by marriage [kēdestai] where kēdos pertains both to family alliances and to funerals/grief). Cf. the pun in Aesch. Ag. 699 on kēdos and also the likely semantic connection between penthos (grief) and penthēros (father-in-law, afterward in-laws). Margaret Alexiou, The Ritual Lament in Greek Tradition (Cambridge 1974), to whose discussion (10–14) I am indebted here, treats the transition from in-laws to the more general category of nonkinsmen, but does not speculate on the reasons for this antiphonal requirement. I suggest that antiphonal lament may be a way to formalize the need for an other who is truly an other (an outsider) to witness and share in the mourner's grief, while the mourner in turn identifies with the one he/she has lost. For a different point of view, see the interesting discussion of self and other in Pietro Pucci, The Violence of Pity in Euripides' "Medea" (Ithaca, N.Y. 1980) 21–32, 226 n. 24.

91   Even his own language betrays this image of body as text, as book, when he opens his hands as one unfolds a scroll (anaptuchai, 601, 1190) and when he urges his father to "unfold" (diaptussō) the matter to get at the truth (985). Anaptussō for unfolding to read: Hdt. 1.125, Eur. 369.6 N^2 and diaptussō, Eur. IT 727, 793; ptuchai as the leaves of the book: Aesch. Suppl. 947, Soph. 144 N^2, Eur. IA 98, 112, IT 760, and Eur. 506.2 N^2. Segal 1979, 155, notes the vocabulary for a different purpose.

92   Théa and theaomai (and theatēs) become technical terms of the theater. Théa: Theophr. Char. 5.7 (spectacle), seat in the theater (Aeschin. de fals. Leg. 2.55, Demos. de Cor. 18.28, Meid. 21.178); theaomai: Ar. Ran. 2, Nub. 518, etc. and Isoc. Paneg. 4.44. Prosōpon is the standard word for mask (persona). It is, unlike the English "face," not that which "faces" you, the other, but the visage, that which you, the other, look at or regard.

93   Schwartz and Kahn (above, n. 76) xiii: "In the continuity of relation between self and other . . . the process is circular and development is the broadening of the circle of possible representations."

94   J.-P. Vernant, Annuaire du Collège de France, 1979–80, Résumé des cours et travaux (Paris 1981) 485, and see his entire discussion, 457–65.

95   It is evident throughout that Hippolytus' agemates do not count in the world of the adults. The text curiously shows him as singular and isolated but also suggests he shares a social life with his peers (cf. 996–1001). These are, it would seem, the ones who are "identical to himself."

96   Reckford 1972, 421. On the rite itself, see Fauth 1959, 389–97.

97   For the intricacies of Phaedra's eukleia, see Loraux 1978.

98   Theog. 237–54. The famous address to Cyrnus is remarkably relevant here; the last part in particular is worth citing: "When you go beneath the hiding places of the earth to the much-lamenting house of Hades, never, although dead, will you

lose your *kleos* but you will be a concern (*melēseis*) for men, possessing an imperishable name (*aphthiton onoma*) forever. . . . The shining gifts of the violet-crowned Muses will send you off, to all those to whom you are a care, and to those yet to come you will be an *aoidē*, a song, as long as earth and sun endure." See also Pl. *Symp.* 208d for the link between the self's longing for immortality and the winning of an *athanatos mnēmē* of *aretē* (immortal commemoration of virtue).

We might also note that, unlike usual finales in Greek tragedy, there is no mention of burial rites to come, as though the cult were to obviate that necessity by replacing perhaps that other ending to Hippolytus' story—resurrection through the agency of Asclepius.

99   Turato 1976 has an excellent discussion of the relationship of rhetoric to seduction in the context of the sophists. More generally, see Marcel Detienne, *Les maîtres de vérité dans la Grèce archaïque* (Paris 1967) 51–80; Kahn (above, n. 13) 119–64.

100 Others who have discussed the mirror include Avery 31 n. 26; C. W. Willink, "Some Problems of Text and Interpretation in the *Hippolytus*, 373–432," *CQ* 18 (1968) 16; and Pigeaud, who offers the most extensive analysis. With the exception of D. J. Conacher, *Euripidean Drama* (Toronto 1967) 36, who speaks of the "prophetic irony of this pretty image," no critic, as far as I know, relates the mirror to both Phaedra and Hippolytus.

101 On the mirror, see Vernant (above, n. 94).

102 See Avery and Segal 1970.

103 See Zeitlin (above, n. 47) 114–35.

104 I partly quote and partly interpret here on the basis of other statements in the play. In this hymn to Eros which follows the nurse's entry into the house with Phaedra's secret, the text gives the play entirely over to the power of Aphrodite. The progress of the ode is significant: first strophe/antistrophe—acknowledgment of Eros and Aphrodite, their substitution for Zeus and Apollo; second strophe/antistrophe—the Dionysiac now enters the scene under the pressures of Aphrodite. Iole, compared to a Bacchant, is given over by Aphrodite to a murderous wedding, and Semele herself, the mother of the twice-born Dionysus, is wed to a bloody doom.

Henceforth, Phaedra herself will be the only signifier, the only bird sign to interpret (759, 827) (see Segal, 1965, 183) and no oath, pledge, or seercraft (1055, 1321) will avail, both because of the passion Theseus acts on as a result of the erotic insult he suffers and because the "double speaking" of eros replaces the "double speaking" of oracles. Eros is, as Plutarch says (Stob. *Flor.* 64.31) an *ainigma duseureton kai dusluton*, an enigma difficult to find a way through, difficult to unbind (resolve), A study of the epistemological language of the play (*oida, katoida, sunoida, gignōskō, epistamai* and related *manthanō, ekmanthanō*) would require too much space here, but the frequency of "I don't know" in one form or another is remarkable (40, 56, 92, 271, 249, 277, 346, 394, 517, 599, 904, 919, 981, 1033, 1091, 1248, 1335).

105 Pigeaud 14–15 rightly links time, the mirror, and the virgin, and understands

204 FROMA I. ZEITLIN

the mirror as both the reflection of the self and reflection on the self as necessary prerequisites for self-knowledge, but he treats Phaedra alone and only as
morally wicked and uses Euripides mainly for comparison with Plato.

106 Northrop Frye's remarks on romance (above, n. 38) 117 are wonderfully appropriate here: "In ordinary life there are two central data of experience that we cannot see without external assistance: our own faces and our own existence in
time. To see the first we have to look in a mirror, and to see the second we have
to look at the dial of a clock. . . . The classical romancers had to make do with
doubles only, as the clock had not been invented."

107 There are many instances in the play of reversed mirror images. The most striking visual one occurs in the prologue where Aphrodite, in speaking of the
temple Phaedra has founded for the goddess because of the eros that struck her
when she saw Hippolytus (27), calls it a *katopsion* of this land (Troezen), that is,
a look-out seen now from the opposite or reverse point of view (cf. 373–74). As
the first play was set in Athens, the early mention of the reversed perspective
may well remind us how much this second play functions as a mirror reversal of
the first.

108 Shakespeare, as usual, says it best (*Troilus and Cressida*, III, iii, 103ff., Achilles
to Ulysses):

The beauty that is borne here in the face
The bearer knows not, but commends itself
To Others' eyes; nor doth the eye itself,
That most pure spirit of sense, behold itself,
Not going from itself; but eye to eye oppos'd
Salutes each other with each other's form;
For speculation turns not to itself
Till it hath travell'd and is mirror'd there
Where it may see itself.

109 It is worth noting that after the disaster to Hippolytus, no one, not Artemis or
Theseus, or Hippolytus, ever says that Phaedra was *kakē*. Instead, bearing in
mind that Theseus too becomes implicated in the action that completes the destruction of all three of them (1403), we find that the terms of Phaedra's "prophecy" about the mirror are explicitly fulfilled in Artemis' words to Theseus. She
says: "In Hippolytus' eyes and in mine you appear (*phainēi*) wicked (*kakos*) [cf.
1316], precisely because you did not wait for pledges or the voice of seers, nor
did you conduct an interrogation, nor did you press an inquiry in the length of
time (*chronōi makrōi*), but swifter than it was necessary, you cast your curses at
your son and killed him" (1320–24). There is one important distinction, however, between Phaedra's text and that of Artemis involving different verbs to
which the prefix *ek-* (connoting full accomplishment of the activity) is applied:
Phaedra speaks of *ek-phainō*, that is, a definitive revelation [of the base self],
while Artemis uses the simpler *phainō* which does not imply a final judgment
of Theseus, since, as she says, his ignorance is what fully absolves (loosens,
ek-luei) him from evil (*kakēs*, 1335). It is Aphrodite, I might add, for whom all
reserve this charge.

110 How can one not invoke here Gorgias' famous statement on tragedy? "Whereas the tragic poet who deceives is juster than he who does not, the deceived is also wiser than the one who is not deceived" (fr. 23 DK).

One might also consider in another perspective the significant features of masculine puberty rites as discussed by Vidal-Naquet (see above, n. 11). The Spartan *krupteia* especially shows elements of "cunning, deception, disorder, and irrationality." These, along with the wearing of female garb in other rituals, are explained as obeying the "law of symmetrical inversion" whereby one sex takes on the characteristics of the other just when entry into adulthood will require conformity to unambiguously masculine hoplite norms. In this sense, boys are actually playing the role of the other—whether that of the savage or of the female. We might go still further. Considering the emphasis on hiding (*krupteia*) and deceit (one etymology of the Athenian festival, the Apatouria), it is tempting to suggest that these activities are essential in themselves for the adolescent male. They teach the self the relations of inside/outside and introduce the ephebes to the ways of the more complex world that awaits them through obliging them to practice the very exercises that characterize that adult perception of reality. Tragedy, in particular, makes use of its theatrical resources to stage this learning process for figures such as Orestes in the *Choephori* and Neoptolemus in the *Philoctetes*. (Vidal-Naquet [above, n. 46] has discussed the significance in these two plays of the ruse and ephebic status but from a different viewpoint.)

111 On language of tripping and stumbling (*sphallō*), see Knox 25–26.

112 On these unhappy loves, see Erwin Rohde, *Der griechische Roman und seine Vorläüfer*[3] (Leipzig 1913) 157.4; Ludwig Radermacher, *Hippolytus und Thekla*, *Sitz. Wien* 182.3 (1916) 3–5; S. Trenkner, *The Greek Novella in the Classical Period* (Cambridge 1958) 26–27 n. 5; and esp. F. Dupont, "Se reproduire ou se métamorphoser," *Topique: revue freudienne* 9–10 (1971) 149; Marcel Detienne, *The Gardens of Adonis* (Eng. trans., Atlantic Highlands, N.J. 1977) 64 (French ed., Paris 1972), and Detienne (above, n. 11) 25–26. In addition, see E. Pellizer, *Favole d'identità, favole di paura: Storie di caccia e altri racconti della Grecia antica* (Rome 1982), which treats the whole question in great detail. We should emphasize that the motif itself of the wrath of Aphrodite as a determining factor of a plot seems to be a rather late development that only fully comes into its own with Hellenistic poetry and romance and owes much, it is thought, to Euripides' eroticizing of the myths. See Fauth 1958, 572–73.

113 See Detienne (above, n. 11) 26–34.

114 See Calame (above, n. 11) 218–21, 416–18.

115 Detienne (above, n. 11) 26, Pellizer (above, n. 112) 22.

116 On Myrrha, see Detienne (above, n. 112) 63–64, 80–83, 90–91. On Leucippus (Parth. *Amat. Narr.* 5) see Pellizer (above, n. 112) 66–69.

117 Pellizer (above, n. 112) e.g. 23–24, 29–30, does not observe this distinction and includes Hippolytus among the other transgressive hunters by saying that he "becomes the victim of a passion contrary to the rules of the family and of kinship." Another story he cites, that of the hunter Tanais, fulfills the pattern exactly (Ps.-Plut. *de Fluviis* 14.1). Son of Berossos and Lysippe (one of the Ama-

zons), Tanais, being very chaste, hated the female race and honored only Ares, the god of war, and naturally held the idea of marriage in great contempt. Aphrodite then inspired in him the desire for his own mother. Tanais first succeeded in resisting such an insane passion, but when bound and constrained by these pangs but still wanting to remain righteous (*eusebēs*), he leaped into the river Amazonios, which henceforth was called the Tanais.

Joseph Fontenrose, *Orion: The Myth of the Hunter and the Huntress* (Berkeley, Calif. 1981) 160–67, also elides the problem because he aims to fit Hippolytus into his construct of the mythic hunter: "Hippolytus . . . is wholly chaste . . . and so cannot be guilty of assault, as Orion and Aktaion were. Hence an accusa-tion of assault must be substituted, and the Potiphar's-wife theme supplies this feature; furthermore, it is not the huntress [i.e., Artemis] but her rival [i.e., Aphrodite/Phaedra] who is the supposed victim." (Note the double inversion Fontenrose needs to make the pattern work.)

In looking at these narrative forms, I am not, of course, including those myths of the reluctant virgins (such as Daphne) which end in metamorphosis, another and very distinct kind of solution for preserving virginity.

118   Glaucus, the son of Poseidon, is especially relevant here in a number of respects (for discussion see Radermacher, above, n. 112, 8–13). His mythology is com-plex and attached to a number of different sites. I therefore select: According to Pausanias 6.20.19, Glaucus drives along the Isthmus of Corinth as a *daimōn* who terrifies the horses, exactly like Poseidon Taraxippos. Servius, commenting on Verg. *G.* 3.268, tells us that since he had spurned the rites of Aphrodite, she maddened his racing mares and they tore him apart with their teeth. A slightly different version, he continues, equates the wrath of Aphrodite with another cause—that Glaucus was torn apart by his mares who were driven out of control by an excess of lust, since he prevented them from coupling in order that they might run more swiftly.

119   Burkert (above, n. 16) 112 sums up the problem: "One may wonder . . . about the curiously complicated method Aphrodite uses to take her revenge: she has Phaedra cause Theseus to pronounce a curse, which moves Poseidon to send a bull from the sea, who in turn causes Hippolytus' horses to go wild, which fi-nally kills the hero. If I were Aphrodite, I would not trust this assassination ma-chine to work properly. At any rate, Aphrodite could have driven the horses wild herself, as she did in the case of Glaukos Potnieus."

On the functions of Poseidon as Taraxippos and Damasippos, see especially the discussion in Detienne and Vernant (above, n. 33) 190–206, which illumi-nates many details in the messenger's narrative of events.

120   Hippolytus himself has affinities in certain respects with many others, including Phaethon, who is specifically named in our text, and even more with Hymenaios, of whom it is told that he disappeared on his wedding night. On all such various elements, see, for example, Radermacher (above, n. 112), Séchan, Tschiedel, Herter (all above, n. 2), Burkert (above, n. 16), and Fauth 1959.

121   If we can take Seneca's *Phaedra* as a reliable guide in this regard, the first play would have invoked the excuse of the wrath of Aphrodite against Phaedra as a female descendant of the Sun because it was Helios who had exposed the adul-

tery of Ares and Aphrodite (Sen. *Phaed.* 124–28). If this were the case, then the nurse's general reference to the "wrath of Aphrodite" (438; cf. 476), as well as Phaedra's own allusions to the unhappy erotic history of the women in her family (337–41), might remind the audience more directly of the previous and quite ·typical relation of cause and effect with respect to Phaedra's passion.

122 On the Potiphar's wife motif in myth and story, see Angelo Brelich, *Gli eroi greci* (Rome 1958) 302–3; Radermacher 4.51; Rohde 33–34; Trenkner 64–66 (all above, n. 112); and Fauth 1958, 565–67. It might be added that none of the other myths and tales of this type include the wrath of Aphrodite as their motivating cause. The wrath leading to the revenge is rather that of the human agent, the woman, and the story is conducted on that level.

In our case, it might be argued that Phaedra is only replicating the role of the goddess. That is, although she is the victim of Aphrodite, at the same time, she becomes her agent and substitute (as I have emphasized throughout) and then passes on this role to Theseus himself. This doubling of goddess/woman may be evidence that this is a secondary stage of the myth's development, in which a shift from divine to human personage has taken place, especially considering the cult relationship between Hippolytus and Aphrodite. From this point of view, even Hippolytus' special relationship with Artemis, which is presented as anomalous within its social context, might resonate to this earlier stratum of the Great Goddess/consort pattern in which the feminine deity is now split into the polar opposites of Artemis and Aphrodite (cf. n. 45, above). Phaedra herself claims origins as child of Zeus (683) and she can be identified with Cretan goddess figures, while Theseus draws upon his divine ancestry from Poseidon to bring about Hippolytus' destruction. (For the fullest discussion of these questions, see Fauth 1959.)

Nevertheless, in this complex of disparate motifs that, for example, combines both hunting and horsemanship for Hippolytus and places him as the new central focus from which his very different relations with other figures radiate out as spokes from a wheel (e.g., Actaeon, Bellerophon, Glaucus, Atalanta, Hymenaios), we must take comprehensive account of the significance of this mythic composite without subordinating or eliminating elements that do not fit a more reductive scheme. We need to approach this new elaboration of the myth, to which Euripides has probably contributed the most, in a way that can uncover the logic of its operations on the level at which it is represented. Certainly, Euripides is playing off divine against human domains and is interweaving the two with the stress falling on the secular and human intrigue.

123· The love that Phaedra bears for Hippolytus and likewise the alleged passion of Hippolytus that "shamed his father's bed" (943–44) are, from the social point of view, obviously unjust (614, 672, 676; 942, 1081, 1171) because both choices of the beloved (whether in truth or not) are transgressive. But there is another kind of "injustice," that of erotic injustice, relevant to the pattern we have been following. This injustice characterizes the refusal on the part of the beloved to reciprocate the affections of the lover. In other words, the lover, by the very fact of loving the other, puts that other under the same obligation to return that love. The typical penalty obeys the law of the talion in prescribing an exchange of

208   FROMA I. ZEITLIN

roles for the future. According to this norm, the *erōmenos* will become in time the *erastēs* (often of still an other) and will experience the same rejection and pain as his/her former *erastēs*. What Phaedra does in contriving to reverse the roles of *erastēs* and *erōmenos* between herself and Hippolytus would then seem *on the surface* to fulfill this rule of reciprocity.

Yet from this erotic viewpoint, our case (the pattern of illicit eros as a penalty for eros refused) might be judged an extreme manifestation of the more usual cycle. Now the *erōmenos* may change or seem to change into the *erastēs* (i.e., Hippolytus), but it is too late to enter into the game. The exchange of roles in this version of erotic justice can only come to a tragic end, because its very initiation (let alone its consummation) constitutes a moral injustice and an offense against the system.

This notion of erotic justice seems to arise in the archaic period as part of a more general set of reflections on alternating cycles of exchange in the world (cf. Anaximander fr. 1 DK) and applies to both heterosexual and homosexual relations (cf. esp. Sappho fr. 1 LP and Theog. 1283–93). For further discussion, see G. A. Privitera, "La rete di Afrodite: Ricerche sulla prima ode di Saffo," *QUCC* 4 (1967) 11–41, and *La rete di Afrodite: Studi su Saffo* (Palermo 1974); Bruno Gentili, "Il 'letto insaziato' di Medea e il tema dell' Adikia a livello amoroso nei lirici (Saffo, Teognide) e nella *Medea* di Euripide," *SCO* 21 (1972) 60–72; M. G. Bonnano, "Osservazioni sul tema della 'giusta' reciprocità da Saffo ai comici," *QUCC* 16 (1973) 110–20; and A. Giacomelli (= Carson), "The Justice of Aphrodite in Sappho Fr. 1," *TAPA* 110 (1980) 135–42.

124   Actaeon as voyeur of Artemis is attested late (Callim. *Hymn* 5.110–16) but he is always a sexual transgressor, as in Stesichorus 236P (Paus. 9.2.3) he seems to incur the wrath of Zeus for attempting to seduce Semele, his aunt. For further discussion, see Segal (above, n. 19) 166 n. 16. On voyeurs in general and their connections with sexual transgression, see R. G. A. Buxton, "Blindness and Limits: Sophocles and the Logic of Myth," *JHS* 100 (1980) 22–37.

125   Aphrodite and Artemis do meet, of course, along with Dionysus and Pan (and other deities) in connection with assaults against the self as a punishment both for too much or too little desire. In this category I include as agents both the maddened animals (such as the hounds of Actaeon and the horses of Hippolytus and Glaucus) as well as those humans who are collectively driven mad and thereby revert to subhuman behavior: Orpheus refuses eros (or at least, heterosexual eros) after his loss of Eurydice and is consequently torn apart by Maenads (Verg. *G.* 4.516–22; Ov. *Met.* 10.78–835; 11.7; cf. Phanocles fr. 1 [Powell] and Hyg. *Poet. Astr.* 2.7). Echo wishes to remain always a virgin and is torn apart at Pan's instigation by maddened shepherds and goatherds who "fall upon the poor girl like enraged wolves or dogs" (Longus 3.23). In the case of Pentheus and his mother in the *Bacchae*, both, of course, have initially refused the worship of Dionysus. (For further discussion on some of these themes, see the splendid study of Ph. Bourgeaud, *Recherches sur le dieu Pan* [Geneva 1979] esp. 124–34, 165–75.) Even in this grouping, Hippolytus' position is odd once again as he requires yet another external agent (the bull) to serve as a catalytic force.

Concepts of Demoralization in the Hecuba

Somewhat revised in 1977, this paper remains close to the oral version presented to the Euripides conference at Duke University on March 18 of that year. It stands in memory of my mother, Janet Reckford Limburg, who died on March 17, 1977, sadly for her family, yet "before falling upon some ugly chance." Today, seven years later, I have supplied English translations but have added no further bibliography or notes. The essay should be read as a product of 1977. I am grateful to Peter Burian for his encouragement.

1   Since L. E. Matthaei's fine essay, *Studies in Greek Tragedy* (Cambridge 1918) 118–57, most critics have accepted the unity and coherence of the *Hecuba* as held together by the experience of the protagonist. The case for unity is well summarized by D. J. Conacher, *Euripidean Drama* (Toronto 1967) 146–65. Differences of concern and emphasis remain. G. M. A. Grube, *The Drama of Euripides* (London 1941) 93–97, 214–28, stresses Hecuba's psychological development and Max Pohlenz her inner transformation (*Die griechische Tragödie*[2] [Göttingen 1954] 277–84). Others such as Walter Zürcher, *Die Darstellung des Menschen in Drama des Euripides* (Basel 1947) 73–84, deny character development and instead study Hecuba's movement from helpless suffering to the revenge action against Polymestor; see Antonio Garzya, "Intorno all' Ecuba di Euripide," *GIF* 7 (1954) 205–12; Walter Kerscher, *Handlungsmotive Euripideischer Dramengestalten* (Munich 1969) 225–36; Albin Lesky, *Greek Tragic Poetry* (trans. Matthew Dillon, New Haven 1983) 241–48 (third German ed. [1972] 329–38); and Wolf Steidle, "Zur *Hekabe* des Euripides," *WS* 79 (1966) 133–42, who opposes any tendency to make Hecuba too passive a victim even in the first part of the play.

Others, while accepting Hecuba's figure as central to the play, have perceived its unity as consisting more in some underlying idea: of human suffering (H. D. F. Kitto, *Greek Tragedy* [London 1939] 216–23), the nature of war and the concentration camp (Ernst L. Abrahamson, "Euripides' Tragedy of Hecuba," *TAPA* 83 [1952] 120–29), human suffering and the examination of *nomos* (G. M. Kirkwood, "Hecuba and Nomos," *TAPA* 78 [1947] 61–68), or the logic of political necessity (William Arrowsmith, introd. to translation in *The Complete Greek Tragedies*, vol. 6, ed. David Grene and Richmond Lattimore [New York 1958] 84–89).

My own interpretation owes much to Jacqueline de Romilly's powerful description (*L'Évolution du pathétique d'Eschyle à Euripide* [Paris 1961]) of human helplessness in Euripidean tragedy and the way people's actions, like Hecuba's revenge (pp. 8off., 114ff.), arise out of an excess of suffering as a "sursaut passioné" (p. 116). My assumptions about Euripidean psychology are closely in accord with those of Albin Lesky, "Psychologie bei Euripides," *Entretiens Hardt* 6:123–50, esp. 151–68. For a good survey of Euripides' empirical psychology in its cultural setting, and for its relation to that of Thucydides, see Friedrich Solmsen's *Intellectual Experiments of the Greek Enlightenment* (Princeton 1975) chap. 5, esp. 129ff., on "assimilation of temper to external conditions."

See also Philip Vellacott, *Ironic Drama* (Cambridge 1975), C. A. E. Luschnig, "Euripides' *HECABE*: The Time Is Out of Joint," *CJ* 71 (1975–76) 227–34, and S. G. Daitz, "Concepts of Freedom and Slavery in Euripides' *Hecuba*," *Hermes* 99 (1971) 217–26.

2   There are exceptions: most notably William Arrowsmith in "A Greek Theatre of Ideas," *Arion* 2 (1963) 32–56; and, on Greek tragedy generally (though mainly Sophocles), Walter Kaufmann, *Tragedy and Philosophy* (Garden City, N.Y. 1968). This essay is the fourth and last in a "loss of innocence" series; thus it draws on and may be supplemented by K. J. Reckford, "Medea's First Exit," *TAPA* 99 (1968) 329–59; "Phaethon, Hippolytus, and Aphrodite," *TAPA* 103 (1972) 405–32; and "Phaedra and Pasiphae: The Pull Backward," *TAPA* 104 (1974) 307–28.

3   Nobody to my knowledge has given a thorough analysis of lines 592–602. Their relevance has generally been accepted since Grube (above, n. 1) argued for it (and for that of comparable passages) in his chapter, "The Problem of Relevance," esp. pp. 95–96. Lines 911–17 from Euripides' *Suppliant Women* offer a good comparison: superficially, because they deal with the question of how morality is taught (this time stressing good upbringing and education); but more important, because Adrastos' claim is so completely discredited by the play taken as a whole (see Peter Burian's essay in this volume). Years later, a discussion of "What is genuine nobility?" proves equally shallow and ironic in the mouth of Orestes, in *El.* 367–85.

4   On Phaedra's great speech (*Hipp.* 373–430) in relation to her moral effort and its failure, see Reckford 1974 (above, n. 2) 313–18; differently, David Claus sees Phaedra's speech as a vindication of the efforts of her *gnōmē* in "Phaedra and the Socratic Paradox," *YCS* 22 (1972) 223–38.

5   For such indications of Hecuba's death-in-life, see lines 231–33, 284, 396, 431, 622–23, 668–69, 683.

6   The central contrast between Polyxena's fate and Hecuba's is drawn with prophetic accuracy by Polyxena as she attempts to console her mother: see lines 211–15, ending *suntuchia kreissōn ekurēsen* ("better luck befell me") and

> Better advise me to die before I meet ugly chances not of my deserving. If a person is unfamiliar with the taste of evils, he can bear them, yes, but it hurts him to put his neck beneath the yoke. One who dies might be luckier than one who goes on living; for to go on living, but not well, is a painful effort. (373–78)

Polyxena's words are followed, ironically, by the chorus' statement, 379–81, that nobility of lineage is "terribly evident" and endures. But compare also Talthybius' remark:

> Alas. Alas. I am old; still, let me die before I fall upon some ugly chance. (497–98)

The point is twofold. Nobility can be "validated," as in Polyxena's case, by right chance and favoring coincidence; but chance, *tuchē*, can also bring a reversal into the ugly-and-shameful—as it will for Hecuba. On the contrast between

Polyxena's fate and Hecuba's, see Conacher (above, n. 1) 154–55. The description of Polyxena's sacrifice and the effects of that "representation" bear closely on the question of tragic catharsis: see Pietro Pucci, "Euripides: The Monument and the Sacrifice," *Arethusa* 10 (1977) 165–95, esp. 168–70 and 180–81.

7   My conviction that Hecuba no longer regards moral principles as real, or as really defensible, is the opposite view from Diego Lanza, "*NOMOS* e *ISON* in Euripide," *Riv. Fil.* 91 (1963) 416–39. Although I agree with Kirkwood (above, n. 1) 66–67 that Hecuba shifts to *peithō* out of disillusionment with *nomos*, I do not place her "moral peripeteia" (as he does) at a single moment within this scene, when she recognizes Agamemnon's moral callousness, but rather see it as evolving gradually after the Odysseus scene. At lines 685–87 Euripides suggests through a play on *nomos* = law/tune that Hecuba has shifted to a "new-learned Bacchic *nomos* out of some avenging power." And even before Agamemnon rejects her, Hecuba speaks with calculation. Surely lines 736ff. are *meant* to be overheard. Although Hecuba may form her plan gradually (as Zürcher well argues [above, n. 1] 80–81), she uses persuasion from the first, and very consciously; cf. Medea's tactics, or Alcmene's. Compare also the later Hecuba of *Troiades* whose devastating rebuttal of Helen's defense (969–1032) proceeds from a radical scepticism or even nihilism that sees no reality in traditional myths or divinities.

My argument, of course, simplifies the conceptual issues involved in the Odysseus-Hecuba and Hecuba-Agamemnon scenes. A. W. H. Adkins, "Basic Greek Values in Euripides' *Hecuba* and *Hercules Furens*," *CQ* n.s. 16 (1966) 193–219, reminds us of how much the conscious judgments of Odysseus and Agamemnon rest on accepted Greek values concerning strength and weakness, the treatment of friends and enemies, and so on. If Adkins is right, then these judgments (or are they rationalizations?) have more force than we usually credit them with today. This would be one more upsetting or confusing element in the play for its Athenian audience, and one more way of involving them in the tragedy.

8   For an Athenian audience the phrase *nomōn graphai* weakens the force of *nomos* by stressing its man-made quality; compare the familiar contrast (with many different implications) between "written" and "unwritten laws."

9   This play includes an unusual number of references to chance: forms of *tuchē* and *tunchanein*, of *eutucheo* and *eutuchēs*, *dustucheo* and *dustuchēs*. For all practical purposes, the rule of *Tuchē* (personified also at 785–86) seems to have replaced the government of Zeus; Talthybius suggests just this conclusion:

Lord Zeus: what shall I say? That you look upon human lives? Or that you have acquired this reputation in vain, and it is chance, mere chance, that oversees all that mortals do? (488–91)

It follows that to "get" the chance you need for good or ill must depend on "chance," on a confluence of favoring events—nothing more.

10   For good discussions of freedom and slavery in this play, see Daitz (above, n. 1) and Vellacott (above, n. 1) 208–14, esp. 211 on the ironic reversal: "for the free and victorious king, guilt and dependence; for the enslaved queen, authority and a freedom bestowed by suffering." But this freedom is only illusory. See de

Romilly (above, n. 1) 117: "Chacun semble prisonnier de cet univers brutal, où les gens rendent coup pour coup, sans être pour autant les vrais maîtres de leurs actes."

11   Odysseus was characterized as *poikilophrōn*, "devious and complex," at 131. Hecuba becomes like Odysseus, just as Medea in her manipulations of intelligence becomes like Jason, Alcmene like Eurystheus, and Phaedra like the nurse. For this last, see Reckford 1974 (above, n. 2) 317 n. 12: Phaedra's resort to tricky, ambiguous language is a precise indication of her deterioration of character from the earlier part of the play.

12   Polymestor himself remarks on the "confusion" of things with hypocritical shock, with an unbeliever's cynicism ("the gods mix everything up . . . so that out of our ignorance we may revere them")—and with an unintentional, very ironic application to Hecuba's plot (as well as his own deed): "Nothing can be trusted . . ." (956–60).

13   See the thoughtful analysis of H.-P. Stahl, *Thukydides* (Munich, 1966). Men's plans fail because of (a) their mistaken behavior and (b) the contingency of chance events (p. 98); indeed, incalculable *tuchē* may arouse man's irrational nature, which then itself becomes an unpredictable factor in history (79–80, on the plague). Stahl's remarks on how Thucydides joins perception of human irrationality with feelings of compassion and sorrow at human *pathēmata* are thoroughly applicable to Euripidean tragedy as well.

14   *Clouds* 1165ff., from *Hecuba* 171–73. (There are other, less obvious borrowings.)

15   The feeling of dependence on fortune, symbolized by movements of wind and wave, appears most powerfully in the concentrated imagery of the choral ode 444ff., beginning *aura, pontias aura*. Compare also lines 28–30 (Polydorus' corpse rolled around by waves—to be brought to the shore for Hecuba to find), 898–901 (the Greeks waiting for a fair wind), and 1289–90.

16   Simone Weil, "L'amour de Dieu et le Malheur," in *Attente de Dieu* (Paris 1950) 107–8. My epigraph is from the same essay, p. 98.

Logos *and* Pathos*: The Politics of the* Suppliant Women

My work on the *Suppliant Women* was furthered by a fellowship from the National Endowment for the Humanities in 1972–73, which I am glad to be able to acknowledge at last with gratitude.

1   For the subject of this play in the orators, see Euripides, *Supplices*, edited with introduction and commentary by Christopher Collard (Groningen 1974) 4 n. 6 (my text is that of this extremely useful edition). The most obvious political interpretation of the *Suppliant Women* is already proposed with admirable brevity in its fragmentary hypothesis: *to de drama engkōmion Athēnōn* (the drama is praise of Athens). Günther Zuntz, *The Political Plays of Euripides* (Manchester 1955), has argued with great subtlety for a version of that view, reading the *Suppliant Women* as praise of an ideal Athens, and he is followed by Collard among others. My own essay may be read as a critique of such interpretations, though I do not here attempt explicit refutation. It should be added, however, that "politi-

cal interpretation" has traditionally meant something far cruder and less re-strained than what Zuntz attempts. Critics have often succumbed to the urge to treat the dramatic text as a repository of allusions, some finding therein an expla-nation for what they regard as deplorable irrelevancies or lapses in judgment, oth-ers quite frankly embracing what they consider the text's real raison d'être, Euripides' burning desire to impart his advice on issues of the moment, at what-ever cost to the drama. It is instructive to compare two such critics at work on a specific passage, the concluding lines of the messenger's battle report which describes "what kind of general should be chosen" (726ff.; cf. below, p. 142). Both Édouard Delebecque, *Euripide et la guerre du Péloponnèse* (Paris 1951) 221–23, and Roger Goossens, *Euripide et Athènes* (Brussels 1962) 440–46, regard it as more or less self-evident that this is Euripides electioneering: for Alcibiades, according to Delebecque, for Nicias, according to Goossens. For Goossens, Alcibiades is too young to be Euripides' choice for *strategos* in 424, which he regards as the certain date of the play. For Delebecque, who dates it to 420, Alkibiades' youth and boldness are the bases of the indentification, as the Theseus of the play is young and bold. Goossens thinks that a recommendation of the pious Nicias is the only possible reason for Euripides' uncharacteristic endorse-ment of oracles and prophecy at 211ff., whereas Delebecque finds a pro-Argive strain in that play that makes recommendation of the pro-Spartan Nicias impos-sible. And so on, through a long series of contradictory positions. The difficulties cannot be resolved by expedients such as the proposal of Vincenzo di Benedetto, *Euripide: teatro e società* (Turin 1971) 158–59, that the electioneering here is not *for* anyone, but *against* Cleon. The real problem is that all these scholars assume that Euripides must be writing not about his ostensible subject but about something else that can only be ferreted out by a kind of allegorical interpretation.

2   On the Proerosia, see H. W. Parke, *Festivals of the Athenians* (London 1977) 73–75; J. D. Mikalson, *The Sacred and Civil Calendar of the Athenian Year* (Princeton 1975) 67–69. Aithra clearly alludes to this festival at 28–29.

3   Cf., e.g., Collard (above, n. 1) *ad* 63–64; W. D. Smith, "Expressive Form in Euripides' *Suppliants*," *HSCP* 71 (1966) 154–55. I have briefly discussed the staging of the initial scene of this play in "The Play before the Prologue: Initial Tableaux on the Greek Stage," in *Ancient and Modern: Essays in Honor of Gerald F. Else*, ed. John H. D'Arms and John W. Eadie (Ann Arbor, Mich. 1977) 84–85.

4   Her treatment of the suppliants' case everywhere goes beyond the expository re-quirements of this speech. Aithra anticipates the mothers' arguments: suppliant status (10), misery (11), the impiety and injustice of the enemy (19). She responds with pity (34) and religious awe (36). While deferring to her son's decision, she states the alternatives in a way that seems almost preemptive (38–40: note esp. *anagkas hikesious* and *hosion ti drasas*).

5   For a useful analysis of the technique of Theseus' entrance, see D. J. Mastronarde, *Contact and Discontinuity* (Berkeley, Calif. 1979) 22–23. Adrastos' case is al-ready perhaps differentiated from that of the suppliant women in Aithra's de-scription of him collapsed in grief at the loss of his armies (22–23); cf. G. M. A. Grube, *The Drama of Euripides* (London 1941) 230.

6 Cf. Smith (above, n. 3) 158.

7 Lines 176–83 are problematic; the whole passage (Dindorf) and parts (177–78 Bothe, 180–83 Reiske) have been excised as interpolated, but in all likelihood the real difficulty is that a lacuna after 179 (Matthiae) has obscured the point of Adrastos' remarks. What remains, however, forms the outline of a speculative argument to which Theseus replies in his answering *rhesis*. Useful discussion and bibliography may be found in Christopher Collard, "Euripides, *Supplices* 176–83," *RFIC* 101 (1973) 411–13.

8 Theseus' notion of "cultural evolution" has been widely discussed in relation to other fifth-century speculations of a similar nature: cf. Collard (above, n. 1, ad 201–13) and (in addition to the literature cited there) E. A. Havelock, *The Liberal Temper in Greek Politics* (London 1957) 70–73; D. J. Conacher, "Prometheus as Founder of the Arts," *GRBS* 18 (1977) 198–200. Gilbert Norwood, *Essays on Euripidean Drama* (Berkeley, Calif. 1954) 144, is the strongest condemnation of the speech's supposed irrelevance. Wilhelm Schmid, *Geschichte der griechischen Literatur* 1, 3 (Munich 1940) 456, perhaps typifies the widespread assumption that Euripides here interrupts the drama to present his own world-view.

9 On the youths (*neoi*) see below, nn. 30 and 41.

10 There are useful comments on the contrast between Aithra's involvement and Theseus' detachment in R. B. Gamble, "Euripides' *Suppliant Women*: Decision and Ambivalence," *Hermes* 98 (1970) 386–93. Gamble overstates his claim, however, when he argues that lines 286–92 show Theseus to be totally devoid of "the notion of a common humanity shared by suppliant and supplicated" (p. 388), and unable to understand it in his mother. This ignores the evidence of 288 (*kame gar diēlthe ti*), which makes it clear that Theseus deliberately suppresses an emotional response dangerous to the conclusions of reason.

11 The relation of Aithra and Theseus is only one of several carefully contrasted examples of the bonds between parents and children in this play: the mothers who mourn their lost sons, the sons' sons who will avenge them, Iphis who must witness the suicide of his daughter Evadne. In this essay I can only touch on the implications of this theme, which requires more attention than it has received to date.

12 Failure to recognize this has contributed to the wide diversity of opinions expressed about Aithra's speech and Theseus' reply. Critics have tended to break the argument down into its heterogeneous components and then to fasten on some at the expense of the rest. "Realist" interpreters, such as L. H. G. Greenwood, *Aspects of Euripidean Tragedy* (Cambridge 1953) 108–12, and J. W. Fitton, "The *Suppliant Women* and the *Heraklidai* of Euripides," *Hermes* 89 (1961) 431–32, emphasize that the bulk of Aithra's speech is devoted to Athens' political reputation and Theseus' personal honor, and that it is to this last argument alone that Theseus seems to respond, with what Greenwood 109 is willing to call "vanity." Zuntz (above, n. 1) 8, the most determinedly "idealist" interpreter, emphasizes. Aithra's insistence on religious duty and the preservation of Panhellenic law, and makes no attempt to cope with Theseus' reply. In between are many critics such as Grube (above, note 5) 233, for whom the details of Euripides' conception are to be explained by a "touch of delightful realism" or "a contemporary reference"

rather than by any coherent artistic purpose. But are not both the "realistic" and "idealistic" elements essential? Aithra's statement of the claims of divine and human law is emphatic and effective, and remains so despite Theseus' lack of direct response to it here. (He does make it his own in the debate with the Theban herald, esp. 531–41.) And yet, the political cost of Aithra's arguments and the crucial role of personal pride in persuading Theseus to act are equally unmistakable. There is no necessary contradiction in this. Part of the point of this scene, and indeed of the whole tortuous movement to the acceptance of the suppliants' suit, is precisely that the issues involved are unavoidably complex and unextricably interlocked. Duty to the gods, public responsibility, personal honor, family ties, all count for something, and all must be taken in account.

13   This untranslatable term may be used favorably to indicate a sort of activism on one's own behalf, censoriously to suggest meddlesomeness in the affairs of others. Victor Ehrenberg, "Polypragmosyne: A Study in Greek Politics," *JHS* 67 (1947) 46–47, shows clearly its use in describing (approvingly or otherwise) the active foreign policy of Pericles and his successors. See also A. W. H. Adkins, "*Polupragmosune* and 'Minding One's Own Business,'" *CP* 71 (1976) 301–27, esp. 311ff.

14   The apparent exception is line 354, in which Theseus announces that he will take Adrastos with him when he goes to win the people's support for his decision. But presenting Adrastos to the Assembly as *deigma tōn emōn logōn* does not imply association with his cause, merely that his presence will be evidence for the account of what has occurred. If the consultation of the Assembly in this play seems perfunctory, especially when contrasted with the similar motif in Aeschylus' *Suppliants* (365–624), the reason is to be sought in the fact that there the king faces a real political dilemma concerning the acceptance of the suppliants' suit which recourse to the Assembly helps render dramatic. Here, no such situation obtains. On Aeschylus' use of the Assembly, see Peter Burian, "Pelasgus and Politics in Aeschylus' Danaid Trilogy," *WS* 8 (1974) 97–113. Euripides seems to be following the Aeschylean model in making Adrastos accompany Theseus, but he reduces the motif to an almost vestigial character. Adrastos plays no role in Theseus' rather casual report of the Assembly's acquiescence in the *ponos* he will undertake (393–94), and indeed line 354 is the sole indication that he does leave the stage (and return) with Theseus.

15   E.g., Grube (above, n. 5) 233: "The main result of the refusal scene would seem to be to keep the Athenian cause pure."

16   Greenwood (above, n. 12) 110; cf. e.g., Norwood (above, n. 8) 155; Fitton (above, n. 12) 432; Henri Grégoire in the Budé edition of Euripides (Paris 1923) 3 : 87.

17   For *agalma* of the dead sons, cf. 631, 1164. The first of these references is noteworthy for foreshadowing their "rehabilitation" in the second half of the play. The herald who reiterates Thebes' refusal to return the bodies has depicted the Seven as impious aggressors whom Zeus rightly destroyed (494–505). The mothers call on Zeus himself to rescue the bodies of the Seven, attributing their sentiments to him by describing their sons as *his* delight and *his* bulwark for the city (*to son agalma, to son idruma poleos*).

18   Plut. *Thes.* 29.4f. states that Aeschylus' *Eleusinioi* had the version in which

Theseus persuades the Thebans to return the bodies and calls it the version that most of his sources follow.

19   Aeschylus' *Suppliants* ends with the war as yet unfought, but obviously imminent. Demophon in Euripides' *Children of Heracles* joins battle against Eurystheus, as does Theseus against Creon in Sophocles' *Oedipus at Colonus* (albeit in a somewhat vestigial form; see Peter Burian, "Suppliant and Saviour: Oedipus at Colonus," *Phoenix* 28 [1974] 421).

20   In Aesch. *Supp.* and Soph. *Oed. Col.*, the enemy enters after the suppliants' suit has been accepted, but at a moment when the king has withdrawn, leaving the suppliants unprotected. In Eur. *Heracl.* the enemy enters before the king has appeared and attempts to wrest the suppliants by force from the altar at which they have taken refuge. In all these instances, there is a sequence of attack—call for help—rescue which is entirely missing from the *Suppliant Women*.

21   Cf. Aesch. *Supp.* 930–33, Eur. *Heracl.* 114 (where the chorus' straightforward answer to the herald's question is in sharp contrast to Theseus' polemics here).

22   Cf. Smith (above, n. 3) 159–60.

23   Hdt. 3. 80–83; for a comparison of this passage with the debate on government in this play, see Jacqueline de Romilly, "Il pensiero di Euripide sulla tirannia," *Dioniso* 43 (1969) 178–79. W. R. Connor, *The New Politicians of Fifth-Century Athens* (Princeton 1971) 199–206, gives a useful survey of opinion on the Herodotean passage, and argues for a date in the late 430s or the 420s, that is, not too far removed from the dates usually preferred for the *Suppliant Women*.

24   Goossens (above, n. 1) esp. 433–36; cf. A. J. Podlecki, "A Pericles *Prosopon* in Attic Tragedy," *Euphrosyne* 7 (1975–76) 22–27.

25   Cf. W. R. Connor, "Theseus in Classical Athens," in A. G. Ward, ed., *The Quest for Theseus* (New York 1970) 152, who says of lines 404ff.: "These are the clichés of the Athenian fifth-century democracy, of which Theseus by Euripides' day had become the symbol and the representative. Moreover, nothing in the play suggests that presenting Theseus as a democratic politician was a particularly radical innovation by Euripides; rather he seems to be working within an already established tradition that held that Theseus' actions were a precedent for the democratic changes of the fifth century. Thus, Theseus, probably quite soon after the end of the tyranny, came to be represented as a democratic leader, and institutions were ascribed to him which were in fact sharp departures from preceding Athenian practice." On Athens' propensity to connect Theseus to important events of their own history, see Hans Herter, "Theseus der Athener," *RhM* 88 (1939) 244–86, 289–326. J. H. Oliver, *Demokratia, the Gods, and the Free World* (Baltimore 1960) 30 n. 29, rightly questions the mid-fourth-century date for the "discovery" of the constitution of Theseus proposed by Eberhard Ruschenbusch, "*PATRIOS POLITEIA,*" *Historia* 8 (1958) 408–15.

26   This evaluation is disputed by those who see satirical intent in the portrayal of "Thesean democracy." Greenwood (above, n. 12) 110–13 argues the case in its strongest form, but fails to convince. His chief contention is that Theseus wins the support of the people for the rescue of the corpses with an ease that proves his

democracy a sham. Greenwood perversely tries to turn Theseus' position as founder of the democratic constitution (352–53) into evidence for despotic intentions. Furthermore, he neglects the demonstration of the opening scenes that Theseus is justified in deciding to aid the suppliants, and the continued insistence on his ideal moderation in pursuing this policy (cf. e.g., 346–48, 385–92, 531–36, 558–63, 723–25). This combination of resolution and moderation reflects upon Theseus the statesmen; and his persuasion (355) of the people could hardly be less like the Theban herald's picture of demagogues flattering and swaying the mob for their own private gain (412–13). The brevity with which the motif of popular ratification is developed hardly discredits Theseus; rather, it shows his strength among the citizens. In this sense, Fitton (above, n. 12) 433 is right to point out that the "paradox of the Thucydidean verdict on Athens under Pericles" (Thuc. 2.65.9: "a democracy in name, in fact the rule of the principle man") is implicit also in the relation of Theseus to his people. This does not, however, justify his description of Theseus as a "rather smooth politician" devoid of respect for the will of the people. That is not implicit in Euripides' portrait of Theseus, or indeed in Thucydides' portrait of Pericles, either.

27 Cf. Goossens (above, n. 1) 420–29. In addition to the Herodotean passage already cited (above, n. 23), roughly contemporary parallels to the language and ideas of the agon include Hdt. 5.78 (on the advantages of Athenian *isēgoria*, a term implying equal right of speech and equality generally); Thuc. 2.65.7 (on the ambition and venality of Pericles' successors) and 5.16.1 (on Cleon's desire for war to cover his own crimes and lend credit to his slanders); Aristophanes' *Knights* 40–65 and *Peace* 632–48 (two of a number of passages that show the people of Athens bamboozled by demagogues).

28 This phrase, as commentators have noticed, has a special immediacy for the Athenian audience as an echo of the formal proclamation by which citizens were invited to speak in the Assembly.

29 Smith (above, n. 3) 160. Fitton (above, n. 12) 433–34 attempts to apply the herald's speech in detail to Theseus and Athens, equating *elpis* (479) with Athenian adventurism, and the lines on the facility with which men vote for war (481–85) with the people's unquestioning support of Theseus. But, as Theseus emphasizes in his reply, he wishes only to bury the dead and has no desire to make war unless compelled to do so (522, 558–60). Nothing in his mission corresponds to the "excess rage" (480) or the desire for domination (491–93) which the herald condemns. On the other hand, it would be wrong to conclude with H. D. F. Kitto, *Greek Tragedy: A Literary Study*³ (London 1961) 222 n. 2, that it is "immaterial" who offers this broad condemnation of war. Greenwood (above, n. 12) 100 is perhaps closer to the mark when he suggests that the herald's pacifism is especially striking because unexpected.

30 Cf. Iphis' pathetic wish for a second cycle of youth and age in which to correct the errors of the first (1081–86), and his decision to "get out of the way of the young" in death (*ekpodōn einai neois*, 1113). There are other occurrences of *neos*, often in the well-attested sense of "strange" or "menacing" (cf. *LSJ* s.v., 2.2): 91, 99, 415, 722, 1032. The elaborate network of references to youth in this play

makes the attempts of scholars interested in supposed political allusions to isolate passages as proof that Euripides favored or opposed Alcibiades all the more
unconvincing.

31 Cf. above, n. 1.

32 Collard (above, n. 1) 273 points out the significance of making the messenger an
Argive.

33 This brings to rest what D. J. Conacher, *Euripidean Drama* (Toronto 1967) 104,
rightly describes as a "minor theme" of this part of the play, introduced when the
Theban herald warns Theseus not to attempt to rescue the bodies of those whom
hubris destroyed (495; the example of Kapaneus follows immediately), and continued in the messenger's image of the *hubristēs laos* which destroys its own happiness (728–30). Collard (above, n. 1) 273 observes the crucial structural juncture
at which this speech is placed, but draws conclusions very different from mine
about its significance. Cf. below, n. 39.

34 On Euripides' invention of this incident, cf. Collard (above, n. 1) *ad loc.* Zuntz
(above, n. 1) 60–62 cogently rejects the widely accepted view of Wilamowitz that
it is an allusion to Spartan peace proposals of 425.

35 The character and implications of the second action furnish the clearest refutation of the view, concisely put by Zuntz (above, n.1) 11 that after the battle is over
the "action has reached its goal; the passion goes on." From such a perspective,
the funeral oration of Adrastos exists to purify the mothers' pathos by linking
it to the civic virtue Athens has embodied; Evadne's death universalizes their
suffering; the children's vision of vengeance in the second kommos is merely part
of the picture of "a family mourning in all its generations" (Collard [above, n. 1]
27, who adopts and develops Zuntz's interpretation). Apart from any other objections, this view simply denies any dynamic relation between the two main parts
of the play, not to mention any serious reflection in the second part of the political themes that dominate the first.

36 Cf. Collard (above, n. 1) 26, Smith (above, n. 3) 153.

37 Smith (above, n. 3) 162. Further: "The distinctions on the basis of which Theseus
undertook the war are blurred and then effaced in the comfortable release of
grief."

38 There is an extended discussion by Christopher Collard, "The Funeral Oration in
Euripides' *Supplices*," *BICS* 19 (1972) 39–53, who offers the most coherent case
for an "uncomplicated view" of the speech. While I sympathize with his efforts
to shore up the text and make sense of it at its face value, I am convinced that he
has had to ignore too many substantial oddities and smooth over too many genuine difficulties to make his case. Even Zuntz (above, n. 1) 23, who offers a ringing
defense of the speech as a laudable attempt to teach civic virtue, must sadly admit that it "sounds awkward, dry, and flat to the point of wrecking the drama."
On the other hand, those who believe that the speech is satirical find it hard to
explain why Euripides should suddenly interrupt and jeopardize his drama for
such a purpose. Norwood (above, n. 8) 126–29 makes his sharp attack on this
speech in the service of a bizarre thesis that much of the text of our play belongs
to a fourth-century closet drama later crudely conflated with genuine Euripides.
Fitton (above, n. 12) 437–40 makes a strong case for an ironic reading but can

only justify it by supposing that Euripides wanted to send up Aeschylus' lost *Eleusinioi*, which he thinks must have attempted a serious reconciliation of heroic and civic ideals.

39 Collard (above, n. 38) 40, 48 sees the importance of this assumption, but his arguments for making it are very thin: (a) Adrastos is on stage throughout the action and has learned from Theseus' management of the sort of moral and political problems at which he did so badly himself; (b) lines 734–49 are a "pathetic reflection [which] marks Adrastos' moral rehabilitation"; (c) Adrastos' death wish at 769 shows consciousness of the suffering he has brought on others. None of these interpretations is compelling, and against them can be argued: (a) Adrastos' silent presence on stage is not in itself an indication that he has learned or changed; (b) 734–49 do not so much show an acceptance of personal responsibility as the generalization of Adrastos' error to make it seem a failing of all mankind (*tous talaiporous brotous*, 734; *ō kenoi brotōn*, 744). This is not unlike the attempt to universalize his misery which Theseus earlier so roundly condemned (cf. 119, 162, 191–92, 195–200), and suggests a persistent moral obtuseness, not rehabilitation; (c) Adrastos' death wish is nowhere related to any suffering but his own and is a token of the extreme emotionalism, entirely like that of the mothers (cf. 770–71), which has characterized him from his first entrance (cf. 104–12 for their indications of his demonstrative misery).

40 Cf. Smith (above, n. 3) 162. Smith regards the extraordinarily irregular entrance of Theseus with an unidentified companion suggested by 838–40 as a device to effect an abrupt change in tone, but the lines effect only confusion. Collard (above, n. 38) 40 gives good reasons to suspect corruption; the text may indeed have suffered mutilation at this point. D. L. Page, *Actors' Interpolations in Greek Tragedy* (Oxford 1934) 69, suggests that the entrance is a product of later tampering.

41 *Neoisin astōn tōnd'* (843): the traditional interpretation refers this to the youth of Athens: "nicely ambivalent of [Theseus'] men and the theatre audience" says Collard (above, n. 1) ad loc. But he perhaps dismisses too hastily the interpretations of Smith (above, n. 3) 169 n. 20, who takes the phrase to mean "the young sons of these, your fellow townsmen," that is, the sons of the fallen heroes, who have been on stage throughout and will receive their fathers' ashes.

42 Zuntz (above, n. 1) 13–19; Collard (above, n. 1) 328.

43 Euripides is not just "suitably supplying some edifying biographical detail passed over by his predecessors" (Zuntz [above, n. 1] 23). Fitton (above, n. 12) 437 is correct to isolate the phrase *euprosēgoron stoma*, "affable in speech," as the point at which Euripides' flouting of the tradition becomes obvious. The death of Amphiaraos is subject to a similar "revisionist" interpretation at 925–27, after having been presented in the traditional way by the Theban herald (500–503). On these apparent contradictions, cf. Gamble (above, n. 10) 403–4.

44 I am inclined to agree with Collard (above, n. 1) *ad* 901–8, that something has gone wrong with our text and 904–8 must be deleted, although it remains a matter of speculation whether marginal notations of parallel passages have here ousted a more coherent and credible original. Collard's grounds for deleting 899–900 (on Parthenopaios' discreet conduct of his love affairs) are another matter. Apart from the much (and inconclusively) discussed problem of *hosas* in

899, the couplet offends only by its seeming frivolity and detraction from what Collard takes to be the intended conclusion of each of these sketches in a comment explicitly relevant to Adrastos' civic theme. The implicit etymology is quite Euripidean (cf. 496–97), and the fact that the etymology is not the "standard" one is in this context perhaps more an argument for authenticity than against.

45 The attempt of Smith (above, n. 3) 163 to restore the manuscripts' attribution of 925–31 to Adrastos, as attractive as it is in many ways, cannot withstand the objections raised by Collard (above, n. 38) 51 n. 22.

46 This need not be an "unorthodox" view of Amphiaraos' fate (cf. Soph. *El.* 836–41, Pind. *Nem.* 9.24–27), but it stands in unmediated opposition to the picture of divine chastisement in the speech of the Theban herald, 500–503. The herald no doubt has a *parti pris*, but it must be said that Zeus' punishment of the Seven is an unchallenged assumption of the play until this scene, and is even granted by their mothers in answer to the herald's speech (511–12). Cf. also Aesch. *Sept.* 609–14, where the prophet's death is treated as divine punishment for his association with evil men.

47 There is nothing here to support the contention of Grube (above, n. 5) 238 that Theseus "truly has had a change of heart." Collard (above, n. 1) *ad* 930–31 comments that Euripides invents the guest-friendship of Polynices "to accommodate him, even if perfunctorily, in praise of all the Seven." But why would Euripides be driven to such an expedient if he really wished Theseus to praise?

48 These lines are often held to be "Euripides . . . speaking for himself" (Greenwood [above, n. 12] 100) to condemn all war, no matter now noble its aims, but in view of the contradictory and unsatisfying nature of Adrastos' moralizing, the choice of vehicle is at least strange. Adrastos surely speaks here as Adrastos, not to convey the poet's private opinion but as part of a dramatic process through which (if at all) that opinion can be given form. Smith (above, n. 3) 164 is nearer the mark: "The play's two examples, of uncivilized ambition and ambition for civilization are made nonsense by the effacement of all distinctions."

49 E.g., Conacher (above, n. 33) 105, who indeed omits the episode from his analysis.

50 E.g., Zuntz (above, n. 1) 12–13.

51 E.g., Jacqueline de Romilly, *L'Évolution du pathétique d'Eschyle à Euripide* (Paris 1961) 37–39.

52 It is worth pointing out that the verb in this phrase is the same one with which Theseus condemned Adrastos' involvement with the Seven: *lampron de tholerōi dōma summeixas to son* (222; cf. 224).

53 In announcing her victory over all women in manly virtue, Evadne explicitly rejects the alternatives Iphis suggests (1062); *ergois Athanas*, that is, the traditional women's work of spinning and weaving, and *phrenōn eubouliai*, the good sense in which Adrastos was so disastrously lacking (161; cf. Smith [above, n. 3] 165).

54 The utter difference in the outlook of father and daughter is presented throughout their brief exchange in a way that blocks any real possibility of dialogue. Evadne does not want at first to answer Iphis' questions for fear of angering him (1050–51), but when she has told him what she plans it is he who urges silence,

she who wants the world to know (1066–67). He argues seemliness and sense (1052, 1056, 1062), she seeks grandeur and fame (1055–61).

55 Cf. above, n. 30 and Smith (above, n. 3) 165.

56 *Tosonde baros* is, as Collard (above, n. 1) ad loc. observes, an echo of the extended figure of heavy ashes at 1123–31, itself a variation of Aesch. *Ag.* 441–44.

57 Zuntz (above, n. 1) 71–78 has useful comments concerning the language of the oath and the historicity of the tripod upon which Athena orders that it be inscribed.

58 Zuntz (above, n. 1) 20.

59 E.g., Greenwood (above, n. 12) 105–6.

60 E.g., Conacher (above, n. 33) 108.

61 Smith (above, n. 3) 166–67 overstates the case, however, when he denies that Athena approves the mission: *sun theōi* (1226) and *chrē* (1219; cf. 1185) are explicit enough on this point.

62 S. E. Fish, *Self-Consuming Artifacts* (Berkeley, Calif. 1972) 1.

63 In the last analysis, the political character of this play, its focus on a dialectic of issues rather than a conflict of wills, seems to be precisely what has led many critics to conclude that it is somehow untragic or even undramatic. Thus, for example, Schmid (above, n. 8) 453 objects: "so interessant die von Euripides geschaffene Theseusfigur im kulturgeschichtlichem Sinn ist, so wenig passt dieser statuarischexemplarisch Idealismus in eine dramatische Bewegung." Evidently Schmid is seeking a different kind of "dramatic movement" from the one Euripides has provided, which Theseus' idealism not only fits but which it in large measure creates by forming one of its poles. On the figure of Theseus, cf. M. H. Shaw, "The *ETHOS* of Theseus in the *Suppliant Women*," *Hermes* 110 (1982) 3–19, which came to my attention too late to take account of, but in which I find many points of agreement.

The Bacchae *as Metatragedy*

This essay appears in a modified form as chapter 7 of my *Dionysiac Poetics and Euripides' "Bacchae"* (Princeton 1982). A summer stipend from the National Endowment for the Humanities in 1977 aided me in putting this material into final form, and I gratefully acknowledge this grant. To the bibliography on this subject should now be added Helene P. Foley's stimulating paper, "The Masque of Dionysus," *TAPA* 110 (1980) 107–33, which appeared while my study was in the course of publication.

1 For the *Frogs* see Charles Segal, "The Character and Cults of Dionysus and the Unity of the *Frogs*," *HSCP* 65 (1961) 207–42, esp. 211f., 225–30; for *Oedipus at Colonus* see Charles Segal, *Tragedy and Civilization: An Interpretation of Sophocles* (Cambridge, Mass. 1981) 406ff.

2 See Charles Segal, "The Two Worlds of Euripides' *Helen*," *TAPA* 102 (1971) 610–12; for Euripides' self-conscious reflection on dramatic conventions see also R. P. Winnington-Ingram, "Euripides: *Poiētēs Sophos*," *Arethusa* 2 (1969) 129–42, esp. 130–32.

3   See Jacqueline de Romilly, "Gorgias et le pouvoir de la poésie," *JHS* 93 (1973) 155–62, esp. 161f.; Segal, "Gorgias and the Psychology of the *Logos*," *HSCP* 66 (1962) 99–155, esp. 112ff., 125ff., 130ff.

4   E. R. Dodds, ed., *Euripides, Bacchae*[2] (Oxford 1960) 149.

5   Gilbert Norwood, *The Riddle of the "Bacchae"* (Manchester 1908); A. W. Verrall, *The "Bacchae" of Euripides and Other Essays* (London 1910). For discussion and criticism see Dodds (above, n. 4) xlviii–l and Victor Castellani, "That Troubled House of Pentheus in Euripides' *Bacchae*," *TAPA* 106 (1976) 61–83, esp. 63–67 with nn. 2–11.

6   See A. M. Dale, "Seen and Unseen on the Greek Stage," *WS* 69 (1956) 96–106, reprinted in *Collected Papers* (Cambridge 1969) 119–29, esp. 124f.; G. M. A. Grube, *The Drama of Euripides* (London 1941) 408–11; Gilbert Murray, *Euripides and His Age* (London 1913) 186f.; R. P. Winnington-Ingram, *Euripides and Dionysus* (Cambridge 1948) 82ff. Castellani (above, n. 5) 68 believes that there was some visual representation of the destruction, perhaps a wooden facade showing a displacement of the entablature corresponding to 591f.; but his attempt to reconcile this with 633f. is not successful, nor does his emendation of 633 (p. 68f. n. 16) commend itself.

7   Note that the syntactical construction of 633f. defines the action of the second verb, *suntethranotai*, in terms of the subjectivity of Pentheus, his perception under the influence of the madness, sent by the god:

συντεθράνωται δ' ἅπαν
πικροτάτους ἰδόντι δεσμοὺς τοὺς ἐμούς.

For the meaning of *suntethranōtai* see Dodds (above, n. 4, ad loc.) and Castellani (above, n. 5) 68f. n. 16. Castellani's view that 633f. is "symbolic utterance" while 591f. is performed action (68f., 75ff.) supports my view of a tension between the two kinds of representation. Hermann Rohdich, *Die Euripideische Tragödie: Untersuchung zu ihrer Tragik* (Heidelberg 1968) 132–37, also stresses the radical contradiction between what is imagined and what is seen, but he interprets this only in the light of the intellectual and religious crisis of the fifth century, as reflecting Euripides' continued concern with the clash of mythical and rational thought, "den Zwiespalt zwischen sophistischem und mythischem Weltverständnis, mit dem er die unüberwindliche Tragik als notwendiges Resultat ihrer Auseinandersetzung aus dem Theater mit sich fortnahm" (p. 135). Through this very contradiction, Rohdich suggests, this scene reenacts and renews on stage the power of Dionysiac inspiration (p. 135f.). The contradiction brings out the mysterious, invisible, and inward power of Dionysus that transcends or defies rational explanation: "Erst dadurch, dass das behauptete Wunder nicht geschieht, zeigt sich das Dionysische als ein Phänomen der menschlichen Seele, das auch den religiösen Skeptiker betrifft" (p. 136). Gilbert Norwood, *Essays on Euripidean Drama* (Berkeley, Calif. 1954) 61–63, appreciated the reference of the palace miracle to the theme of "stage illusion" (p. 61), but pulled back from the logical conclusion of his argument: "In precisely the same way the Athenian choristers pretend to be mastered by glamour, and so to believe that the house falls; the spectator believes them thus possessed, but does not believe that it falls. He cannot, for he sees that it is unchanged, just as he sees that the head is in fact the king's. The miracle, in short, is effected, but not the downfall: it is the divinely induced belief in the downfall; and Euripides shows the method by which glamour may be created—that and nothing more" (p. 62).

8 See Norwood (above, n. 7) 62: "Through Dionysus he [Euripides] casts on his Maenads the spell that every competent playwright casts on his audience." For some suggestions about possible relations between the illusionistic element in the play and the ecstatic character of Dionysiac cult see Winnington-Ingram (above, n. 6) 164f. and M. R. Glover, "The *Bacchae*," *JHS* 49 (1929) 84ff.

9 See René Girard, *Violence and the Sacred*, trans. P. Gregory (Baltimore 1977) 162ff., 166–68, esp. 168 (original French ed. [1972] 225ff., 232–34): "Masks stand at that unequivocal frontier between the human and the 'divine,' between a differentiated order in the process of disintegration and its final undifferentiated state—the point where all differences, all monstrosities are concentrated, and from which a new order will emerge" (p. 168).

10 Walter F. Otto, *Dionysus, Myth and Cult* (Bloomington, Ind. 1965) 90f. For the cult significance of the Dionysiac mask see also Margarete Bieber, s.v. "Maske," *RE* 14.2 (1930) 2113.

11 For the double reference of *sophia* to both poetry and religion see Winnington-Ingram (above, n. 6) 167f. The meaning of *sophia* in the play has been much discussed: see Winnington-Ingram, 62f.; Marylin Arthur, "The Choral Odes of the *Bacchae* of Euripides," *YCS* 22 (1972) 176–79; William Arrowsmith's introduction to his translation (1959) in David Grene and Richmond Lattimore, eds., *The Complete Greek Tragedies*, Modern Library Edition, vol. 7 (New York, n.d.) 347f.; Hans Diller, "Die *Bakchen* und ihre Stellung im Spätwerk des Euripides," *Ak. der Wiss. u. Lit. in Mainz, Abh. des Geistes- u. Sozialwiss. Kl.* 5 (1955), reprinted in E.-R. Schwinge, ed., *Euripides, Wege der Forschung* 89 (Darmstadt 1968) 482–84 with the literature there cited.

12 Cf. the use of the verb *mousoō* in a literary context in Ar. *Lys.* 1127.

13 This scene (lines 912–76), as Dodds (above, n. 4) 192 observes, also shows the increasing power of Dionysus as a god both of religious ecstasy and dramatic illusion, for Dionysus' robing of Pentheus answers Pentheus' attempt to disrobe the stranger at 493–97. The mortal's attempt to remove the god's signs of power are now echoed by the god, who puts his own characteristic ritual dress on his antagonist.

14 For this monstrous side of Pentheus and its implications see Charles Segal, "Euripides' *Bacchae*: Conflict and Mediation," *Ramus* 6 (1977) 103–20, esp. 108–10.

15 For the spatial dimension of the conflicts see Segal (above, n. 14) 112–14; also Castellani (above, n. 5) 72f.; Hans Diller, "Umwelt und Masse als dramatische Faktoren bei Euripides," *Entretiens Hardt* 103f.; William Scott, "Two Suns over Thebes: Imagery and Stage Effects in the *Bacchae*," *TAPA* 105 (1975) 342f.; H. J. Tschiedel, "Natur und Mensch in den *Bakchen* des Euripides," *A&A* 23 (1977) 64–76, esp. 67–70.

16 See J. C. Kamerbeek, "Mythe et réalité dans l'oeuvre d'Euripide," *Entretiens Hardt* 8: "Tout le charme enivrant du plus cruel mythe hellénique s'exhale de leur poésie en contrepoint avec l'horreur provoquée par le spectacle de la ruine des humains." On the ambiguity of the chorus see also Arthur (above, n. 11) 145–77; Norwood (above, n. 7) 67; Walter Kranz, *Stasimon* (Berlin 1933) 235; Hans Bogner, *Der tragische Gegensatz* (Heidelberg 1947) 242f.; Diller (above, n. 11) 472.

17 Victor Castellani has called to my attention the possibility that *prosōpon* in 1277 might refer to the tragic mask, and I am indebted to him for this suggestion. The word may carry some such reference also at *Cyclops* 227 and *Orestes* 224. Eur. *El.* 855ff. provides a possible parallel: when Orestes returns to the stage with the severed head of Aegisthus, he, like Agave, very probably carries the mask of the actor who played that unfortunate character's role. Jeanne Roux, *Euripide, Les Bacchantes* (Paris 1972) 2:610f. (ad loc.) makes an interesting observation on the word and its scenic effect: "Plus frappant que *kephalē* parce que le visage implique à la fois une expression humaine et une identité. Le mot contient aussi l'indication d'un jeu de scène: jusque là, Agavé tenait la tête par la chevelure et ne pouvait voir le visage que Cadmos l'invite ici à examiner" (p. 610).

18 The translation of 1020–23 is that of Winnington-Ingram (above, n. 6) 126, with Tyrrell's emendation. For the problem of the text and translation of these lines see Dodds (above, n. 4) and Roux (above, n. 17).

19 See Winnington-Ingram (above, n. 6) 127: "The irony of it [the hunter as hunted beast] will be pleasant to Dionysus, and he will smile, not for the first time. Now at last the meaning of that enigmatic smile with which the 'gentle beast' surrendered to his captors (439) is made clear."

20 For some psychoanalytic approaches to the play see Philip Slater, *The Glory of Hera* (Boston 1968) chaps. 9 and 10; William Sale, "The Psychoanalysis of Pentheus in the *Bacchae* of Euripides," *YCS* 22 (1972) 63–82; George Devereux, "The Psychotherapy Scene in Euripides' *Bacchae*," *JHS* 90 (1970) 35–48. For further discussion see Castellani (above, n. 5) 67 n. 13; Charles Segal, "Pentheus and Hippolytus on the Couch and on the Grid: Psychoanalytic and Structuralist Readings of Greek Tragedy," *CW* 72 (1978) 129–48.

21 See Roux (above, n. 17) 2.241 (ad v. 4). Cf. also lines 296, 302, 477f., 607, 618f., 944, 1266, 1329f., and so on. For other aspects of these *meta*-compounds in the play see B. M. W. Knox, "Second Thoughts in Greek Tragedy," *GRBS* 7 (1966) 229.

22 See Roux (above, n. 17) ad loc.

23 For the extraordinary quality of Dionysus' presence on stage see Henri Jeanmaire, *Dionysos* (Paris 1951) 139f.

24. See, e.g., Felix Wassermann, "Die Bakchantinnen des Euripides," *NJbb* 5 (1929) 274:

> Die Doppelgestaltigkeit des Gottes, die es ihm erlaubt, aus einer Sphäre in die andere hinüberzuwechseln, wird aus seinem eigenen Wort deutlich, dass die dem menschlichen Auge des Zuschauers sich unmittelbar bietende Gestalt eigentlich nur Maske ist (4, 53). Verkörperung des Grundprinzips des mit seinem Kult verknüpften dramatischen Spiels, erscheint der Gott selbst

als Schauspieler und dadurch dann sein Gegner als ein Mensch, der nur die *eine* anthropomorphe Gestalt des göttlichen Schauspielers erkennt und in der Maske Wirklichkeit sieht, um dadurch in sein Verderben zu sturzen.

25 Devereux (above, n. 20) views the scene as a return to "reality" in a psychological sense, as presenting a kind of psychotherapy that returns Agave to a normal state of mind.

26 See Arrowsmith (above, n. 11) 355f.; B. M. W. Knox, "The Hippolytus of Euripides," *YCS* 13 (1952) 30f.; R. P. Winnington-Ingram, "Hippolytus: A Study in Causation," *Entretiens Hardt* 190f.

27 See in general Jacqueline de Romilly, "Le thème du bonheur dans les *Bacchantes*," *REG* 76 (1963) 361–80.

28 For the ambiguity of the play as a *pharmakon* see Pietro Pucci, "Euripides: The Monument and the Sacrifice," *Arethusa* 10 (1977) 165–95, esp. 167f., 178.

29 Gorgias 82 B23 DK.

Selected Bibliography of Euripidean Criticism since World War II

What follows is a sampling of the vast literature on Euripides that has appeared since World War II. Editions and commentaries have been excluded, as have purely philological studies (e.g., works on transmission of the text, chronology, metrics, as well as textual notes). Those interested in more complete listings should consult *L'Année Philologique*. What has been included here is designed to give access to a wide range of literary studies of high quality. No "school" or tendency has been privileged at the expense of any other, the goal being rather to illustrate the variety of directions Euripidean criticism has taken in the last four decades. Abbreviations and short titles used in the Bibliography will be found preceding the Notes, pp. 175–76.

I. General Studies Devoted in Part to Euripides

Diller, Hans. "Erwartung, Enttäuschung und Erfüllung in der griechischen Tragödie." *Serta Aenipontana Philol.* (Innsbruck 1962) 93–115. Reprinted in H.-J. Newiger and H. Seyffert, eds. *Kleine Schriften zur antiken Literatur* 304–34. Munich 1971.

Ferguson, John. *A Companion to Greek Tragedy.* Austin, Tex. 1972.

Jens, Walter, ed. *Die Bauformen der griechischen Tragödie. Poetica* Beiheft 6 (Munich 1971).

Jones, John. *On Aristotle and Greek Tragedy.* London 1962.

Kitto, H. D. F. *Greek Tragedy: A Literary Study*[3]. London 1961.

Knox, B. M. W. "Second Thoughts in Greek Tragedy." *GRBS* 7 (1966) 213–32. Reprinted in *Word and Action* 231–249.

Lattimore, Richmond. *Story Patterns in Greek Tragedy.* Ann Arbor, Mich. 1964.

Lesky, Albin. *Greek Tragic Poetry.* Translated from the 3d German edition by Matthew Dillon. New Haven, Conn. 1983.

———. *Greek Tragedy.* Translated from the 3d German edition by H. A. Frankfort. London 1965.

Parry, Hugh. *The Lyric Poems of Greek Tragedy.* Toronto 1978.

Pohlenz, Max. *Die griechische Tragödie*[2]. Göttingen 1954.

Romilly, Jacqueline de. *L'évolution du pathétique d'Eschyle à Euripide.* Paris 1961.

Rosenmeyer, T. G. *The Masks of Tragedy.* Austin, Tex. 1963.

Spira, Andreas. *Untersuchungen zum Deus ex Machina bei Sophokles und Euripides.* Kallmünz 1960.

Steidle, Wolfgang. *Studien zum antiken Drama: Unter besonderer Berücksichtigung des Bühnenspiels.* Munich 1968.

Taplin, Oliver. *Greek Tragedy in Action.* Berkeley, Calif. 1978.

Vickers, Brian. *Towards Greek Tragedy: Drama, Myth, Society.* London 1973.

Walsh, G. B. *The Varieties of Enchantment: Early Greek Views of the Nature and Function of Poetry.* Chapel Hill, N.C. 1984.

II. General Studies on Euripides

Arnott, W. G. "Euripides and the Unexpected." *G&R* 20 (1973) 49–63.

———. "Red Herrings and Other Baits, A Study in Euripidean Techniques." *MPL* 3 (1978).

Arrowsmith, William. "A Greek Theater of Ideas." *Arion* 2 no. 3 (1963) 32–56. Reprinted slightly abridged in E. Segal, ed. *Euripides* 13–33.

Barlow, S. A. *The Imagery of Euripides.* London 1971.

Benedetto, Vincenzo di. *Euripide: teatro e società.* Turin 1971.

Bergson, Leif. *Die Relativität der Werte im Frühwerk des Euripides.* Stockholm 1971.

Burnett, A. P. *Catastrophe Survived: Euripides' Plays of Mixed Reversal.* Oxford 1971.

Buttrey, T. V. "Tragedy as Form in Euripides." *Michigan Quarterly Rev.* 15 (1976) 155–72.

Collard, Christopher. "Formal Debates in Euripides' Drama." *G&R* 22 (1975) 58–71.

Conacher, D. J. *Euripidean Drama.* Toronto 1967.

———. "Rhetoric and Relevance in Euripidean Drama." *AJP* 102 (1981) 3–25.

Diller, Hans. "Umwelt und Masse als dramatische Faktoren bei Euripides." *Entretiens Hardt* 89–121. Reprinted in H.-J. Newiger and H. Seyffert, eds. *Kleine Schriften zur antiken Literatur* 335–58. Munich 1971.

Eisner, Robert. "Euripides' Use of Myth." *Arethusa* 7 (1979) 153–74.

Erbse, Hartmut. *Studien zum Prolog der euripideischen Tragödie.* Berlin 1984.

Foley, H. P. *Ritual Irony: Poetry and Sacrifice in Euripides.* Ithaca, N.Y. 1985.

Friedrich, W. H. *Euripides und Diphilos: Zur Dramaturgie der Spätformen.* Zetemata 5 (Munich 1953).

Garzya, Antonio. *Pensiero e tecnica drammatica in Euripide: Saggio sul motivo della salvazione nei suoi drammi.* Naples 1962.

Grube, G. M. A. *The Drama of Euripides.* London 1941.

Hamilton, Richard. "Prologue and Plot in Four Plays of Euripides." *AJP* 99 (1978) 277–302.

Hourmouziades, N. C. *Production and Imagination in Euripides: Form and Function of the Scenic Space.* Athens 1965.

Jens, Walter. "Euripides." Introduction to Euripides, *Sämtliche Tragödien,* vol. 1, vii–xxxix. Stuttgart 1958. Reprinted in Schwinge, ed. *Euripides* 1–35.

Kamerbeek, J. C. "Mythe et realité dans l'oeuvre d'Euripide." *Entretiens Hardt* 1–25.

Knox, B. M. W. "Euripidean Comedy." In Alan Cheuse and Richard Koffler, eds. *The*

Rarer Action, Essays in Honor of Francis Fergusson. New Brunswick, N.J. 1971. Reprinted in *Word and Action* 250–74.

Lesky, Albin. "Psychologie bei Euripides." *Entretiens Hardt* 125–50. Reprinted in Walther Kraus, ed. *Gesammelte Schriften* (Bern 1966) 247–63 and in Schwinge, ed. *Euripides* 79–101.

Martin, Victor. "Euripide et Menandre face à leur publique." *Entretiens Hardt* 243–83.

Matthiessen, Kjeld. *Elektra, Taurische Iphigenie, und Helena.* Hypomnemata 4 (Göttingen 1964).

Pucci, Pietro. "Euripides: The Monument and the Sacrifice." *Arethusa* 10 (1977) 165–95.

Reinhardt, Karl. "Die Sinneskrise bei Euripides." *Eranos Jb* 26 (1957) 279–317. Reprinted in Carl Becker, ed. *Tradition und Geist: Gesammelte Essays zur Dichtung* (Göttingen 1960) 227–56 and in Schwinge, ed. *Euripides* 507–42.

Rivier, André. *Essai sur le tragique d'Euripide*². Paris 1975.

Rohdich, Hermann. *Die Euripideische Tragödie: Untersuchungen zu ihrer Tragik.* Heidelberg 1968.

Sale, William. *Existentialism and Euripides.* *Ramus* monograph. Berwick, Victoria, Australia 1977.

Schwinge, E.-R. *Die Verwendung der Stichomythie in den Dramen des Euripides.* Heidelberg 1968.

Segal, Charles. "Pentheus and Hippolytus on the Couch and on the Grid: Psychoanalytic and Structuralist Renderings of Greek Tragedy." *CW* 72 (1978) 129–48.

Stahl, H. P. "On 'Extra-Dramatic' Communication of Characters in Euripides." *YCS* 25 (1977) 159–76.

Strohm, Hans. *Euripides: Interpretationen zur dramatischen Form.* Zetemata 15 (1957).

———. "Trug und Täuschung in der euripideischen Dramatik." *Wurzburger Jb für die Altertumswiss.* 4 (1949–50) 140–56. Reprinted in Schwinge, ed. *Euripides* 345–72.

———. "Zum Problem der Einheit des euripideischen Bühnenwerkes." *WS* 15 (1981) 135–55.

———. "Zur Gestaltung euripideischen Prologreden." *Grazer Beiträge* 6 (1977) 113–32.

Vellacott, Philip. *Ironic Drama: A Study of Euripides' Method and Meaning.* Cambridge 1975.

Walsh, G. B. "Public and Private in Three Plays of Euripides." *CP* 74 (1979) 294–309.

Webster, T. B. L. "Euripides: Traditionalist and Innovator." In D. C. Allen and H. T. Rowell, eds. *The Poetic Tradition* 27–45. Baltimore 1968.

———. *The Tragedies of Euripides.* London 1967.

Whitman, C. H. *Euripides and the Full Circle of Myth.* Cambridge, Mass. 1974.

Winnington-Ingram, W. P. "Euripides: Poiētēs Sophos." *Arethusa* 2 (1969) 127–42.

Wolff, Christian. "Euripides." In *Ancient Writers: Greece and Rome* 1:233–66. New York 1982.

Zürcher, Walter. *Die Darstellung des Menschen im Drama des Euripides.* Basel 1947.

Zuntz, Günther. "Contemporary Politics in Euripides." *Acta Congressus Madvigiani* 1 (1958) 155–62. Reprinted in *Opuscula Selecta* 54–61. Manchester 1972.

III. Individual Plays
ALCESTIS

Arrowsmith, William. "Introduction." In Euripides, *Alcestis*, trans. William Arrowsmith, 3–29. New York 1974.
Beye, C. R. "Alcestis and Her Critics." *GRBS* 2 (1959) 109–27.
Burnett, A. P. "The Virtues of Admetus." *CP* 60 (1965) 240–55. Reprinted without notes in E. Segal, ed. *Euripides* 51–69.
Castellani, Victor. "Notes on the Structure of Euripides' *Alcestis*." *AJP* 100 (1979) 487–96.
Erbse, Hartmut. "Euripides' *Alkestis*." *Philologus* 116 (1972) 32–52.
Fritz, Kurt von. "Euripides' *Alkestis* und ihre modernen Nachahmer und Kritiker." *A&A* 5 (1956) 27–69. Reprinted in *Antike und Moderne Tragödie* 256–321. Berlin 1962.
Gregory, Justina. "Euripides' *Alcestis*." *Hermes* 107 (1979) 259–70.
Kullmann, Wolfgang. "Zum Sinngehalt der euripideischen *Alkestis*." *A&A* 13 (1967) 127–49.
Lesky, Albin. "Der angeklagte Admet." *Maske und Kothurn* 10 (1964) 203–16. Reprinted in Walther Kraus, ed. *Gesammelte Schriften* 281–94. Bern 1966.
Nielsen, R. M. "Alcestis: A Paradox in Dying." *Ramus* 5 (1976) 92–102.
Paduano, Guido. *La formazione del mondo ideologico e poetico di Euripide: Alcesti-Medea*. Pisa 1968.
Smith, W. D. "The Ironic Structure in *Alcestis*." *Phoenix* 14 (1960) 127–45.
Sutton, D. F. "Satyric Elements in the *Alcestis*." *RSC* 21 (1973) 384–91.

ANDROMACHE

Albini, Umberto. "Un dramma d'avanguardia: l'*Andromaca* di Euripide." *Maia* 26 (1974) 83–95.
Boulter, P. N. "Sophia and Sophrosyne in *Andromache*." *Phoenix* 20 (1966) 51–58.
Erbse, Hartmut. "Euripides' *Andromache*." *Hermes* 94 (1966) 276–97. Reprinted in Schwinge, ed. *Euripides* 275–304.
Kovacs, P. D. *The "Andromache" of Euripides*. American Classical Studies 6 (1980).
Lee, K. H. "Euripides' *Andromache*: Observations on Form and Meaning." *Antichthon* 9 (1975) 4–16.
Lesky, Albin. "Der Ablauf der Handlung in der *Andromache* des Euripides." *Anzeiger der Ak. der Wiss. in Wien* 84 (1947) 99–115. Reprinted in Walther Kraus, ed. *Gesammelte Schriften* 144–55. Bern 1966.

BACCHAE

Arrowsmith, William. "Introduction to *The Bacchae*." In David Grene and Richmond Lattimore, eds. *The Complete Greek Tragedies* 4:530–41. Chicago 1959.
Arthur, M. B. "The Choral Odes of the *Bacchae* of Euripides." *YCS* 22 (1972) 145–80.
Burnett, A. P. "Pentheus and Dionysus: Host and Guest." *CP* 75 (1970) 15–29.
Castellani, Victor. "That Troubled House of Pentheus in Euripides' *Bacchae*." *TAPA* 106 (1976) 61–83.

Devereux, George. "The Psychotherapy Scene in Euripides' *Bacchae.*" *JHS* 90 (1970) 35–48.

Diller, Hans. "Die *Bakchen* und ihre Stellung im Spätwerk des Euripides." *Ak. der Wiss. u. Lit. in Mainz, Abh. der Geistes- u. Sozialwiss. Kl.* 5 (1955) 453–71. Reprinted in H.-J. Newiger and H. Seyffert, eds. *Kleine Schriften zur antiken Literatur* (Munich 1971) 369–87, and in Schwinge, ed. *Euripides* 469–92.

Dyer, R. R. "Image and Symbol. The Link Between the Two Worlds of the *Bacchae.*" *AUMLA* 21 (1964) 15–26.

Foley, H. P. "The Masque of Dionysus." *TAPA* 110 (1980) 107–33.

Glenn, Justin. "Pentheus and the Psychologists: Some Recent Views of the *Bacchae.*" *RSC* 27 (1979) 5–10.

Gold, B. K. "*EUKOSMIA* in Euripides' *Bacchae.*" *AJP* 98 (1977) 3–15.

Podlecki, A. J. "Individual and Group in Euripides' *Bacchae.*" *AC* 43 (1947) 143–65.

Romilly, Jacqueline de. "Le thème du bonheur dans les *Bacchantes.*" *REG* 76 (1963) 361–80.

Sale, William. "The Psychoanalysis of Pentheus in the *Bacchae* of Euripides." *YCS* 22 (1972) 63–82.

Scott, W. C. "Two Suns Over Thebes: Imagery and Stage Effects in the *Bacchae.*" *TAPA* 105 (1975) 333–46.

Seaford, Richard. "Dionysiac Drama and the Dionysiac Mysteries." *CQ* 31 (1981) 252–75.

Segal, Charles. *Dionysiac Poetics and Euripides' "Bacchae".* Princeton 1982.

———. "Euripides' *Bacchae*: Conflict and Mediation." *Ramus* 6 (1977) 103–20.

———. "The Menace of Dionysus: Sex Roles and Reversals in Euripides' *Bacchae.*" *Arethusa* 11 (1978) 185–202.

Seidensticker, Bernd. "Comic Elements in Euripides' *Bacchae.*" *AJP* 99 (1978) 303–20.

———. "Pentheus." *Poetica* 5 (1972) 35–63.

———. "Sacrificial Ritual in the *Bacchae.*" *Arktouros* 181–90.

Winnington-Ingram, R. P. *Euripides and Dionysus: An Interpretation of the "Bacchae".* Cambridge 1948.

CYCLOPS

Arnott, W. G. "Parody and Ambiguity in Euripides' *Cyclops.*" *Antidosis*, Festschrift Kraus = *WS* Beiheft 5 (1972) 21–30.

Chalkia, Irène. "Fonctions narratives et substitutions dans le *Cyclope* d'Euripide." *Hellenica* 31 (1979) 293–315.

Hamilton, Richard. "Euripides' Cyclopean Symposium." *Phoenix* 33 (1979) 287–92.

Konstan, David. "An Anthropology of Euripides' *Cyclops.*" *Ramus* 10 (1981) 87–103.

Rossi, L. E. "Il *Ciclope* di Euripide come *KOMOS* 'mancato.'" *Maia* 23 (1971) 10–38.

Sutton, D. F. "Euripides' *Cyclops* and the *Kyôgen Esashi Jûô.*" *QUCC* 32 (1979) 53–64.

Ussher, R. G. "The *Cyclops* of Euripides." *G&R* 18 (1971) 166–79.

ELECTRA

Arnott, W. G. "Double the Vision: A Reading of Euripides' *Electra.*" *G&R* 27 (1981) 179–92.

Bond, G. W. "Euripides' Parody of Aeschylus." *Hermathena* 118 (1974) 1–14.

Gellie, G. H. "Tragedy and Euripides' *Electra*." *BICS* 28 (1981) 1–12.

Kubo, Masaaki. "The Norm of Myth: Euripides' *Electra*." *HSCP* 71 (1966) 15–31.

Mirto, M. S. "Il Sacrificio tra metafora e mechanema nell' *Elettra* di Euripide." *CCC* 1 (1980) 299–329.

Morwood, J. H. W. "The Pattern of the Euripidean *Electra*." *AJP* 102 (1981) 362–70.

O'Brien, M. J. "Orestes and the Gorgon: Euripides' *Electra*." *AJP* 85 (1964) 13–39.

Pucci, Pietro. "Euripides Heautontimoroumenos." *TAPA* 98 (1967) 365–71.

Schwinge, E.-R. "Abermals die Elektren." *RhM* 62 (1969) 1–13.

Solmsen, Friedrich. "Electra and Orestes: Three Recognitions in Greek Tragedy." *Mededelingen der Koninkl. Nederlandse Ak. van Wettenschappen*, Afd. Letterk. 30, 2 (1967) 31–62.

Stoessl, Franz. "Die *Electra* des Euripides." *RhM* 99 (1956) 47–92.

Tarkow, T. A. "The Scar of Orestes: Observations on a Euripidean Innovation." *RhM* 74 (1981) 143–53.

Theiler, Willy. "Die ewigen Elektren." *WS* 79 (1966) 102–12.

Walsh, G. B. "The First Stasimon of Euripides' *Electra*." *YCS* 25 (1977) 277–89.

Zeitlin, F. I. "The Argive Festival of Hera and Euripides' *Electra*." *TAPA* 101 (1970) 645–69.

HECUBA

Abrahamson, E. L. "Euripides' Tragedy of Hecuba." *TAPA* 83 (1952) 120–29.

Adkins, A. W. H. "Basic Greek Values in Euripides' *Hecuba* and *Hercules Furens*." *CQ* n.s. 16 (1966) 192–219.

Daitz, S. G. "Concepts of Freedom and Slavery in Eurpides' *Hecuba*." *Hermes* 99 (1971) 217–26.

Gellie, G. H. "*Hecuba* and Tragedy." *Antichthon* 14 (1980) 30–44.

Luschnig, C. A. E. "Euripides' *Hecabe*: The Time is Out of Joint." *CJ* 71 (1976) 227–34.

Meridor, Ra'anana. "Hecuba's Revenge." *AJP* 99 (1978) 28–35.

Rosivach, V. J. "The First Stasimon of the *Hecuba*." *AJP* 96 (1975) 349–62.

Steidle, Wolf. "Zur *Hekabe* des Euripides." *WS* 74 (1966) 133–42.

HELEN

Alt, Karin. "Zur Anagnorisis in der *Helena*." *Hermes* 90 (1962) 6–24.

Burnett, A. P. "Euripides' *Helen*, a Comedy of Ideas." *CP* 55 (1960) 151–63.

Dimock, G. E., Jr. "God or not God, or between the two?—Euripides' *Helen*." Engel Lecture, Smith College, Northampton, Mass. 1977.

Segal, Charles. "The Two Worlds of Euripides' *Helen*." *TAPA* 102 (1971) 553–614.

Wolff, Christian. "On Euripides' *Helen*." *HSCP* 77 (1973) 61–84.

Zuntz, Günther. "On Euripides' *Helena*: Theology and Irony." *Entretiens Hardt* 201–27.

HERACLES

Adkins, A. W. H. "Basic Greek Values in Euripides' *Hecuba* and *Hercules Furens*." *CQ* n.s. 16 (1966) 192–219.

Arrowsmith, William. "Introduction to *Heracles*." In David Grene and Richmond Lattimore, eds. *The Complete Greek Tragedies* 3:266–81. Chicago 1959.

Barlow, S. A. "Structure and Dramatic Realism in Euripides' *Herakles*." *G&R* 29 (1982) 115–25.

Chalk, H. H. O. "*ARETE* and *BIA* in Euripides' *Herakles*." *JHS* 82 (1962) 7–18.

Gregory, Justina. "Euripides' *Heracles*." *YCS* 25 (1977) 259–75.

Kamerbeek, J. C. "Unity and Meaning of Euripides' *Herakles*." *Mnem.* 19 (1966) 1–16.

Pachet, Pierre. "Le bâtard monstrueux." *Poétique* 12 (1972) 531–43.

Romilly, Jacqueline de. "Le refus du suicide dans l'*Héraclès* d'Euripide." *Archaiognosia* 1 (1980) 1–10.

Ruck, Carl. "Duality and the Madness of Herakles." *Arethusa* 9 (1976) 53–75.

HERACLIDAE

Avery, H. C. "Euripides' *Heracleidai*." *AJP* 92 (1971) 539–65.

Burian, Peter. "Euripides' *Heraclidae*: An Interpretation." *CP* 72 (1977) 1–21.

Burnett, A. P. "Tribe and City, Custom and Decree in *Children of Heracles*." *CP* 71 (1976) 4–26.

Fitton, J. W. "The *Suppliant Women* and the *Heraklidai* of Euripides." *Hermes* 89 (1961) 430–61.

Stoessl, Franz. "Die *Herakliden* des Euripides." *Philologus* 100 (1956) 207–34.

Zuntz, Günther. "Is the *Heraclidae* Mutilated?" *CQ* (1947) 46–52. Reprinted in *Opuscula Selecta* 43–53. Manchester 1972.

———. *The Political Plays of Euripides*. Manchester 1955.

HIPPOLYTUS

Dimock, G. E., Jr. "Euripides' *Hippolytus*, or Virtue Rewarded." *YCS* 25 (1977) 239–258.

Fauth, Wolfgang. *Hippolytos und Phaidra: Bemerkungen zu religiösen Hintergrund eines tragischen Konflikts*, parts 1 and 2. Ak. der Wiss. u. der Lit. in Mainz, *Abh. der Geistes- u. Sozialwiss. Kl.* 9 (1958), 8 (1959).

Fitzgerald, G. J. "Misconception, Hypocrisy, and the Structure of Euripides' *Hippolytus*." *Ramus* 2 (1973) 20–40.

Herter, Hans. "Hippolytos und Phaidra." In Ernst Vogt, ed. *Kleine Schriften* 119–56. Munich 1975.

Knox, B. M. W. "The *Hippolytus* of Euripides." *YCS* 13 (1952) 3–31. Reprinted in *Word and Action* 205–30, and without notes in E. Segal, ed. *Euripides* 90–114.

Kovacs, P. D. "Shame, Pleasure, and Honor in Phaedra's Great Speech (Euripides, *Hippolytus* 375–87)." *AJP* 101 (1980) 287–303.

Reckford, K. J. "Phaedra and Pasiphae: The Pull Backward." *TAPA* 104 (1974) 307–28.

———. "Phaethon, Hippolytus, and Aphrodite." *TAPA* 103 (1972) 405–32.

Segal, Charles. "Curse and Oath in Euripides' *Hippolytus*." *Ramus* 1 (1972) 165–80.

———. "Euripides, *Hippolytus* 108–112: Tragic Irony and Tragic Justice." *Hermes* 97 (1969) 297–305.

———. "Shame and Purity in Euripides' *Hippolytus*." *Hermes* 98 (1970) 278–99.

———. "Solar Imagery and Tragic Heroism in Euripides' *Hippolytus*." *Arktouros* (1979) 151–61.

———. "The Tragedy of the *Hippolytus*: The Waters of Ocean and the Untouched Meadows." *HSCP* 70 (1965) 117–69.

Smith, W. D. "Staging in the Central Scene of the *Hippolytus*." *TAPA* 91 (1960) 162–77.

Turato, Fabio. "L'*Ippolito* di Euripide tra realtà e suggestioni di fuga." *BIFG* 1 (1974) 136–63.

———. "Seduzione della parola e dramma dei segni nell' *Ippolito* di Euripide." *BIFG* 3 (1976) 159–83.

Winnington-Ingram, R. P. "Hippolytus: A Study in Causation." *Entretiens Hardt* 169–97.

ION

Burnett, A. P. "Human Resistance and Divine Persuasion in Euripides' *Ion*." *CP* 57 (1962) 89–103.

Gauger, Barbara. *Gott und Mensch im "Ion" des Euripides: Untersuchungen zum 3. Epeisodion des Dramas.* Bonn 1977.

Imhof, Marx. *Eurpides' "Ion": Eine literarische Studie.* Bern 1966.

Immerwahr, H. I. "Athenian Images in Euripides' *Ion*." *Hellenica* 25 (1972) 277–97.

Loraux, Nicole. "Créuse autochthone." In *Les enfants d'Athéna: idées athéniennes sur la citoyenneté et la division des sexes* 197–253. Paris 1981.

Mastronarde, D. J. "Iconography and Imagery in Euripides' *Ion*." *CSCA* 8 (1975) 163–76.

Mueller, Gerhard. "Beschreibung von Kunstwerken im *Ion* des Euripides." *Hermes* 103 (1975) 25–44.

Rosivach, V. J. "Earthborns and Olympians: The Parodos of the *Ion*." *CQ* 27 (1977) 284–94.

Walsh, G. B. "Rhetoric of Birthright and Race in Euripides' *Ion*." *Hermes* 106 (1978) 301–15.

Wolff, Christian. "The Design and Myth in Euripides' *Ion*." *HSCP* 69 (1965) 169–94.

IPHIGENIA IN AULIS

Bain, David. "The Prologues of Euripides' *Iphigeneia in Aulis*." *CQ* 27 (1977) 10–26.

Dimock, G. E., Jr. "Introduction." In Euripides, *Iphigeneia at Aulis*, trans. W. S. Merwin and G. E. Dimock, Jr., 3–21. New York 1978.

Foley, H. P. "Marriage and Sacrifice in Euripides' *Iphigeneia in Aulis*." *Arethusa* 15 (1982) 159–80.

Knox, B. M. W. "Euripides' *Iphigenia in Aulide* 1–163 (in that order)." *YCS* 22 (1972) 239–62. Reprinted in *Word and Action* 274–94.

Smith, W. D. "Iphigenia in Love." *Arktouros* 173–80.

Vretska, Karl. "Agamemnon in Euripides' *Iphigenie in Aulis*." *WS* 74 (1961) 18–39.

IPHIGENIA IN TAURIS

Caldwell, Richard. "Tragedy Romanticized: The *Iphigenia Taurica*." *CJ* 70 (1974) 23–40.

Ebener, Dietrich. "Der humane Gehalt der *Taurischen Iphigenie*." *Alterum* 12 (1966) 97–103.

Sansone, David. "The Sacrifice Motif in Euripides' *IT*." *TAPA* 105 (1975) 283–95.

MEDEA

Bongie, E. B. "Heroic Elements in the *Medea* of Euripides." *TAPA* 107 (1977) 27–56.

Burnett, A. P. "*Medea* and the Tragedy of Revenge." *CP* 68 (1973) 1–24.

Buttrey, T. V. "Accident and Design in Euripides' *Medea*." *AJP* 79 (1958) 1–17.

Easterling, P. E. "The Infanticide in Euripides' *Medea*." *YCS* 25 (1977) 177–91.

Ebener, Dietrich. "Zum Motiv des Kindermordes in der *Medeia*." *RhM* 104 (1961) 213–24.

Erbse, Hartmut. "Über die Aigeusszene der euripideischen *Medea*." *WS* 79 (1966) 120–33.

Flory, Stewart. "Medea's Right Hand: Promises and Revenge." *TAPA* 108 (1978) 69–74.

Friedrich, W. H. "Medeas Rache." *Nachr. der Ak. der Wiss. in Göttingen, Philol.-hist. Kl.* 4 (1960) 67–111. Reprinted in *Vorbild und Neugestaltung* (Göttingen 1967) 7–56 and in Schwinge, ed. *Euripides* 177–237.

Fritz, Kurt von. "Die Entwicklung der Iason-Medea-Sage und die *Medea* des Euripides." *A&A* 8 (1959) 33–160. Reprinted in *Antike und moderne Tragödie* 322–429. Berlin 1962.

Knox, B. M. W. "The *Medea* of Euripides." *YCS* 25 (1977) 193–225. Reprinted in *Word and Action* 295–322.

Mills, S. P. "The Sorrows of Medea." *CP* 75 (1980) 289–96.

Musurillo, Herbert. "Euripides' *Medea*: A Reconsideration." *AJP* 87 (1966) 52–74.

Paduano, Guido. *La formazione del mondo ideologico e poetico di Euripide: Alcesti-Medea*. Pisa 1968.

Pucci, Pietro. *The Violence of Pity in Euripides' "Medea"*. Ithaca, N.Y. 1980.

Reckford, K. J. "Medea's First Exit." *TAPA* 99 (1968) 329–59.

Schlesinger, Eilhard. "Zu Euripides' *Medea*." *Hermes* 94 (1966) 26–53. Trans. and slightly abridged in E. Segal, ed. *Euripides* 70–89.

ORESTES

Biehl, Werner. "Zur Darstellung des Menschen in Euripides' *Orestes*: Ein Beitrag zur Interpretation." *Helikon* 8 (1968) 197–221.

Burkert, Walter. "Die Absurdität der Gewalt und das Ende der Tragödie: Euripides' *Orestes*." *A&A* 20 (1974) 97–109.

Erbse, Hartmut. "Zum *Orestes* des Euripides." *Hermes* 103 (1975) 434–59.

Falkner, T. M. "Coming of Age in Argos: Physis and Paideia in Euripides' *Orestes*." *CJ* 78 (1983) 289–300.

Greenberg, N. A. "Euripides' *Orestes*: An Interpretation." *HSCP* 66 (1962) 157–92.

Parry, Hugh. "Euripides' *Orestes*: The Quest for Salvation." *TAPA* 100 (1969) 337–53.

Rawson, Elizabeth. "Aspects of Euripides' *Orestes*." *Arethusa* 5 (1972) 155–68.

Smith, W. D. "Disease in Euripides' *Orestes*." *Hermes* 95 (1967) 291–307.

Wolff, Christian. "*Orestes*." In E. Segal, ed. *Euripides* 132–49.

Zeitlin, F. I. "The Closet of Masks: Role-playing and Myth-making in the *Orestes* of Euripides." *Ramus* 9 (1980) 51–77.

PHOENICIAN WOMEN

Arthur, M. B. "The Curse of Civilization: The Choral Odes of the *Phoenissae*." *HSCP* 81 (1977) 163–85.
Burian, Peter. "Introduction." In Euripides, *The Phoenician Women*, trans. Peter Burian and Brian Swann, 3–17. New York 1981.
Conacher, D. J. "Themes in the Exodus of Euripides' *Phoenissae*." *Phoenix* 21 (1967) 92–101.
Podlecki, A. J. "Some Themes in Euripides' *Phoenissae*." *TAPA* 93 (1962) 355–73.
Rawson, Elizabeth. "Family and Fatherland in Euripides' *Phoenissae*." *GRBS* 11 (1970) 109–27.
Romilly, Jacqueline de. "*Phoenician Women* of Euripides: Topicality in Greek Tragedy." *Bucknell Rev.* 15, 3 (1967) 108–32.

RHESUS

Kitto, H. D. F. "The *Rhesus* and Related Matters." *YCS* 25 (1977) 317–50.
Paduano, Guido. "Ettore e la frustrazione del piano eroico." *SCO* 23 (1974) 5–30.
———. "Funzioni drammatiche nella struttura del *Reso*." *Maia* 25 (1973) 3–29.
Parry, Hugh. "The Approach of Dawn in the *Rhesus*." *Phoenix* 18 (1964) 283–93.
Ritchie, William. *The Authenticity of the "Rhesus" of Euripides*. Cambridge 1964.
Rosivach, V. J. "Hector in the *Rhesus*." *Hermes* 104 (1978) 54–73.
Strohm, Hans. "Beobachtungen zum *Rhesos*." *Hermes* 87 (1959) 257–74.

SUPPLIANT WOMEN

Collard, Christopher. "The Funeral Oration in Euripides' *Supplices*." *BICS* 19 (1972) 39–53.
Fitton, J. W. "The *Suppliant Women* and the *Heraklidai* of Euripides." *Hermes* 89 (1961) 430–61.
Gamble, R. B. "Euripides' *Suppliant Women*: Decision and Ambivalence." *Hermes* 98 (1970) 385–405.
Shaw, M. H. "The *ETHOS* of Theseus in *The Suppliant Women*." *Hermes* 110 (1982) 3–19.
Smith, W. D. "Expressive Form in Euripides' *Suppliants*." *HSCP* 71 (1966) 151–70.
Zuntz, Günther. *The Political Plays of Euripides*. Manchester 1955.

TROJAN WOMEN

Burnett, A. P. "*Trojan Women* and the Ganymede Ode." *YCS* 25 (1977) 291–316.
Gilmartin, Kristine. "Talthybius in the *Trojan Women*." *AJP* 91 (1970) 213–22.
Havelock, E. A. "Watching the *Trojan Women*." In E. Segal, ed. *Euripides* 115–27.
Poole, Adrian. "Total Disaster: Euripides' *The Trojan Women*." *Arion* 3 (1976) 257–87.
Scodel, Ruth. *The Trojan Trilogy of Euripides*. Hypomnemata 60 (Göttingen 1980).

Contributors

Peter Burian, Associate Professor of Classical Studies at Duke University, has published a number of essays on the Greek tragic poets as well as a translation, in collaboration with Brian Swann, of Euripides' *Phoenician Women* (1981).

Anne Pippin Burnett, Professor of Classics at the University of Chicago, is the author of *Catastrophe Survived: Euripides' Plays of Mixed Reversal* (1971), a translation and commentary of Euripides' *Ion* (1970), and numerous articles on Euripides, Aeschylus, and the lyric poets. Her latest book is *Three Archaic Poets: Archilochus, Alcaeus, Sappho* (1983).

Bernard Knox, Director of the Center for Hellenic Studies, Washington, D.C., has collected his essays on the ancient theater in *Word and Action* (1979). Among his other publications are the two Sophoclean studies *Oedipus at Thebes* (1957) and *The Heroic Temper* (1964).

Kenneth J. Reckford, Professor of Classics at the University of North Carolina, Chapel Hill, has written extensively on Latin poets, including a book on *Horace* (1969), as well as on the Greek theater, notably Euripides and Aristophanes. His translation, with Janet Lembke, of Euripides' *Hecuba* is scheduled to appear in 1985.

Charles Segal, Benedict Professor of Classics and Comparative Literature at Brown University, has published widely on almost every aspect of ancient literature. His books include *Landscape in Ovid's "Metamorphoses"* (1969), *The Theme of the Mutilation of the Corpse in the "Iliad"* (1971), *Poetry and Myth in Ancient Pastoral: Essays in Theocritus and Vergil* (1981), *Tragedy and Civilization: An Interpretation of Sophocles* (1981), and *Dionysiac Poetics and Euripides' "Bacchae"* (1982).

Froma I. Zeitlin, Professor of Classics at Princeton University, is the author of *Under the Sign of the Shield: Semiotics and Aeschylus' "Seven against Thebes"* (1982), as well as studies of Aeschylus, Euripides, Aristophanes, and Petronius.